D0728486

Society, Solitude, and Community

Melissa M

Lynchburg College Symposium Readings

Third Edition

2006

Volume IV

Society, Solitude, and Community

Edited by

Phillip H. Stump, Ph.D.

Copyright © 2006 by Lynchburg College.

Library of Congress Control Number: 2006901905
ISBN: Hardcover   1-4257-1109-X
                               Softcover   1-4257-1108-1

All rights reserved. No part of this book may be reproduced or transmitted in any form or by any means, electronic or mechanical, including photocopying, recording, or by any information storage and retrieval system, without permission in writing from the copyright owner.

This book was printed in the United States of America.

To order additional copies of this book, contact:
Xlibris Corporation
1-888-795-4274
www.Xlibris.com
Orders@Xlibris.com
23027

CONTENTS

ACKNOWLEDGEMENTS

The editors acknowledge with appreciation the permissions granted by these holders of the respective copyrights.

From *Sacred Books of Confucius & Other Confucian Classics* by Winberg Chai, copyright ©1965 by Bantam, a division of Random House, Inc. Used by permission of Bantam Books, a division of Random House, Inc.

Excerpts from *Patterns of Culture* by Ruth Benedict. Copyright 1934 by Ruth Benedict; copyright renewed (c) 1961 by Ruth Valentine. Reprinted by permission of Houghton Mifflin Company. All rights reserved.

The Iliad of Homer, R. Lattimore, Trans. Copyright © 1951. University of Chicago Press. Reprinted by permission. pp. 59-75.

Zahan, Dominique. *The Religion, Spirituality, and Thought of Traditional Africa.* Copyright © 1979. The University of Chicago Press. Reprinted by permission. pp. 36-52.

After Virtue: A Study of Moral Theory © 1981 Alasdair MacIntyre. Reprinted by permission of University of Notre Dame Press.

The Lais of Marie de France, translated by R. Hanning and J. Ferrante. New York: E.P. Dutton Copyright © 1978, a division of Baker Publishing Group. Reprint by permission.

The Heptaméron by Marguerite de Navarre, translated with an introduction by P.A. Chilton (Penguin Books, 1984). Copyright © P.A. Chilton, 1984. pp. 83-101, 108-114, 503-506, 510-512.

Entire chapter, pp.315-337 Perennial Classics edition from
One Hundred Years of Solitude by Gabriel Garcia Marquez.
English translation copyright (c) 1970 by Harper & Row
Publishers, Inc. Reprinted by permission of HarperCollins
Publishers.

The Labyrinth of Solitude by Octavio Paz, translated by Lysander
Kemp. Copyright © 1962 by Grove Press, Inc. Used by
permission of Grove/Atlantic, Inc.

The editors further acknowledge with thanks the
dedicated work of Elizabeth Giglio, English major, '05 and
Rachel Moore, Communication Studies major, '08 for their
dedicated work and editorial assistance.

LYNCHBURG COLLEGE SYMPOSIUM READINGS, SENIOR SYMPOSIUM, AND THE LCSR PROGRAM

The ten-volume series, Lynchburg College Symposium Readings, has been developed by Lynchburg College faculty for use in the Senior Symposium and the Lynchburg College Symposium Readings Program (SS/LCSR). Each volume presents primary source material organized around interdisciplinary, liberal arts themes.

In 1976, the College developed the Senior Symposium as a two-hour, interdisciplinary course, required of all graduating seniors. On Mondays students in all sections of the course come together for public lectures, given by invited guest speakers. On Wednesdays, Symposium students meet in their sections for student-led discussions and presentations on associated readings from the LCSR series. The course requires students, who have spent their later college years in narrowing the scope of their studies, to expand their fields of vision within a discussion group composed of and led by their peers. Students can apply analytical and problem-solving capabilities learned in their major fields of study to issues raised by guest speakers and classical readings.

This approach works against convention in higher education, which typically emphasizes the gradual exclusion of subject areas outside of a student's major field. But Senior Symposium leads students, poised for graduation, into their post-College intellectual responsibilities. They gain experience in taking their liberal education into real world problems, using it to address contemporary problems thoughtfully and critically. In order to do this successfully, students must abandon their habitual posture as docile receptors of authoritative information for a much more skeptical attitude toward opinion, proof, reasoning, and authoritative experience. The effort to think constructively through a variety of conflicting opinions—on a weekly basis—prepares them well for the mature, independent, well-reasoned points of view expected of educated adults.

The LCSR Program's primary goals are to foster an appreciation of the connection between basic skills and interdisciplinary knowledge, and to promote greater cross-disciplinary communication among faculty and students. General education core courses or courses that serve other program requirements may be classified as "LCSR," as long as they fulfill certain speaking and writing activities connected to LCSR readings. The effect of the program has been to help create the atmosphere of a residential academic community; shared learning creates a climate in which teaching and learning take root more forcefully.

Since its inception, the SS/LCSR Program has helped create opportunities for faculty interaction across the disciplines in "pre-service" and "in-service" workshops. Each May, the LCSR Program sponsors a four-day pre-service workshop to which all new full-time and part-time faculty members are invited. Participants receive individual sets of the Lynchburg College Symposium Readings, which they make their own by using them during the workshop in exercises designed to promote familiarity with a wide variety of the readings. The goals of the workshop are several: for those unfamiliar with the program, to begin planning an LCSR course; for new faculty, to become acquainted with those they have not met and get to know their acquaintances better; for other faculty of various experiential levels, to share their pedagogical successes; for new teachers, to ask questions about teaching, about the College, and about the students in an informal setting; for experienced teachers to re-visit some of their assumptions, pedagogies, and strategies; to inspire strong scholarship, creative teaching, risk-taking, and confidence among all participants.

Another opportunity comes with the "in-service" workshops, which occur each month during the school year. The LCSR Program sponsors luncheons and dinners at which faculty teaching in the program give informal presentations on their use of specific teaching strategies or reading selections. Attendance is voluntary, but many try to be present for every session. For those involved in the LCSR program, teaching has become what Lee Schulman, President of the Carnegie Foundation, calls "community property."

On the Lynchburg College campus, there is evidence of a systematic change in teaching effectiveness as well as sustained faculty commitment to the program. By the 2002-2003 academic year, nearly two-thirds of all full-time faculty members and more than half of all part time faculty members had completed the workshop at some time during their time at Lynchburg College. In any given semester, roughly ten to fifteen percent of the total class enrollments are in LCSR courses, not counting the required Senior Symposium. An important feature of this program is that participation is voluntary on the part of the faculty and, except for the required Senior Symposium, on the part of students. The program's influence quietly pervades the campus community, improving teaching and scholarship. Many see the LCSR Program as the College's premier academic program.

The Senior Symposium/LCSR program publishes *The Agora*, an in-house journal that features the best of student writings responding to LCSR texts. The journal selections by students must integrate classical ideas and issues with contemporary ones. Faculty may also submit writings that address innovative teaching strategies. The journal takes its title from the marketplace at the heart of classical Athens, where much of Athenian public life was carried on: mercantile exchange, performance, political debate, athletic contests, and the public worship of deities—all took place within the hustle and bustle of the Athenian agora. Similarly, the journal seeks to be a marketplace for compelling ideas and issues. Faculty members and students serve together on the editorial committee.

Since 1976, the Senior Symposium and the LCSR Program have affected the academic community both on and beyond the Lynchburg College campus. In 1991, Professor Richard Marius from Harvard University's writing center in reviewing the program favorably said, "I have seldom in my life been so impressed by an innovation in college education. I suppose the highest compliment that I could pay to the program was that I wished I could teach in it." Also in 1991, Professor Donald Boileau of George Mason University's communication studies department wrote, "what I discovered was a sound program that not only enriches the education of students at Lynchburg College, but what I hope can be a model for many other colleges and universities throughout our country." In spring 2003, in an article titled, "Whither the Great Books," Dr. William Casement described the LCSR program as the "most fully organized version" of the recent growth of great-books programs that employ an "across-the-disciplines structure." According to him, this approach perhaps encourages the use of the great books across the curriculum, which can be less isolating than even interdisciplinary programs. The Senior Symposium and LCSR Programs have received national acclaim in such publications as Loren Pope's Colleges *That Change Lives* and

Charles Sykes and Brad Miner's *The National Review of College Guide, America's 50 Top Liberal Arts Schools.*

Society, Solitude, and Community is the fourth volume of the third edition of the Lynchburg College Symposium Readings series. The first edition, published in the early 1980s, included several selections also printed here in this volume. Dr. Stump has served as the faculty editor for all three editions of this volume. The Senior Symposium was the creation of Dr. James Huston, Dean of the College, Emeritus (1972-1984); he and Dr. Michael Santos, Professor of History, co-founded the LCSR program. Dean Huston served as the first series editor, and with Dr. Julius Sigler, Professor of Physics, as co-editor of the second series. All four remain committed to the program today, and for this we are grateful.

Peggy A. Pittas, Ph.D.
Katherine Gray, Ph.D.
Series Co-Editors

INTRODUCTION

Tension between the individual and society has been a major theme in Western culture and has often become an outright conflict, while in non-Western cultures harmony between individual and society has more often been the ideal. In his book *The Lonely Crowd* David Riesman argued that Western society has passed through three phases, in which people were first tradition-directed, then inner-directed, and finally other-directed. Ironically, as modern Westerners have become more other-directed, they have often become more isolated and lonely. Earlier cultures knew solitude, but not the solitude of the crowd; in these earlier cultures the power of society over the individual, though it could become oppressive, also led to more tight-knit communities. But modern Western society seems to be in danger of losing both individuality and community. The classic writings in this volume explore the themes of the individual and society, solitude, and community.

The volume opens with works from the traditional societies of ancient Greece and China—works that are in fact cornerstones of the Western and Eastern classical traditions: the Homeric epics and the Confucian classics. Both transmitted oral traditions and were themselves originally composed orally. Oral traditions are the creations of societies rather than individuals; yet, both Homer and Confucius were individual creators of great genius. The tension between society and individual creativity is one of the major themes of this volume; it existed already in these early societies, whose moral demands had vastly more power over individuals than any society today. Individuals who resisted these early societies' unwritten expectations suffered terrible consequences of shame and loss of honor. Confucius recognized that this shame was a much more powerful sanction than any formal laws or penalties. Anthropologists have referred to such societies as "shame cultures," distinguishing them from later "guilt cultures," in which an individual's acts are judged by a God or by personal religious values so that one experiences personal guilt for one's sins, even if they remain hidden from society.

The norms of Homeric Greece and China were very different, although both were shame cultures. The world of the *Iliad* was one in which warriors fought together against a common foe, but also competed with each other for honor in warfare and in speech by showing military skill, courage, and ability to persuade and dominate in public debate. The setting was the Trojan War, but the central conflict of the epic was between two Greeks—Achilles, the greatest warrior, and Agamemnon, the nominal leader of the expedition. Achilles believed he had been wronged by Agamemnon and in anger he withdrew from battle, wanting the Greeks to lose, and they began to do so. Scholars still debate whether or not Achilles was rejecting the norms of his society and seeking an individual greatness beyond its pale. But in any case he was the prototypical solitary hero, and his actions introduce the theme of solitude to this volume. In the society Confucius envisions, on the other hand, conflict is to be avoided, the ultimate goal is harmony, and solitude plays little or no role. Honor is preserved and shame avoided when rulers lead the people by example and exert moral influence, and when the people act humanely toward one another and observe the proper rituals.

The great sociologist, Max Weber, believed that these Confucian values were not conducive to the development of modern, capitalistic, industrial society, which, he argued, could only have begun in the West, for numerous reasons. In the third excerpt below he examines what he believes to be one of the most important reasons, one which originated in the "guilt culture" of Christianity, in the ascetic mentality with which Christians sought to deal with their guilt. He finds the roots of this asceticism in the teachings of medieval monastic life, which called men and women to reject the world, its pleasures, and its wealth. Monastic life became a curious fusion of solitude and community, to which Protestants, according to Weber, added a further twist by taking asceticism out of the cloister into the secular "callings" of the world of work. For them the accumulation of wealth through success at work was now not only acceptable, but became a sign of God's grace. However, the ascetic spirit dictated that the wealth could not be enjoyed, so the Protestant entrepreneurs systematically reinvested their wealth, thus furthering their capital accumulation. All this contributed mightily, according to Weber, to the rationalizing of society and the overcoming of traditional ways that made possible modern, Western, capitalist society. Yet, recent successes of Asian nations in developing thriving capitalistic economies may call Weber's theories into question. Asian scholars point to Confucian writings like the opening passage of *The Great Learning*, which stresses the cultivation of individual morality as the basis for all social harmony, and they even speak of a "Confucian work ethic."

The next two readings look at American Indian and African societies; they are the works of anthropologists, based on their investigation of the rich oral and artistic traditions of these societies, traditions which, unlike those of Homer and Confucius, were not committed to writing. We will find some similarities to the Homeric and Confucian societies; for example, all of them were shame societies. In the first reading, Ruth Benedict argues that each culture develops its own unique pattern of cultural norms and illustrates this theory by analyzing the patterns of two quite different American Indian cultures—the Kwakiutl nation of the Northwest Pacific coast and the Zuñi people of the U.S. Southwest. The contrasts are in some ways curiously similar to those between the Homeric and Confucian cultures. The Kwakiutl engage in constant competition for honor and dominance like the Homeric Greeks, while the Zuñi are a ceremonious people who seek social harmony and non-offensiveness like the Confucians. Ancient Greek culture was complex, however, and Benedict found parallels in it to both of these American Indian cultures, which she labeled Dionysian and Apollonian, respectively, drawing on terminology coined by Nietzsche.

An excerpt from the work of another anthropologist, Dominique Zahan, is included in this volume because of the insights it affords into the diverse cultures on the continent that was both the cradle of civilization and the cradle of humanity itself—Africa. As in the traditional societies of China, Greece, and North America, we find in African cultures a pervasive humanism and a sense of community, but with their own unique accents. The selection from Zahan focuses on African views of death and time. Death is in many ways the ultimate solitude. But in the societies depicted in the excerpt the dead are often still present in society as respected ancestors. The role of the ancestor is closely tied to concepts of tradition and time which are very different from modern Western ones. "Tradition is above all the collective experience of the community" over time. In such a view progress becomes a retrospective attempt to realize in the present the greatness of the ideal past of the ancestors.

Zahan's excerpt should be read in conjunction with the excerpt from Olaudah Equiano's biography, which gives unique insight into one early African society—the Igbo people of West Africa—provided by a member of that society who recorded the happy memories of his childhood in the eighteenth century before he was captured by slave traders. Equiano's memoirs also reveal the differences between African slavery and slavery in the European colonies and the horrifying reality of the "Middle Passage." He describes the terrible solitude of being wrenched out of the community he so loved and transported to an unknown world, where he was treated as a material possession rather than a human being. He thus raises the theme of the solitude of oppression, but also the solitude of self-reliance. Equiano actually gained his freedom and became a successful seaman, and later, a leading abolitionist in Britain.

These two interlocking themes of solitude are also explored in three excerpts from women authors: Mary Wollstonecraft, Maria Stewart, and Elizabeth Cady Stanton. Mary Wollstonecraft issued the challenge of self-reliance with special force. Elizabeth Cady Stanton took it up in one of her final speeches, "The Solitude of Self," in which she conjured up the paradigmatic image of Robinson Crusoe on his desert island. The use of the novel *Robinson Crusoe* by Rousseau to teach self-reliance to his young pupil Émile (see LCSR Volume 1) had already impressed Mary Wollstonecraft, but she brilliantly criticized Rousseau for teaching self-reliance only to males while teaching women to be weak and dependent men-pleasers. Interestingly, Stanton made her Robinson Crusoe and Friday into women.

Maria Stewart, the first woman to deliver public lectures in America, based her call for self-reliance and her demands for equal rights on her own experiences as an African American and a woman. She also drew deeply from the well of her spirituality, comparing the experiences of her people to those of another oppressed people, biblical Israel. On the other hand, Mary Wollstonecraft expressed her vision of equal rights in terms of the Enlightenment's commitment to universal human rights. She wrote *Vindication of the Rights of Man* to defend the French Revolution's struggle for human rights. Two years later, she took the Enlightenment ideas of equal rights to their logical conclusion in *Vindication of the Rights of Women*. Equiano and Stewart similarly extended the Enlightenment arguments to argue for the abolition of slavery and equal rights for former slaves.

Some post-Enlightenment scholars have called into question the idea of universal codes of rights or morality. Recently, "communitarian" thinkers have pointed to the diversity of moral codes in different cultures, a fact which is supported by anthropological studies like that of Ruth Benedict (see above). One such thinker (though he eschews the communitarian label) argues against universal moral codes and rights but at the same time seeks to find the basis for a universal morality founded on virtues rather than codes. In his book *After Virtue* excerpted below, Alasdair MacIntyre argues that we can find a number of such universal virtues— especially truthfulness, justice, and courage—that enable us to attain goals in a wide variety of different practices, even though these practices might be different in different cultures and even though each culture might have a different code of justice, truthfulness, and courage. MacIntyre goes on to argue that these virtues must exist in individuals who live in communities, and he suggests that it is the narrative of an individual's entire life—his or her actions and interactions with the community—that gives coherence and integrity to the life of both individual and community.

One might indeed almost say that narrative makes possible community. It does so in at least four ways: 1) by linking the past with the present; 2) by recording interaction among individuals; 3) by placing individual human actions in their contexts; and 4) by giving voice to alternate views, thus reconciling conflicting perspectives. When MacIntyre speaks of narratives he is referring to historical narratives. But in some ways, fictional narrative is even more effective in creating community because of the ways in which it unites reality and aspiration, reminding us that even "historical" narratives may be told differently from the perspectives of different individual participants. In addition to the historical narrative of Olaudah Equiano and the epic narrative of Homer's *Iliad*, we have excerpts in this volume from two sets of tales and one novel.

Both sets of tales are authored by French women, separated by four centuries, Marie de France and Marguerite de Navarre. The difference in the social settings is striking. De France describes the ideal and partly magical world of medieval knights and ladies, whereas de Navarre portrays the much more worldly and even cynical realities of Renaissance life. De Navarre's tales explore the possibilities of narrative in very complex ways with multiple perspectives. Like plays within a play, her collection of tales (the *Heptaméron*), is framed within a larger narrative, because the tales are told by ten storytellers. After each tale the storytellers discuss the tale, revealing much about their own personalities and interactions. The storytellers are fictional characters, but they are modeled on a circle of de Navarre's own friends, and they agree that the stories they tell will all be true stories (and some indeed are true). Fictional narratives like de Navarre's explore the importance of truthfulness in creating community because they address the interplay between truth and fiction and the devastating effects of suppressing the truth.

The excerpt from Gabriel García Márquez's novel, *One Hundred Years of Solitude*, dramatically explores these themes. The novel is the history of multiple generations of a large extended family, the Buendías, in a Colombian village named Macondo. The pristine isolation of the village is abruptly terminated by the arrival of a North American banana company that brings with it all the good and bad of modern society. It brings much superficial wealth, but terrible conditions of exploitation for the workers. The workers resist, taking the company to court, but the company evades legal action by claiming it has no workers (they were all subcontracted.) Even more disastrous events and denials of truth follow when the workers strike. The whole episode in the novel becomes increasingly surreal, but ironically it is based on the facts of a real historical banana strike that took place in Colombia against the United Fruit Company in 1928. The event marks the turning point in the novel as the banana company withdraws, taking with it the superficial prosperity and plunging Macondo into an even deeper, more hopeless solitude.

In probing the inter-relationship between truth and fiction, García Márquez makes consummate use of a technique known as "magical realism," by which he introduces fantastical events into everyday life using a straightforward narrative style. When de France similarly introduces marvelous events into her narratives, it is often to redeem the more bitter reality of life and the many types of solitude it brings—the solitude of Tristan and Iseult's forbidden love in *Chevrefeuil*, the solitude of adolescence in *Guigemar*, and the solitude of abandonment in *Le Frêne*. Solitude would seem to play a lesser role in the vibrant society of the *Heptaméron*, but the crucial fourth tale suggests otherwise. It tells the story of the attempted rape of a princess by a "gentleman" who was entertaining the princess and her brother at his château. Though the princess successfully fights him off, her lady in waiting advises her not to reveal the rape for fear the princess's own reputation will be tarnished. Most scholars believe that the princess in the tale was Marguerite de Navarre herself, and the solitude of living alone with the memory of the trauma and injustice may have played a powerful role in shaping the entire *Heptaméron*.[1]

In writing about the solitude of Macondo, García Márquez was really writing about the way in which Colombia, indeed

---

[1] See the intriguing interpretation by Patricia Cholakian, *Rape and Writing in the* Heptaméron *of Marguerite de Navarre* (Carbondale, IL: Southern Illinois University Press, 1991).

all Latin America, has been reduced to solitude. In his Nobel Prize acceptance speech he held out the hope of a different world, in which "no one will be able to decide for others how they die, where love will prove true and happiness be possible, and where the races condemned to one hundred years of solitude will have, at last and forever, a second opportunity on earth." Like García Márquez, Octavio Paz explores the varieties of solitude, but in the discursive format of a book of essays, rather than the narrative of a novel. Paz draws together almost all the themes touched on in this volume. He shows how solitude can be a positive part of life's dynamic in the solitude of the adolescent, the hero, the prophet, and the saint, and how it can be part of a healthy process of withdrawal and return. But he also underlines the varieties of solitude that are oppressive, signs of the sickness of our society; his diagnosis of the pathology is reminiscent of Weber's pessimistic assessment of the alienation which the "progress" of our modern rationalistic, capitalistic, bureaucratic society has produced. As a contrast Paz holds up the Mexican fiesta, which destroys solitude and chronometric time; allowing its participants to experience a universal present where they find community and even communion.

In the Western views of chronometric time we have too often forgotten what the African cultures discussed by Zahan know so well—that progress is not linear, but moves forward by looking back. In his beautiful work of poetic sociology, W.E.B. Du Bois calls into question the narrow Western idea of time and progress and argues that if America is to progress and flourish it will do so through the "gifts" of the African American. The veil of race has created solitude for African Americans, but it has also "gifted" them with a "second sight," the ability to see oneself and others through one's own eyes and also through the others'. Through this second sight, Du Bois saw that if true community is to exist in America, it must be possible for the African American to be both African and an American, thus rending the veil.

Some have seen a conflict between the individual and society, arguing that an overemphasis on individual rights and freedoms has weakened communal ties. But precisely the opposite seems to be true for the future. The creation of true community can only occur when each individual is free to experience his or her fullest development, when solitude will not be a state of oppression to which people are subjected, but part of a healthy interchange between the individual and the community. I hope the classic readings in this volume have provided some ideas about how this might occur.

Phillip H. Stump, Ph. D.
Professor of History

CONFUCIUS

(551-479 B.C.E.)

CONFUCIAN CLASSICS

Ironically, Confucius saw himself as a failure, but he is among a handful of the most influential persons in world history. Like Buddha and Jesus he did not write anything. The *Analects* were written down later by disciples, but they record many of his sayings. "Analects" is the English word for the Chinese *Lun Yü*, which means, roughly, "sayings." They also include sayings of his disciples and records of short dialogues between Confucius and other people.

At the time of his birth China was in a period of political breakdown. The once great Zhou Dynasty had become very weak, and power was in the hands of regional lords. Even the duke of Lu, Confucius's ruler, was a figurehead, whose power had been usurped by the wealthy Ji family. Confucius dreamed of restoring the golden age of the early Zhou dynasty, when he believed China had been united by strong leaders like the emperors Wen and Wu and the duke of Chou, who led by humaneness and moral influence and set the example for their people. Confucius hoped to hold office in order to put his ideas into practice, but all he ever held were relatively minor posts, such as supervisor of granaries. He resigned from his last post in frustration and spent many years traveling and teaching.

He had many students, who were deeply impressed by his ideas of virtue and good rule. These disciples did become officials and eventually his ideas became the basis for the educational system of China. The rigorous system of examinations for Chinese officials (a merit-based civil service system which existed hundreds of years before anything like it in the West) was based on Confucian thought. The core texts for the exam were the *Analects, The Great Learning, the Doctrine of the Mean,* and the *Book of Mencius.* Excerpts from the first three of these are included below, and an excerpt from the Book of Mencius is in another LCSR volume. *The Great Learning* and the *Doctrine of the Mean* were originally chapters in the *Record of Rituals* (or *The Book of Rites*), which was probably first compiled in the first century B.C.E.

Confucius was three when his father died, and he was raised by his mother. She was either a second wife or a concubine to his father, and was not accepted by his father's family, so she had little money. Later writers embellished Confucius's ancestry by saying he was descended from an old noble family, but this is unlikely. When Confucius began teaching he accepted students regardless of their ability to pay, as long as they wanted to learn. He believed that all had the capacity to learn.

From an early age Confucius was interested in ritual and music. He eventually developed an expertise in these that placed him in considerable demand as an advisor and teacher. For Confucius, ritual (*li*) was much more than rote ceremony. The rituals were to be performed with sincerity and engagement, and they permeated all kinds of social interactions. At age fifteen Confucius began to study. For him learning was of great importance his whole life; he believed one did not only learn from books, but from interactions with others and from students. He and his disciples held intense, argumentative discussions.

Confucius believed that people can live together in harmony if they follow ritual and learn to act humanely toward each other. *Jen* (humaneness) is possibly the central Confucian concept. *Jen* is represented by the Chinese characters for "man" and "two"; so it refers to the proper relationship between two people. It is not just altruism, but has a reciprocal component. For the person who acts humanely good things result; and one acts humanely because that is how one wants to be treated. Confucius calls a person who acts according to *jen* a *chün-tzu* (gentleman or superior man).

The *Analects* are divided into twenty books, each of which is divided into chapters. The chapters are individual sayings or short narratives or dialogues, with little or no logical connection between the chapters. The excerpts below have been reorganized topically; after each chapter the numbers in square brackets identify the book and chapter numbers in the complete *Analects*. Many scholars identify earlier and later layers in the *Analects*. Generally, Books 3-9 are considered to be the earliest written, followed by 1-2 and 10, then 11-15, and finally 16-20. Books 3-9 are the most likely to reflect Confucius's own teaching rather than that of his disciples.

SOURCE

The Sacred Books of Confucius and other Confucian Classics. Ch'u Chai and Winberg Chai, Eds. New Hyde Park, New York: University Books, 1965.

Selections from:
>*The Confucian Analects* (excerpted 25-28, 29-30, 41-42, 43-45, 48-50, 52-55)
>*The Great Learning*, Part I: The General Statement (294-295)
>*The Doctrine of the Mean* (excerpted 306-309)

The Confucian Analects

PART ONE:

THE TEACHINGS OF CONFUCIUS

1. The Master said: "Clever words and flattering looks seldom speak of *jen* (humanity)." [I-3]

2. The Master said: "It is best to live in the company of *jen*. If a man chooses not to live where *jen* prevails, how can he be considered wise?" [IV-1]

3. The Master said: "Without *jen*, a man cannot long endure adversity, nor can he long endure prosperity. A man of *jen* rests in *jen*; a man of wisdom finds it beneficial." [IV-2]

4. The Master said: "It is only a man of *jen* who knows how to love people and how to hate people." [IV-3]

5. The Master said: "If a man is devoted to *jen*, he will be free from evil." [IV-4]

6. The Master said: "Riches and honor are what one likes, but if they come contrary to the *Tao*[1] they should not be retained. Poverty and lowliness are what one detests, but if they come contrary to the *Tao*, they should not be evaded. If a *chün-tzu* departs from *jen*, he is unworthy of such a name. Not even from the space of a single meal, should a *chün-tzu* act contrary to *jen*. In moments of haste, he cleaves to it; in times of difficulty, he cleaves to it." [IV-5]

7. The Master said: "I have not yet seen a man who loves *jen* nor a man who detests what is contrary to *jen*. He who loves *jen* esteems nothing else above it. He who detests what is contrary to *jen* seeks to be *jen*-minded so that he will not let anything contrary to *jen* appear

---

[1] *Tao*—a way of life—as used here, is ethical in meaning, denoting the principle of truth.

in his person. Is there anyone who is able even for a single day to apply his energy to *jen?* Well, I have not seen a man whose energy was not equal to it. Should there be any such man, I have not met him." [IV-6]

8. The Master said: "A man's faults are measured by his associates. Observe his faults and you may know whether he is *jen*-minded." [IV-7]

9. The Master said: "The wise delight in water; the *jen*-minded delight in mountains. The wise are active; the *jen*-minded are placid. The wise are happy; the *jen*-minded endure." [VI-21]

10. The Master said: "Is *jen* really so far away? I desire *jen*, and, see, it is by." [VII-29]

11. The Master said: "The wise man is free from perplexity; the *jen*-minded man is free from anxiety; the brave man is free from fear." [IX-28]

12. The Master said: "One who is firm of spirit, resolute in character, simple in manner, and slow of speech is near to *jen*." [XIII-27]

13. The Master said: "A man of virtue is sure to be good in speech, but one who is good in speech may not be virtuous. A man of *jen* is sure to be brave, but one who is brave may not be *jen*-minded." [XIV-5]

14. The Master said: "The strong-willed scholars and *jen*-minded men will not seek life at the expense of *jen*, but rather sacrifice their lives to preserve their *jen*." [XV-8]

15. The Master said: "*Jen* is more essential to man than fire and water. I have seen men die from stepping into fire and water, but I have never seen a man die from stepping into *jen*." [XV-34]

16. The Master said: "In attaining *jen*, a man need not defer to his teacher." [XV-35]

17. Fan Ch'ih asked about wisdom, and the Master said: "Devote yourself to the proper duty due to man, and respect the ghosts and spirits, but keep away from

them; this may be called wisdom." Then he asked about *jen*, and the master said: "A man of *jen* first concentrates on what is difficult and then on rewards; this may be called *jen*." [VI-20]

18. Tsai Wo asked: "Suppose a man of *jen* were told, 'There is a man down in the well,' would he go down after the man?" "Why should he do so?" said the master. "A *chün-tzu* might be induced [to go to the well] but not be trapped [in it]. He might be deceived, but not led astray." [VI-24]

19. Tzu Kung said: "Suppose there were a prince who conferred benefits far and wide upon the people and who was able to succor the multitude, what might you say of him? Could he be called *jen*-minded?" "Would it be merely a matter of *jen*?" said the Master. "Would he also be a sage? Even Yao and Shun fell short of it. A man of *jen* is one who, in seeking to establish himself, finds a foothold for others and who, desiring attainment for himself, helps others to attain. To be able from one's own self to draw a parallel in dealing with others is indeed the way of achieving *jen*." [VI-28]

20. Yen Yuen asked about the *jen*, and the Master said: "*Jen* consists in submitting oneself to *li* for one day and everybody will accord you in *jen*. For is *jen* to begin in one's self, or is it to begin in others?" "May I beg for details?" asked Yen Yuen. The Master said: "Look not at what is contrary to *li*, listen not to what is contrary to *li*, speak not what is contrary to *li*, and make no movement that is contrary to *li*." "Though I am slow-witted," said Yen Yuen, "I shall try to live up to the lesson taught by this saying." [XII-1]

21. Chung Kung asked about *jen*, and the Master said: "When abroad, behave as if you were meeting an honored guest; in employing the people, act as if you were officiating in the grand sacrifice. What you do not wish to yourself, do not do to others. Then neither

in the country nor in the family, will there be any resentment against you." "Though I am slow-witted," said Chung Kung, "I shall try to live up to the lesson taught in this saying." [XII-2]

22. Szu-ma Niu asked about *jen*, and the Master said: "A man of *jen* is wary of speech." "Wary of speech?" echoed Szu-ma Niu, "is this what is meant by *jen*?" The Master said: "When a man feels the difficulty of achievement, can he help but be wary in speaking about it?" [XII-3]

23. Fan Chi asked about *jen*, and the Master said: "Love men." Then he asked about wisdom, and the Master said: "Know men." Fan Chi did not understand. The Master said: "Employ the upright and set aside the crooked, so can the crooked be made upright." Fan Chi, after leaving the Master, met Tzu Hsia and said: "Just now I was with the master and asked about wisdom. He said, 'Employ the upright and set aside the crooked, so the crooked can be made upright.' What did he mean?" "Truly rich is this saying!" said Tzu Hsia. "When shun [sage king] ruled the world, choosing from among the multitude, he employed Kao Yao and those devoid of *jen* disappeared. When T'ang [founder of the Shang dynasty] ruled the world, choosing from among the multitude, he employed Yin Yi and those devoid of *jen* disappeared." [XII-22]

24. Fan Chi asked about *jen*, and the Master said: "It is, in private life, to be courteous; in business, to be attentive; in all human relations, to be honest. And it should never be abandoned, even though one goes to live amid the barbaric tribes of the east or north." [XIV-19]

25. Hsien asked: ". . . If a man refrains from domineering, boasting, resentment, and desire, this may be counted to him as *jen*?" "This may be counted as difficult," said the Master, "but whether as *jen*, I do not know." [XIV-2]

26. Tzu Kung asked how to achieve *jen*, and the Master said: "When a workman wishes to do a good job, he must first

sharpen his tools. So when you stay in a state, serve only the worthy among its ministers, and make friends with those scholars who are *jen*-hearted." [XV-9]

27. Tzu Chang asked Master K'ung about *jen*, and Master K'ung said: "To be able to practice the five virtues in the world constitutes *jen*." Upon being asked what they were, the Master said: "They are respect, magnanimity, sincerity, earnestness, and kindness. With respect, you will avoid insult; with magnanimity, you will win over the multitude; with sincerity, men will trust you; with earnestness, you will have achievements; and with kindness, you will be fitted to command others." [XVII-6]

28. The Master said: "When a man's father is alive, observe his purpose. When his father is dead, observe his conduct. If for the three years of mourning he does not change from the ways of his father, he is indeed deemed to be filial." [I-11]

37. Tsai Wo, asking about the three years' mourning, suggested that one year was long enough. "If," said he, "a gentleman for three years abstains from ceremonial observances, ceremonies will certainly degenerate; if for three years he abstains from the use of music, music will certainly go to ruin. [In a year] the old crops are consumed, and the new crops have come up; the fire-striking sticks have been changed—a year would be long enough." "Would you then feel at ease in eating good rice and wearing fine clothes?" said the Master. "Quite at ease," was the reply. "If you feel at ease, then do so. But a gentleman, when in mourning, does not relish good food when he eats it; nor does he enjoy music when he hears it; nor does he feel at ease when he lives in a comfortable dwelling. Therefore he abstains from those things. But now if you would feel at ease, then go and do them." When Tsai Wo went out, the Master said: "What lack of *jen* is in Yü [i.e., Tsai Wo]! Only when a child is three years old, does he leave his parents'

arms; so must three years' mourning be the universal mourning period everywhere below heaven. And Yü, did he not enjoy the loving care of his parents for three years?" [XVII-21]

38. The Master said: "In the morning I hear the *Tao*, then may I let myself die in the evening." [IV-8]

39. The Master said: "Ts'ang! there is one central idea that runs through all my teachings." "Yes," answered Tseng Tzu. After the Master left, the disciples asked: "What did the Master mean?" "Our Master's doctrine," said Tseng Tzu "is simply this: chung [loyalty] and shu [altruism]." [IV-15]

40. The Master said: "Who can go out [of the house] except by the door: Likewise, who can get along without following the *Tao*?" [VI-15]

41. The Master said: "Tz'u, do you think I am one who knows because of extensive learning?" "Yes, is it not so?" "No," said the Master, "there is one central idea that runs through all my teachings." [XV-2]

42. The Master said: "A man can enlarge the *Tao*, but the *Tao* cannot enlarge the man." [XV-28]

43. Tzu Kung said: "What I do not want others to do to me, I would not do to others." "Oh, Ssu!" said the Master, "you are not up to that!" [V-13]

44. Tzu Kung asked: "Is there a single word that one can live by all one's life?" "Is not *shu* [altruism] such a word?" said the Master. "Do not do to others what you do not want done to yourself." [XV-23]

45. The Master said: "Virtue dwells not alone but will always have neighbors." [IV-25]

46. The Master said: "Perfect indeed is the virtue which is in accord with the doctrine of Chun-Yung. For a long time few have had the capacity for it." [VI-27]

47. The Master said: "I have never seen a man who loves virtue as much as he loves a woman's beauty." [IX-17, XV-12]

48. The Master said: "A well-bred horse is praised not for its might but for its good qualities." [XIV-35]
49. The Master said: "Yu, those who know virtue are few." [XV-3]
50. The Master said: "The good careful villagers are the simulators of virtue." [XVII-13]

• • •

153. The Master said: "It is difficult to be poor without complaint; it is easy to be rich without arrogance." [XIV-11]
154. Tzu Lu asked how to serve a prince. The Master said: "Do not impose on him, but rather resist him." [XIV-23]
155. The Master said: "Do not worry about lack of fame; worry about lack of ability." [XIV-32]
156. The Master said: "A man should not anticipate fraud, nor expect falsehood; yet if he is conscious of this beforehand—is he not a man of worth?" [XIV-33]
157. Someone asked: "What may be said of requiting injury with kindness?" "How will you then requite kindness?" said the Master. "Requite injury with justice, and kindness with kindness." [XIV-36]
158. The Master said: Some men of worth retire from the world; those next to them withdraw from their fatherland; the next from uncongenial looks; and the next from uncongenial words." [XIV-39] The Master said: "There are seven men who have retired." [XIV-40]
159. Tzu Chang asked how a man should conduct himself. The Master said: "Let him be faithful and true in his words; let him be sincere and reverent in his actions; and then he will conduct himself even among barbarians. But if he is not faithful and true in his words, nor sincere and reverent in his actions, even among his own villagers, how can he be expected to conduct himself? When standing, see these precepts in front of

you; when in a carriage, see them on the yoke. Then you may conduct yourself well wherever you go." Tzu Chang inscribed this down on his sash. [XV-5]

160. The Master said: "Not to speak with a man who can be spoken with is to lose a man. To speak with a man who cannot be spoken with is to waste words. He who is truly wise never loses a man; he, too, never wastes his words." [XV-7]

• • •

173. The Master said: "At fifteen I set my mind on learning; at thirty I could stand; at forty I had no doubts; at fifty I knew the Fate; at sixty I was already obedient [to the Fate]; and at seventy I could follow my heart's desires without transgressing the standards of right." [II-4]

174. The Master said: "I transmit but I do not create; I have faith in, and a passion for, ancient studies. In this respect, I venture to compare myself to Lao P'eng." [VII-1]

175. The Master said: "Knowing through silent reflection, learning without satiety, and teaching others without becoming weary—these are merits which I can claim." [VII-2]

176. The Master said: "As to being a sage or even a man of *jen*, how dare I make such claims? But it may be said of me that I have strived to learn without satiety and to teach others without becoming weary." Kung Hsi Hua said: "This is what we disciples fail to learn." [VII-33]

177. The Master said: "Is it true that *chün-tzu*, widely learned in culture, properly conducted in propriety, may not be far wrong?" [VI-25]

178. The Master said: "Were I to be given a few more years, I would give fifty to the study of *Yi*; only then might I be free from grave faults." [VII-16]

179. The Duke of Yeh asked Tzu Lu about Master K'ung, and Tzu Lu did not answer him. The Master said: "Why

didn't you tell him that I am a person who forgets to eat when he is in pursuit of knowledge, forgets all worries when he is in his enjoyment of it, and is not aware that old age is coming on?" [VII-18]

180. The Master said: "There are those who act without knowing why. But I am not like that. To hear much and then to select the good and follow it; to see much and then to ponder it—this comes next to true knowledge." [VII-27]

181. The Master said: "I am not one born with the possession of knowledge, but being fond of antiquity, I assiduously pursue it." [VII-19]

182. The Master said: "Sometimes I have passed a whole day without eating and a whole night without sleep, giving myself in thought. But it was of no avail. It is better to learn." [XV-30]

183. The Master said: "Study without thought is labor lost; thought without study is perilous." [II-15]

184. The Master said: "A youth should be filial at home and fraternal when abroad. He should be earnest and sincere, feeling an affection for all and a disposition toward *jen*. If, when all is done, he still has any energy to spare, then let him study the polite arts." [I-6]

185. The Master said: "The study of heterodox doctrines is injurious indeed." [II-16]

186. The Master said: "*Chün-tzu* does not seek satiety in his food, or comfort in his home, but he is earnest in his work and cautious in his speech; he still seeks the company of the righteous for reification of his conduct. Such a man may rightly be said to be fond of learning." [I-14]

187. The Master said: "Learn as though you would never be able to master it; hold it as though you would be in fear of losing it." [VIII-17]

188. The Master said: "In old days, men studied only for their own improvement; nowadays men study for approbation of others." [XIV-25]

189. The Master said: "In education there is no class distinction." [XV-38]

190. The Master said: "By nature men are nearly alike, but through experience they grow wide apart." [XVII-2]

191. The Master said: "To those who are above average, it is possible to discourse on the high doctrines. To those who are below average, it is impossible to do so." [VI-19]

192. The Master said: "Those who are born wise are the highest type of men; those who become wise through learning are next; those who are dull-witted and yet strive to learn come after that. Those who are dull-witted and yet make no effort to learn are the lowest type of men." [XVI-9]

193. The Master said: "The one who never changes is either the wisest of the wise or the dullest of the dull." [XVII-3]

194. The Master said: "From him who has brought his simple present of dried meat seeking to enter my school, I have never withheld instruction." [VII-7]

195. The Master said: "I won't teach a man who is not eager to learn, nor will I explain to one incapable of forming his own ideas. Nor have I anything to say to those who, after I have made clear one corner of the subject, cannot deduce the other three." [VII-8]

196. The Master said: "To be able to acquire new knowledge while reviewing the old qualifies one as an instructor of men." [II-11]

197. The themes on which the Master frequently discoursed were: the *Shih* [Odes], the *Shu* [History], and performance of the Rites. Of these he frequently discoursed. [VII-17]

198. The Master took four subjects for his teaching: belles-letters and conduct, loyalty and truth. [VII-24]

• • •

211. The Master said: "Personal cultivation begins with poetry, is established by rites, and is perfected by music." [VIII-8]

212. Chen K'ang asked of P'o Yü: "Have you learned anything different from what we all have had?" "No," replied P'o Yü, "but once when I was hurrying across the hall, where my father was standing alone, he said to me, 'Have you learned the *Odes*?' I answered, 'Not yet.' 'If you do not learn them,' he admonished, 'you will have no hold on words.' Then I retired and studied the *Odes*. On another occasion, as he was again standing by himself, I hurried across the hall to greet him. 'Have you learned the Rites?' he asked. 'Not yet,' I answered. 'Without learning the Rites,' he said, 'you will not be able to establish yourself.' So I retired and studied the Rites. Only these two things have I heard from him." Chen K'ang turned away and in delight, said: "I asked one thing and got three. I have learned about the *Odes* and the Rites; and I have learned too that *chün-tzu* is reserved toward his son." [XVI-13]

213. The Master said: "If I should summarize the three hundred *Odes* in one sentence, I would say: 'Wayward thoughts are absent.'" [II-2]

214. The Master said: "[In the *Odes*, the first piece] *Kuan-chü* expresses joy without being licentious and grief without being injurious." [III-20]

215. The Master said: "A man may learn the three hundred odes by heart, but if he proves himself incompetent when given a government post, or if he cannot make a speech unaided when sent abroad on mission, then of what use to him is all his learning?" [XIII-5]

216.   The flowers of a cherry tree
       Flutter on every spray.
   It is not that I do not think of thee,
     But that thou art far away!

[Commenting on these lines], the Master said: "He did not really think of her, what does the distance mean to him?" [IX-30]

217. The Master said: "My pupils, why don't you study the *Odes*? The *Odes* are evocative of thoughts; they are material for introspection; they contribute to social intercourse, they alleviate one's frustration. From the *Odes*, one learns the immediate duty of serving one's father and the remote duty of serving one's prince. And in the *Odes* one may be better acquainted with the names of birds and beasts, plants and trees." [VII-9]

218. The Master said to P'o Yü: "Have you ever learned the odes *Chou-nan* and *Shao-nan*? A man who has not ever learned them is like one who stands with his face against the wall; is he not so?" [XIII-10]

219. Tzu Hsia asked: "What is the meaning of the following verse?

How bewitching her artful smiles!
How clear her beautiful eyes!
There must be plain background
For the application of colors!"

"The painting comes after the plain groundwork," said the Master. "Then rituals and etiquette (*li*) are secondary?" said Tzu Hsia. "It is Shang who can open new vistas to me," said the Master. "In this way, I can begin to discuss the *Odes* with him." [III-8]

220. The Master said: "A man without *jen*—what has he to do with rites? A man without *jen*—what has he to do with music?" [III-3]

221. Lin Fang asked about the basic principles of rites, and the Master said: "A great question indeed! In ceremonials at large, it is better to be sparing than extravagant; and as for mourning rites, there should be deep grief rather than minute attention to details." [III-4]

222. The Master said: "Ceremonials! Ceremonials! Do they mean no more than offerings of jade and silk? Music! Music! Does it mean no more than bells and drums?" [XVII-11]

• • •

244. The Master said: "To rule a state of a thousand chariots, there must be reverent attention to duties and sincerity, economy in expenditure and love for the people, working them only at the proper seasons." [I-5]

245. The Master said: "One who governs by virtue is comparable to the polar star, which remains in its place while all the stars turn towards it." [II-1]

246. The Master said: "Govern the people by laws and regulate them by penalties, and the people will try to do no wrong, but they will lose the sense of shame. Govern the people by virtue and restrain them by rules of propriety, and the people will have a sense of shame and be reformed of themselves." [II-3]

247. Duke Ai asked: "What should I do to secure the submission of the people?" "Promote the upright and banish the crooked," said the Master; "then the people will be submissive. Promote the crooked and banish the upright; then the people will not be submissive." [II-19]

248. Chi Kang Tzu asked: "What should be done to make the people respectful and be encouraged to cultivate virtues?" "Approach the people with dignity," said the Master, "and they will be respectful. Show filial piety and kindness, and they will be loyal. Promote those who are worthy, and train those who are incompetent; and they will be encouraged to cultivate virtues." [II-20]

249. Duke Ting asked how a prince should employ his ministers and how ministers should serve their prince. Master K'ung said: "A prince should employ his

ministers with propriety; ministers should serve their prince with loyalty." [III-19]

250. The Master said: "If a prince governs his state with propriety and courtesy, what difficulty will he have? But if not, of what use are rituals?" [IV-13]

251. The Master said: "Yung would be a ruler." Then Chung Kung [Yung] asked about Tzu-sang Po-tzu. "He would be, too," said the Master, "but he is lax." "Such a man might be a ruler," said Chung Kung, "if he were scrupulous with his own conduct and lax only in his dealing with the people. But a man who is lax in his own conduct as well as in government would be too lax." The Master said: "What Yung says is true." [VI-1]

252. [Alluding to the States of Ch'i and Lu], the Master said: "Ch'i, by one change, might attain to the level of Lu; and Lu, by one change, might attain to the level of *Tao!*" [VI-22]

253. The Master said: "A cornered vessel that has no corners. What a cornered vessel! What a cornered vessel!" [VI-23]

254. The Master said: "The people may be made to follow but not to understand." [VIII-9]

255. Tzu Kung asked about government, and the Master said: "The essentials [of good government] are sufficient food, sufficient arms, and the confidence of the people." "But," asked Tzu Kung, "if you have to part with one of the three, which would you give up?" "Arms," said the Master. "But suppose," said Tzu Kung, "one of the remaining two has to be relinquished, which would it be?" "Food," said the Master. "From time immemorial, death has been the lot of all men, but a people without confidence is lost indeed." [XII-7]

256. Duke Ching asked Master K'ung about government, and Master K'ung said: "Let the ruler be ruler; the minister, minister; the father, father, and the son, son." "Good!" said the Duke. "For truly if the ruler

be not ruler, the minister not minister; if the father be not father, and the son be not son, then with all the grain in my possession, should I be able to relish it?" [XII-11]

257. The Master said: "In hearing lawsuits I am no better than other men, but my aim is to bring about the end of lawsuits." [XII-13]

258. Tzu Chang asked about government, and the Master said: "Attend to his affairs untiringly, and carry it out loyally." [XII-14]

259. Chi Kang Tzu asked Master K'ung about government, and Master K'ung said: "To govern means to rectify. If you, Sir, lead the people in rectitude, who dares not to be rectified?" [XII-17]

260. Chi Kang Tzu, being troubled by burglars, asked Master K'ung what he should do, and Master K'ung said: "If only you, Sir, are free from desire [for wealth], they will not steal even though you pay them." [XII-18]

261. Chi Kang Tzu asked Master K'ung about government, saying: "Suppose I kill the *Tao*-less for the good of the *Tao*-abiding, what do you think of it?" "What need, Sir," said Master K'ung, "is there of killing in your administration? Let you desire good, and the people will be good. The virtue of the prince [*chün-tzu*] is the wind, and that of the common people [*hsiao-jen*] the grass. The grass bends in the direction of the wind." [XII-19]

262. Tzu Lu asked about government, and the Master said: "Go before the people and be diligent in their affairs." When asked for further instruction, the Master said: "Be not weary." [XIII-1]

263. Chung Kung, chief minister of the Chi family, asked about government, and the Master said: "Employ first the services of your men, overlook minor faults, and then promote men of worth and talents." "How do I know a man of worth and talents in order to promote him?" said Chung Kung. "Promote those whom you

know," said the Master. "Those whom you do not know others will certainly not neglect." [XIII-2]

264. Tzu Lu said: "The prince of Wei is awaiting you, Sir, to join his government. What will you do first, Sir?"

The Master said: "The first thing needed is the rectification of names."

"So, indeed!" said Tzu Lu. "How pedantic it sounds! Why must there be such rectification?" "Yu! How rude you are!" said the Master. "*Chün-tzu* abstains from what he does not know. If names are not correct, then words are inappropriate; when the words are inappropriate, then things cannot be accomplished. Then rites and music will not flourish, punishments will not be properly administered, and the people have nowhere to put hand or foot. Therefore *chün-tzu* designates what can be properly stated, and only speaks of what can properly be carried into effect. *Chün-tzu*, in what he says, leaves nothing that is remiss." [XIII-3]

265. The Master said: "If a prince himself is upright, all will go well without orders. But if he himself is not upright, even though he gives orders, they will not be obeyed." [XIII-6]

266. The Master said: "In their governments, Lu and Wei are still brothers." [XIII-7]

267. When the master went to Wei, Jan Yu acted as driver of his carriage. The Master said: "How thriving is the population here!" "Since it is so thriving," asked Jan Yu, "what more shall be done for the people?" "Enrich them!" was the Master's reply. "And when they are enriched, what more shall be done?" "Educate them!" said the Master. [XIII-9]

268. The Master said: "Were any prince to employ me, in a year something could be done; in three years, the work could be completed." [XIII-10]

269. The Master said: "'Only if good men were to govern a country for one hundred years, would it really be

possible to transform the evil and do away with killings.'
How true is the saying!" [XIII-11]

270. The Master said: "If a prince has rendered himself
upright, he will have no difficulty in governing the
people. But if he cannot rectify himself, how can he
hope to rectify the people?" [XIII-13]

271. The Master said: "If a sage-king were to arise, *jen* would
prevail within one generation." [XIII-12]

• • •

❧ The Ta Hsüeh

PART ONE:

THE GENERAL STATEMENT

The General Statement of the *Ta Hsüeh* consists of the
Three Guiding Principles, of the three "main cords," and the
Eight Ethical-Political Items, or the eight "minor wires." The
Three Guiding Principles are (1) "manifestation of illustrious
virtue," (2) "loving the people," (3) "rest in the highest good."
The Eight Ethical-Political Items are (1) "investigation of
things," (2) "extension of knowledge," (3) "sincerity in one's
thoughts," (4) "rectification of one's heart," (5) "cultivation
of one's person," (6) "regulation of one's family," (7) "the
governing of one's state," and (8) "insurance of world peace."

❧   ☙

CHAPTER 1.

THE THREE GUIDING PRINCIPLES

1. The *Tao* of the Great Learning is to manifest illustrious
virtue, to love the people, and to rest in the highest good.

2. Only when one knows where one is to rest can one have a fixed purpose. Only with a fixed purpose can one achieve calmness of mind. Only with calmness of mind can one attain a tranquil repose. Only in a tranquil repose can one devote oneself to careful deliberation. Only through careful deliberation can one attain to the highest good.

CHAPTER II.

THE EIGHT ETHICAL-POLITICAL ITEMS

3. Everything has its roots and branches. Affairs have their end and beginning. To know what comes first and what comes last is to be near to the *Tao*.
4. The ancients who wished clearly to manifest illustrious virtue throughout the world would first govern their own states well. Wishing to govern their states well, they would first regulate their families. Wishing to regulate their families they would first cultivate their own persons. Wishing to cultivate their own persons, they would first rectify their hearts. Wishing to rectify their hearts, they would first seek sincerity in their thoughts. Wishing for sincerity in their thoughts, they would first extend their knowledge. The extension of knowledge lay in the investigation of things.
5. Only when many things are investigated is knowledge extended; only when knowledge is extended are thoughts sincere; only when thoughts are sincere are hearts rectified; only when hearts are rectified are our persons cultivated; only when our persons are cultivated are our families regulated; only when our families are regulated are states well governed; only when states are well governed can the world be at peace.
6. From the Son of Heaven down to the common people, all must consider the cultivation of the person as the root. When the root is in disorder, the branches cannot

grow in order. To treat the important as unimportant and to treat the unimportant as important—this should never be.

7. This is called knowing the root; this is called the perfection of knowledge.

• • •

ℰℴ The Chung Yung

CHAPTER I:

GENERAL STATEMENT

• • •

1. That which Heaven confers is called "man's nature"; the development of this nature is called the *Tao;* the cultivation of the *Tao is* called "culture."

   The *Tao* cannot be disregarded even for a moment. If it may be disregarded, it is not the *Tao.* Hence the *chün-tzu* is ever cautious regarding matter not yet seen and stands in awe of things not yet heard. There is nothing more evident than that which is hidden; there is nothing more manifest than what is minute. Therefore the *chün-tzu* is watchful even when he is alone.

2. To have none of the passions, such as pleasure and anger, sorrow and joy, surging up, is called being in a state of equilibrium [*chung*]. To have these passions surging up, but all in due time, is called being in a state of harmony. This state of equilibrium is the supreme root of the great universe, and this state of harmony is its far-reaching *Tao.* Once equilibrium and harmony are achieved, Heaven and earth shall maintain their proper positions and all things receive their full nourishment.

Chapter II:

THE DOCTRINE OF CHUNG YUNG

3. Chung-ni [i.e., Confucius] said: "The *chün-tzu* lives in accordance with the mean while the *hsiao-jen* lives contrary to it; the *chün-tzu* lives in accordance with the mean because he is the noble man and holds the timely mean; the *hsiao-jen* [lives contrary to] the mean because he is the common man, and knows no restraint."

4. The Master said: "Perfect indeed is the mean! For long people seldom had the capacity for it."

5. The Master said: "I know now why the *Tao* is not observed. The wise overlook it, and the foolish fall short of it. I know now why the *Tao* is not understood. Men of worth overlook it, and the unworthy fall short of it. There is no one who does not eat or drink, but there are few who can distinguish flavors."

6. The Master said: "How is the *Tao* neglected?"

7. The Master said: "Shun indeed was profoundly wise! He was fond of making inquiries and studying casual remarks of men. Then he withheld what was bad and displayed what was good. When he was confronted with two extremes, he held to the mean in dealing with the people. It was by acting this way that he was Shun!"

8. The Master said: "Men all say, 'I am wise,' but when driven and taken in a net, a trap, or a pitfall, they know not how to escape. Men all say, 'I am wise,' but when they choose the mean, they can hardly hold to it for a round month."

9. The Master said: "Hui [Confucius's disciple] was a man who chose to abide by the mean. When he found something good, he would hold to it firmly and never lose it."

10. The Master said: "The world, state, and family may be well governed; honors and emoluments may be declined; naked weapons may be trampled; but the mean can hardly be attained to."

11. Tzu Lu [Confucius's disciple] asked about courage. The Master said: "Do you mean the courage of the southern people or the courage of the northern people? Or do you mean the courage [one should cultivate]? of the brave man? To be patient and gentle in teaching others and not to revenge an injustice is the courage of the southern people. This is what the *chün-tzu* abides by. To take up arms and meet death without regret is the courage of the northern people. This is what the brave man abides by. "Therefore, the *chün-tzu* accords with others without being coerced. How firm is he in his courage! He maintains his mean position without throwing his weight to either side. How firm is he in his courage! When the *Tao* prevails in the country, he does not deviate from the principles he maintained in retirement. How firm is he in his courage! When the *Tao* fails to prevail in the country, he holds fast to his principle even if it means death. How firm is he in his courage!"

12. The Master said: "There are men who pursue what is abstruse and practice what is eccentric, so that they may be known to posterity. This is what I do not do.

    "Again, there are men who try to pursue the *Tao* but abandon it halfway. This is what I cannot do.

    "But the *chün-tzu* accords with the mean. Though he may be unknown and neglected by the world, he feels no regret. Indeed, only the sage was able enough for this."

CHAPTER III:

THE EXPOSITION OF THE TAO

13. The *Tao* of the *chün-tzu* is pervading and yet is concealed. Common men and women, however ignorant, may know it; yet in its ultimate development there is something which even the sage does not know. Common men and

women, however worthless, may practice it; yet in its ultimate development there is something which even the sage cannot practice. Vast as Heaven and earth are, men still find something therein to disparage. Hence, when the *chün-tzu* speaks of the *Tao* in greatness, the world cannot embrace it; when he speaks of it in its minuteness, the world cannot split it.

In the *Shih* it is said:

> Up to the heaven flies the hawk;
> Fishes leap in the deep.

This is to say that the *Tao* operates high up in the Heaven and down below on the earth. The *Tao* of the *chün-tzu* begins with the relationship of common men and women, but in its ultimate development it pervades Heaven and earth.

1.

THE SUBSTANCE OF THE TAO

14. The Master said: "The *Tao is* not far from man. When men try to pursue a *Tao* which is far from man, it is not the *Tao*. In the *Shih* it is said:

> In hewing an ax-shaft, in hewing an ax-shaft,
> The pattern is not far off.

"We grasp one ax-handle to hew the other; but if we look from one to the other, we still consider them as apart. Therefore the *chün-tzu* governs men by men; and as soon as they change [what is wrong], he stops.

"*Chung* [conscientiousness to others] and *shu* [altruism] are not far from the *Tao*. What you do not like done to yourself, do not do to others.

"In the *Tao* of the *chün-tzu* there are four things, none of which I have attained to. To serve my father as I would have my son serve me; I am not yet able to do that. To serve my sovereign as I would have my minister serve me; I am not yet able to do that. To serve my elder brother as I would have my younger brother serve me; I am not yet able to do that. To set an example in behaving to a friend as I would have him behave to me; I am not yet able to do that. The *chün-tzu* practices the ordinary virtues and pays attention to ordinary words. When there is deficiency, he never fails to make further efforts; when there is excess, he dares not go to the limit. His words must conform to his actions, and his actions must conform to his words. Is not the *chün-tzu* characterized by being cautious and earnest?"

15. The *chün-tzu* acts in accord with his station in life and does not desire what is beyond it. If he is wealthy and honorable, he acts like one wealthy and honorable; if poor and lowly, he acts like one poor and lowly. If he is among the barbarians, he does what one does among the barbarians; if he is in trouble or danger, he does what one does in trouble or danger. There is no situation in which the *chün-tzu is* not at ease with himself.

In a superior position he does not abuse his inferiors; in an inferior position he does not lean on his superiors. He rectifies himself and seeks nothing from others, and so he has no complaint. He does not complain against Heaven, nor does he grumble against men.

Thus the *chün-tzu* lives at ease and calmly awaits the Fate, whereas the *hsiao-jen* walks in danger and looks for lucky occurrences.

The Master said: "In the archer there is something like the *chün-tzu*. When he misses the target, he turns inward to look for the cause of his failure."

HOMER

THE ILIAD

(*ca.* 730 B.C.E.)

For the Greeks, who had no canon of sacred scriptures, the *Iliad* played a role in some ways analogous to the role of the Bible and the Qur'an for Jews, Christians, and Muslims. Many a Greek youth had to learn it by memory. Though it became an important source of lore concerning the Greek gods, the *Iliad* was principally a human drama, the story of a great ten-year war between the early Greeks and their enemy Troy (or Ilium). Upon closer inspection the *Iliad* focuses on a forty-day period in the last year of that war, and it is really the story of one great warrior, Achilleus (Achilles), and of the results of his own personal conflict with the leader of the Greek forces, King Agamemnon of Mycenae. The excerpt below tells the story of how that quarrel began and of Achilleus's resulting self-isolation.

Throughout the *Iliad* there are allusions to the other events of the war, which are told in other poems of the epic cycle. The ancient Greeks believed that the Trojan War was caused by the abduction of Helen, the beautiful wife of King Menelaus of Sparta (Agamemnon's brother), by Paris, son of the king of Troy. According to ancient calculations, the war occurred about four hundred years before Homer's day. However, there is no direct evidence for the war, and by the early 1800s modern scholars had come to doubt that it ever occurred. Then in the later nineteenth century an amateur German archeologist, Heinrich Schliemann, discovered and excavated Troy and Mycenae (Agamemnon's palace). Now many scholars agree that a war between the Mycenaean Greeks and Troy did occur sometime in the later thirteenth century B.C.E. By this time early Greek civilization had reached a peak of development under the strong influence of Egyptians, Phoenicians, and the "Minoans" of Crete. Soon after the supposed time of the Trojan War, this magnificent early state of civilization began to decline, probably from a combination of internal warfare and external marauders. For three to four centuries Greece was plunged into a Dark Age, in which even the art of writing was lost. But memories of the heroic times were transmitted orally by professional singers of tales.

The ancients believed that a single great poet composed the *Iliad* (and also the *Odyssey*). But two centuries ago scholars began to question this assumption, arguing instead that both works were pieced together by later compilers from materials composed orally by different anonymous poets over time. Thus arose the famous "Homeric Question," which pitted "Analysts" (multiple-author thesis) against "Unitarians" (single-author thesis). Most scholars today follow a solution first proposed by Milman Parry in the 1930s—that a person named Homer stands at the end of a long line of earlier bards, and that he composed the *Iliad* orally, drawing on their accumulated traditions, but weaving them into his own coherent and uniquely beautiful creation.

We know amazingly little about Homer's life. Most scholars today believe that he lived in the eighth century B.C.E. and that his home was most likely the island of Chios off the western shore of Asia Minor, where mainland Greeks had migrated during the Dark Age, taking with them the memories of the heroic age. According to one ancient tradition, Homer was blind; if so, sensory compensation may have heightened his sensitivity to his aural-oral form of art.

Homer's poem was one of the first signs of the great revival and flourishing of Greek civilization after the Dark Age. Homer deliberately placed the setting of his poem in the past, suppressing elements of his own surroundings which he knew did not exist in the times of Agamemnon. At the time he composed, the concept of a common Greek identity was still forming, so the Greeks in the *Iliad* are referred to as Achaeans, Danaans, or Argives. Homer had little inkling of the way people actually lived more than four hundred years before his time (in fact they lived in elaborately organized, bureaucratic palace societies), so most of the ways of life in the *Iliad* reflect the simpler life of Homer's more recent past—the Dark Age.

SOURCE

Homer. ca. 730 B.C.E. *Illiad*, In the Illiad of Homer. Trans. Richard Lattimore. Chicago and London: The University of Chicago Press. 1951.

Selections from: Book 1 (59-75)

BOOK ONE

SING, goddess, the anger of Peleus' son Achilleus [Achilles]
and its devastation, which put pains thousandfold upon the Achaians,
hurled in their multitudes to the house of Hades strong souls
of heroes, but gave their bodies to be the delicate feasting
of dogs, of all birds, and the will of Zeus was accomplished
since that time when first there stood in division of conflict
Atreus' son the lord of men and brilliant Achilleus.
      What god was it then set them together in bitter collision?
Zeus' son and Leto's, Apollo, who in anger at the king drove
the foul pestilence along the host, and the people perished,
since Atreus' son had dishonoured Chryses, priest of Apollo,
when he came beside the fast ships of the Achaians to ransom

back his daughter, carrying gifts beyond count and holding
in his hands wound on a staff of gold the ribbons of Apollo
who strikes from afar, and supplicated all the Achaians,
but above all Atreus' two sons, the marshals of the people:
'Sons of Atreus and you other strong-greaved Achaians,
to you may the gods grant who have their homes on Olympos
Priam's city to be plundered and a fair homecoming thereafter,
but may you give me back my own daughter and take the ransom,
giving honour to Zeus' son who strikes from afar, Apollo.'
    Then all the rest of the Achaians cried out in favour
that the priest be respected and the shining ransom be taken;
yet this pleased not the heart of Atreus' son Agamemnon,
but harshly he drove him away with a strong order upon him:
'Never let me find you again, old sir, near our hollow
ships, neither lingering now nor coming again hereafter,
for fear your staff and the god's ribbons help you no longer.
The girl I will not give back; sooner will old age come upon her
in my own house, in Argos, far from her own land, going
up and down by the loom and being in my bed as my companion.
So go now, do not make me angry; so you will be safer.'
    So he spoke, and the old man in terror obeyed him
and went silently away beside the murmuring sea beach.
Over and over the old man prayed as he walked in solitude
to King Apollo, whom Leto of the lovely hair bore: 'Hear me,
lord of the silver bow who set your power about Chryse
and Killa the sacrosanct, who are lord in strength over Tenedos,
Smintheus, if ever it pleased your heart that I built your temple,
if ever it pleased you that I burned all the rich thigh pieces
of bulls, of goats, then bring to pass this wish I pray for:
let your arrows make the Danaans pay for my tears shed.'
    So he spoke in prayer, and Phoibos [Phoebus] Apollo heard him,
and strode down along the pinnacles of Olympos, angered
in his heart, carrying across his shoulders the bow and the hooded
quiver; and the shafts clashed on the shoulders of the god walking
angrily. He came as night comes down and knelt then
apart and opposite the ships and let go an arrow.

Terrible was the clash that rose from the bow of silver.
First he went after the mules and the circling hounds, then let go
a tearing arrow against the men themselves and struck them.
The corpse fires burned everywhere and did not stop burning.
    Nine days up and down the host ranged the god's arrows,
but on the tenth Achilleus called the people to assembly;
a thing put into his mind by the goddess of the white arms, Hera,
who had pity upon the Danaans when she saw them dying.
Now when they were all assembled in one place together,
Achilleus of the swift feet stood up among them and spoke forth:
'Son of Atreus, I believe now that straggling backwards
we must make our way home if we can even escape death,
if fighting now must crush the Achaians and the plague likewise.
No, come, let us ask some holy man, some prophet,
even an interpreter of dreams, since a dream also
comes from Zeus, who can tell why Phoibos Apollo is so angry,
if for the sake of some vow, some hecatomb he blames us,
if given the fragrant smoke of lambs, of he goats, somehow
he can be made willing to beat the bane aside from us.'
    He spoke thus and sat down again, and among them stood up
Kalchas, Thestor's son, far the best of the bird interpreters,
who knew all things that were, the things to come and the things past,
who guided into the land of Ilion the ships of the Achaians
through that seercraft of his own that Phoibos Apollo gave him.
He in kind intention toward all stood forth and addressed them:
'You have bidden me, Achilleus beloved of Zeus, to explain to
you this anger of Apollo the lord who strikes from afar. Then
I will speak; yet make me a promise and swear before me
readily by word and work of your hands to defend me,
since I believe I shall make a man angry who holds great kingship
over the men of Argos, and all the Achaians obey him.
For a king when he is angry with a man beneath him is too strong,
and suppose even for the day itself he swallow down his anger,
he still keeps bitterness that remains until its fulfilment
deep in his chest. Speak forth then, tell me if you will protect me.'
    Then in answer again spoke Achilleus of the swift feet:

'Speak, interpreting whatever you know, and fear nothing.
In the name of Apollo beloved of Zeus to whom you, Kalchas,
make your prayers when you interpret the gods' will to the Danaans,
no man so long as I am alive above earth and see daylight
shall lay the weight of his hands on you beside the hollow ships,
not one of all the Danaans, even if you mean Agamemnon,
who now claims to be far the greatest of all the Achaians.'
    At this the blameless seer took courage again and spoke forth:
'No, it is not for the sake of some vow or hecatomb he blames us,
but for the sake of his priest whom Agamemnon dishonoured
and would not give him back his daughter nor accept the ransom.
Therefore the archer sent griefs against us and will send them
still, nor sooner thrust back the shameful plague from the Danaans
until we give the glancing-eyed girl back to her father
without price, without ransom, and lead also a blessed hecatomb
to Chryse; thus we might propitiate and persuade him.'
    He spoke thus and sat down again, and among them stood up
Atreus' son the hero wide-ruling Agamemnon
raging, the heart within filled black to the brim with anger
from beneath, but his two eyes showed like fire in their blazing.
First of all he eyed Kalchas bitterly and spoke to him:
'Seer of evil: never yet have you told me a good thing.
Always the evil things are dear to your heart to prophesy,
but nothing excellent have you said nor ever accomplished.
Now once more you make divination to the Danaans, argue
forth your reason why he who strikes from afar afflicts them,
because I for the sake of the girl Chryseis would not take
the shining ransom; and indeed I wish greatly to have her
in my own house; since I like her better than Klytaimestra
my own wife, for in truth she is no way inferior,
neither in build nor stature nor wit, not in accomplishment.
Still I am willing to give her back, if such is the best way.
I myself desire that my people be safe, not perish.
Find me then some prize that shall be my own, lest I only
among the Argives go without, since that were unfitting;
you are all witnesses to this thing, that my prize goes elsewhere.'

Then in answer again spoke brilliant swift-footed Achilleus:
'Son of Atreus, most lordly, greediest for gain of all men,
how shall the great-hearted Achaians give you a prize now?
There is no great store of things lying about I know of.
But what we took from the cities by storm has been distributed;
it is unbecoming for the people to call back things once given.
No, for the present give the girl back to the god; we Achaians
thrice and four times over will repay you, if ever Zeus gives
into our hands the strong-walled citadel of Troy to be plundered.'
Then in answer again spoke powerful Agamemnon:
'Not that way, good fighter though you be, godlike Achilleus,
strive to cheat, for you will not deceive, you will not persuade me.
What do you want? To keep your own prize and have me sit here
lacking one? Are you ordering me to give this girl back?
Either the great-hearted Achaians shall give me a new prize
chosen according to my desire to atone for the girl lost,
or else if they will not give me one I myself shall take her,
your own prize, or that of Aias [Ajax], or that of Odysseus,
going myself in person; and he whom I visit will be bitter.
Still, these are things we shall deliberate again hereafter.
Come, now, we must haul a black ship down to the bright sea,
and assemble rowers enough for it, and put on board it
the hecatomb, and the girl herself, Chryseis of the fair cheeks,
and let there be one responsible man in charge of her,
either Aias or Idomeneus or brilliant Odysseus,
or you yourself, son of Peleus, most terrifying of all men,
to reconcile by accomplishing sacrifice the archer.'
Then looking darkly at him Achilleus of the swift feet spoke:
'O wrapped in shamelessness, with your mind forever on profit,
how shall any one of the Achaians readily obey you
either to go on a journey or to fight men strongly in battle?
I for my part did not come here for the sake of the Trojan
spearmen to fight against them, since to me they have done nothing.
Never yet have they driven away my cattle or my horses,
never in Phthia where the soil is rich and men grow great did they
spoil my harvest, since indeed there is much that lies between us,

the shadowy mountains and the echoing sea; but for your sake,
o great shamelessness, we followed, to do you favour,
you with the dog's eyes, to win your honour and Menelaos'
from the Trojans. You forget all this or else you care nothing.
And now my prize you threaten in person to strip from me,
for whom I laboured much, the gift of the sons of the Achaians.
Never, when the Achaians sack some well-founded citadel
of the Trojans, do I have a prize that is equal to your prize.
Always the greater part of the painful fighting is the work of
my hands; but when the time comes to distribute the booty
yours is far the greater reward, and I with some small thing
yet dear to me go back to my ships when I am weary with fighting.
Now I am returning to Phthia, since it is much better
to go home again with my curved ships, and I am minded no longer
to stay here dishonoured and pile up your wealth and your luxury.'

    Then answered him in turn the lord of men Agamemnon:
'Run away by all means if your heart drives you. I will not entreat
you to stay here for my sake. There are others with me
who will do me honour, and above all Zeus of the counsels.
To me you are the most hateful of all the kings whom the gods love.
Forever quarrelling is dear to your heart, and wars and battles;
and if you are very strong indeed, that is a god's gift.
Go home then with your own ships and your own companions,
be king over the Myrmidons. I care nothing about you.
I take no account of your anger. But here is my threat to you.
Even as Phoibos Apollo is taking away my Chryseis,
I shall convey her back in my own ship, with my own
followers; but I shall take the fair-cheeked Briseis,
your prize, I myself going to your shelter, that you may learn well
how much greater I am than you, and another man may shrink back
from likening himself to me and contending against me.'

    So he spoke. And the anger came on Peleus' son, and within
his shaggy breast the heart was divided two ways, pondering
whether to draw from beside his thigh the sharp sword, driving away
all those who stood between and kill the son of Atreus,
or else to check the spleen within and keep down his anger.

Now as he weighed in mind and spirit these two courses
and was drawing from its scabbard the great sword, Athene descended
from the sky. For Hera the goddess of the white arms sent her,
who loved both men equally in her heart and cared for them.
The goddess standing behind Peleus' son caught him by the fair hair,
appearing to him only, for no man of the others saw her.
Achilleus in amazement turned about, and straightway
knew Pallas Athene and the terrible eyes shining.
He uttered winged words and addressed her: 'Why have you come now,
o child of Zeus of the aegis, once more? Is it that you may see
the outrageousness of the son of Atreus Agamemnon?
Yet will I tell you this thing, and I think it shall be accomplished.
By such acts of arrogance he may even lose his own life.'

Then in answer the goddess grey-eyed Athene spoke to him:
'I have come down to stay your anger—but will you obey me?—
from the sky; and the goddess of the white arms Hera sent me,
who loves both of you equally in her heart and cares for you.
Come then, do not take your sword in your hand, keep clear of fighting,
though indeed with words you may abuse him, and it will be that way.
And this also will I tell you and it will be a thing accomplished.
Some day three times over such shining gifts shall be given you
by reason of this outrage. Hold your hand then, and obey us.'

Then in answer again spoke Achilleus of the swift feet:
'Goddess, it is necessary that I obey the word of you two,
angry though I am in my heart. So it will be better.
If any man obeys the gods, they listen to him also.'

He spoke, and laid his heavy hand on the silver sword hilt
and thrust the great blade back into the scabbard nor disobeyed
the word of Athene. And she went back again to Olympos
to the house of Zeus of the aegis with the other divinities.

But Peleus' son once again in words of derision
spoke to Atreides, and did not yet let go of his anger:
'You wine sack, with a dog's eyes, with a deer's heart. Never
once have you taken courage in your heart to arm with your people
for battle, or go into ambuscade with the best of the Achaians.
No, for in such things you see death. Far better to your mind

is it, all along the widespread host of the Achaians
to take away the gifts of any man who speaks up against you.
King who feed on your people, since you rule nonentities;
otherwise, son of Atreus, this were your last outrage.
But I will tell you this and swear a great oath upon it:
in the name of this sceptre, which never again will bear leaf nor
branch, now that it has left behind the cut stump in the mountains
nor shall it ever blossom again, since the bronze blade stripped
bark and leafage, and now at last the sons of the Achaians
carry it in their hands in state when they administer
the justice of Zeus. And this shall be a great oath before you:
some day longing for Achilleus will come to the sons of the Achaians,
all of them. Then stricken at heart though you be, you will be able
to do nothing, when in their numbers before man-slaughtering Hektor
they drop and die. And then you will eat out the heart within you
in sorrow, that you did no honour to the best of the Achaians.'
　　　Thus spoke Peleus' son and dashed to the ground the sceptre
studded with golden nails, and sat down again. But Atreides
raged still on the other side, and between them Nestor
the fair-spoken rose up, the lucid speaker of Pylos,
from whose lips the streams of words ran sweeter than honey.
In his time two generations of mortal men had perished,
those who had grown up with him and they who had been born to
these in sacred Pylos, and he was king in the third age.
He in kind intention toward both stood forth and addressed them:
'Oh, for shame. Great sorrow comes on the land of Achaia.
Now might Priam and the sons of Priam in truth be happy,
and all the rest of the Trojans be visited in their hearts with gladness,
were they to hear all this wherein you two are quarrelling,
you, who surpass all Danaans in council, in fighting.
Yet be persuaded. Both of you are younger than I am.
Yes, and in my time I have dealt with better men than
you are, and never once did they disregard me. Never
yet have I seen nor shall see again such men as these were,
men like Peirithoös, and Dryas, shepherd of the people,
Kaineus and Exadios, godlike Polyphemos,

or Theseus, Aigeus' son, in the likeness of the immortals.
These were the strongest generation of earth-born mortals, the
    strongest, and they
fought against the strongest, the beast men
living within the mountains, and terribly they destroyed them.
I was of the company of these men, coming from Pylos,
a long way from a distant land, since they had summoned me.
And I fought single-handed, yet against such men
no one of the mortals now alive upon earth could do battle. And also
these listened to the counsels I gave and heeded my bidding.
Do you also obey, since to be persuaded is better.
You, great man that you are, yet do not take the girl away
but let her be, a prize as the sons of the Achaians gave her
first. Nor, son of Peleus, think to match your strength with
the king, since never equal with the rest is the portion of honour
of the sceptred king to whom Zeus gives magnificence. Even
though you are the stronger man, and the mother who bore you
    was immortal,
yet is this man greater who is lord over more than you rule.
Son of Atreus, give up your anger; even I entreat you
to give over your bitterness against Achilleus, he who
stands as a great bulwark of battle over all the Achaians.'
    Then in answer again spoke powerful Agamemnon:
'Yes, old sir, all this you have said is fair and orderly.
Yet here is a man who wishes to be above all others,
who wishes to hold power over all, and to be lord of
all, and give them their orders, yet I think one will not obey him.
And if the everlasting gods have made him a spearman,
yet they have not given him the right to speak abusively.'
    Then looking at him darkly brilliant Achilleus answered him:
'So must I be called of no account and a coward
if I must carry out every order you may happen to give me.
Tell other men to do these things, but give me no more
commands, since I for my part have no intention to obey you.
And put away in your thoughts this other thing I tell you.
With my hands I will not fight for the girl's sake, neither

with you nor any other man, since you take her away who gave her.
But of all the other things that are mine beside my fast black
ship, you shall take nothing away against my pleasure.
Come, then, only try it, that these others may see also;
instantly your own black blood will stain my spearpoint.'
     So these two after battling in words of contention
stood up, and broke the assembly beside the ships of the Achaians.
Peleus' son went back to his balanced ships and his shelter
with Patroklos, Menoitios' son, and his own companions.
But the son of Atreus drew a fast ship down to the water
and allotted into it twenty rowers and put on board it
the hecatomb for the god and Chryseis of the fair cheeks
leading her by the hand. And in charge went crafty Odysseus.
     These then putting out went over the ways of the water
while Atreus' son told his people to wash off their defilement.
And they washed it away and threw the washings into the salt sea.
Then they accomplished perfect hecatombs to Apollo,
of bulls and goats along the beach of the barren salt sea.
The savour of the burning swept in circles up to the bright sky.
     Thus these were busy about the army. But Agamemnon
did not give up his anger and the first threat he made to Achilleus,
but to Talthybios he gave his orders and Eurybates
who were heralds and hard-working henchmen to him: 'Go now
to the shelter of Peleus' son Achilleus, to bring back
Briseis of the fair cheeks leading her by the hand. And if he
will not give her, I must come in person to take her
with many men behind me, and it will be the worse for him.'
     He spoke and sent them forth with this strong order upon them.
They went against their will beside the beach of the barren
salt sea, and came to the shelters and the ships of the Myrmidons.
The man himself they found beside his shelter and his black ship
sitting. And Achilleus took no joy at all when he saw them.
These two terrified and in awe of the king stood waiting
quietly, and did not speak a word at all nor question him.
But he knew the whole matter in his own heart, and spoke first:
'Welcome, heralds, messengers of Zeus and of mortals.

Draw near. You are not to blame in my sight, but Agamemnon
who sent the two of you here for the sake of the girl Briseis.
Go then, illustrious Patroklos, and bring the girl forth
and give her to these to be taken away. Yet let them be witnesses
in the sight of the blessed gods, in the sight of mortal
men and of this cruel king, if ever hereafter
there shall be need of me to beat back the shameful destruction
from the rest. For surely in ruinous heart he makes sacrifice
and has not wit enough to look behind and before him
that the Achaians fighting beside their ships shall not perish.'
      So he spoke, and Patroklos obeyed his beloved companion.
He led forth from the hut Briseis of the fair cheeks and gave her
to be taken away; and they walked back beside the ships of the Achaians,
and the woman all unwilling went with them still. But Achilleus
weeping went and sat in sorrow apart from his companions
beside the beach of the grey sea looking out on the infinite water.
Many times stretching forth his hands he called on his mother:
'Since, my mother, you bore me to be a man with a short life,
therefore Zeus of the loud thunder on Olympos should grant me
honour at least. But now he has given me not even a little.
Now the son of Atreus, powerful Agamemnon,
has dishonoured me, since he has taken away my prize and keeps it.'
      So he spoke in tears and the lady his mother heard him
as she sat in the depths of the sea at the side of her aged father,
and lightly she emerged like a mist from the grey water.
She came and sat beside him as he wept, and stroked him
with her hand and called him by name and spoke to him: 'Why then,
child, do you lament? What sorrow has come to your heart now?
Tell me, do not hide it in your mind, and thus we shall both know.'
      Sighing heavily Achilleus of the swift feet answered her:
'You know; since you know why must I tell you all this?
We went against Thebe, the sacred city of Eëtion,
and the city we sacked, and carried everything back to this place,
and the sons of the Achaians made a fair distribution
and for Atreus' son they chose out Chryseis of the fair cheeks.
Then Chryses, priest of him who strikes from afar, Apollo,

came beside the fast ships of the bronze-armoured Achaians to ransom
back his daughter, carrying gifts beyond count and holding
in his hands wound on a staff of gold the ribbons of Apollo
who strikes from afar, and supplicated all the Achaians,
but above all Atreus' two sons, the marshals of the people.
Then all the rest of the Achaians cried out in favour
that the priest be respected and the shining ransom be taken;
yet this pleased not the heart of Atreus' son Agamemnon,
but harshly he sent him away with a strong order upon him.
The old man went back again in anger, but Apollo
listened to his prayer, since he was very dear to him, and let
the wicked arrow against the Argives. And now the people
were dying one after another while the god's shafts ranged
everywhere along the wide host of the Achaians, till the seer
knowing well the truth interpreted the designs of the archer.
It was I first of all urged then the god's appeasement;
and the anger took hold of Atreus' son and in speed standing
he uttered his threat against me, and now it is a thing accomplished.
For the girl the glancing-eyed Achaians are taking to Chryse
in a fast ship, also carrying to the king presents. But even
now the heralds went away from my shelter leading
Briseus' daughter, whom the sons of the Achaians gave me.
You then, if you have power to, protect your own son, going
to Olympos and supplicating Zeus, if ever before now
either by word you comforted Zeus' heart or by action.
Since it is many times in my father's halls I have heard you
making claims, when you said you only among the immortals
beat aside shameful destruction from Kronos' son the dark-misted,
that time when all the other Olympians sought to bind him,
Hera and Poseidon and Pallas Athene. Then you,
goddess, went and set him free from his shackles, summoning
in speed the creature of the hundred hands to tall Olympos,
that creature the gods name Briareus, but all men
Aigaios' son, but he is far greater in strength than his father.
He rejoicing in the glory of it sat down by Kronion,

and the rest of the blessed gods were frightened and gave up
    binding him.
Sit beside him and take his knees and remind him of these things
now, if perhaps he might be willing to help the Trojans,
and pin the Achaians back against the ships and the water,
dying, so that thus they may all have profit of their own king,
that Atreus' son wide-ruling Agamemnon may recognize
his madness, that he did no honour to the best of the Achaians.'
    Thetis answered him then letting the tears fall: 'Ah me,
my child. Your birth was bitterness. Why did I raise you?
If only you could sit by your ships untroubled, not weeping,
since indeed your lifetime is to be short, of no length.
Now it has befallen that your life must be brief and bitter
beyond all men's. To a bad destiny I bore you in my chambers.
But I will go to cloud-dark Olympos and ask this
thing of Zeus who delights in the thunder. Perhaps he will do it.
Do you therefore continuing to sit by your swift ships
be angry at the Achaians and stay away from all fighting.
For Zeus went to the blameless Aithiopians at the
Ocean yesterday to feast, and the rest of the gods went with him.
On the twelfth day he will be coming back to Olympos,
and then I will go for your sake to the house of Zeus, bronze-founded,
and take him by the knees and I think I can persuade him.'
    So speaking she went away from that place and left him
sorrowing in his heart for the sake of the fair-girdled woman
whom they were taking by force against his will. But Odysseus
meanwhile drew near to Chryse conveying the sacred hecatomb.
These when they were inside the many-hollowed harbour
took down and gathered together the sails and stowed them in
    the black ship,
let down mast by the forestays, and settled it into the mast crutch
easily, and rowed her in with oars to the mooring.
They threw over the anchor stones and made fast the stern cables
and themselves stepped out on to the break of the sea beach,
and led forth the hecatomb to the archer Apollo,

and Chryseis herself stepped forth from the sea-going vessel.
Odysseus of the many designs guided her to the altar
and left her in her father's arms and spoke a word to him:
'Chryses, I was sent here by the lord of men Agamemnon
to lead back your daughter and accomplish a sacred hecatomb
to Apollo on behalf of the Danaans, that we may propitiate
the lord who has heaped unhappiness and tears on the Argives.'

He spoke, and left her in his arms. And he received gladly
his beloved child. And the men arranged the sacred hecatomb
for the god in orderly fashion around the strong-founded altar.
Next they washed their hands and took up the scattering barley.
Standing among them with lifted arms Chryses prayed in a great voice:
'Hear me, lord of the silver bow, who set your power about
Chryse and Killa the sacrosanct, who are lord in strength over
Tenedos; if once before you listened to my prayers
and did me honour and smote strongly the host of the Achaians,
so one more time bring to pass the wish that I pray for.
Beat aside at last the shameful plague from the Danaans.'

So he spoke in prayer, and Phoibos Apollo heard him.
And when all had made prayer and flung down the scattering barley
first they drew back the victims' heads and slaughtered them
        and skinned them,
and cut away the meat from the thighs and wrapped them in fat,
making a double fold, and laid shreds of flesh upon them.
The old man burned these on a cleft stick and poured the gleaming
wine over, while the young men with forks in their hands stood
        about him.
But when they had burned the thigh pieces and tasted the vitals,
they cut all the remainder into pieces and spitted them
and roasted all carefully and took off the pieces.
Then after they had finished the work and got the feast ready
they feasted, nor was any man's hunger denied a fair portion.
But when they had put away their desire for eating and drinking,
the young men filled the mixing bowls with pure wine, passing
a portion to all, when they had offered drink in the goblets.
All day long they propitiated the god with singing,

chanting a splendid hymn to Apollo, these young Achaians,
singing to the one who works from afar, who listened in gladness.
  Afterwards when the sun went down and darkness came onward
they lay down and slept beside the ship's stern cables.
But when the young Dawn showed again with her rosy fingers,
they put forth to sea toward the wide camp of the Achaians.
And Apollo who works from afar sent them a favouring stern wind.
They set up the mast again and spread on it the white sails,
and the wind blew into the middle of the sail, and at the cutwater
blue wave rose and sang strongly as the ship went onward.
She ran swiftly cutting across the swell her pathway.
But when they had come back to the wide camp of the Achaians
they hauled the black ship up on the mainland, high up
on the sand, and underneath her they fixed the long props.
Afterwards they scattered to their own ships and their shelters.
  But that other still sat in anger beside his swift ships,
Peleus' son divinely born, Achilleus of the swift feet.
Never now would he go to assemblies where men win glory,
never more into battle, but continued to waste his heart out
sitting there, though he longed always for the clamour and fighting.
  But when the twelfth dawn after this day appeared, the gods who
live forever came back to Olympos all in a body
and Zeus led them; nor did Thetis forget the entreaties
of her son, but she emerged from the sea's waves early
in the morning and went up to the tall sky and Olympos.
She found Kronos' broad-browed son apart from the others
sitting upon the highest peak of rugged Olympos.
She came and sat beside him with her left hand embracing
his knees, but took him underneath the chin with her right hand
and spoke in supplication to lord Zeus son of Kronos:
'Father Zeus, if ever before in word or action
I did you favour among the immortals, now grant what I ask for.
Now give honour to my son short-lived beyond all other
mortals. Since even now the lord of men Agamemnon
dishonours him, who has taken away his prize and keeps it.
Zeus of the counsels, lord of Olympos, now do him honour.

So long put strength into the Trojans, until the Achaians
give my son his rights, and his honour is increased among them.'
      She spoke thus. But Zeus who gathers the clouds made no answer
but sat in silence a long time. And Thetis, as she had taken
his knees, clung fast to them and urged once more her question:
'Bend your head and promise me to accomplish this thing,
or else refuse it, you have nothing to fear, that I may know
by how much I am the most dishonoured of all gods.'
      Deeply disturbed Zeus who gathers the clouds answered her:
'This is a disastrous matter when you set me in conflict
with Hera, and she troubles me with recriminations.
Since even as things are, forever among the immortals
she is at me and speaks of how I help the Trojans in battle.
Even so, go back again now, go away, for fear she
see us. I will look to these things that they be accomplished.
See then, I will bend my head that you may believe me.
For this among the immortal gods is the mightiest witness
I can give, and nothing I do shall be vain nor revocable
nor a thing unfulfilled when I bend my head in assent to it.'
      He spoke, the son of Kronos, and nodded his head with
            the dark brows,
and the immortally anointed hair of the great god
swept from his divine head, and all Olympos was shaken.
      So these two who had made their plans separated, and Thetis
leapt down again from shining Olympos into the sea's depth,
but Zeus went back to his own house, and all the gods rose up
from their chairs to greet the coming of their father, not one had courage
to keep his place as the father advanced, but stood up to greet him.
Thus he took his place on the throne; yet Hera was not
ignorant, having seen how he had been plotting counsels
with Thetis the silver-footed, the daughter of the sea's ancient,
and at once she spoke revilingly to Zeus son of Kronos:
'Treacherous one, what god has been plotting counsels with you?
Always it is dear to your heart in my absence to think of
secret things and decide upon them. Never have you patience
frankly to speak forth to me the thing that you purpose.'

Then to her the father of gods and men made answer:
'Hera, do not go on hoping that you will hear all my
thoughts, since these will be too hard for you, though you are my wife.
Any thought that it is right for you to listen to, no one
neither man nor any immortal shall hear it before you.
But anything that apart from the rest of the gods I wish to
plan, do not always question each detail nor probe me.'
      Then the goddess the ox-eyed lady Hera answered:
'Majesty, son of Kronos, what sort of thing have you spoken?
Truly too much in time past I have not questioned nor probed you,
but you are entirely free to think out whatever pleases you.
Now, though, I am terribly afraid you were won over
by Thetis the silver-footed, the daughter of the sea's ancient.
For early in the morning she sat beside you and took your
knees, and I think you bowed your head in assent to do honour
to Achilleus, and to destroy many beside the ships of the Achaians.'
      Then in return Zeus who gathers the clouds made answer:
'Dear lady, I never escape you, you are always full of suspicion.
Yet thus you can accomplish nothing surely, but be more
distant from my heart than ever, and it will be the worse for you.
If what you say is true, then that is the way I wish it.
But go then, sit down in silence, and do as I tell you,
for fear all the gods, as many as are on Olympos, can do nothing
if I come close and lay my unconquerable hands upon you.'
      He spoke, and the goddess the ox-eyed lady Hera was frightened
and went and sat down in silence wrenching her heart to obedience,
and all the Uranian gods in the house of Zeus were troubled.
Hephaistos the renowned smith rose up to speak among them,
to bring comfort to his beloved mother, Hera of the white arms:
'This will be a disastrous matter and not endurable
If you two are to quarrel thus for the sake of mortals
and bring brawling among the gods. There will be no pleasure
in the stately feast at all, since vile things will be uppermost.
And I entreat my mother, though she herself understands it,
to be ingratiating toward our father Zeus, that no longer
our father may scold her and break up the quiet of our feasting.

For if the Olympian who handles the lightning should be minded
to hurl us out of our places, he is far too strong for any.
Do you therefore approach him again with words made gentle,
and at once the Olympian will be gracious again to us.'

He spoke, and springing to his feet put a two-handled goblet
into his mother's hands and spoke again to her once more:
'Have patience, my mother, and endure it, though you be saddened,
for fear that, dear as you are, I see you before my own eyes
struck down, and then sorry though I be I shall not be able
to do anything. It is too hard to fight against the Olympian.
There was a time once before now I was minded to help you,
and he caught me by the foot and threw me from the magic threshold,
and all day long I dropped helpless, and about sunset
I landed in Lemnos, and there was not much life left in me.
After that fall it was the Sintian men who took care of me.'

He spoke, and the goddess of the white arms Hera smiled at him,
and smiling she accepted the goblet out of her son's hand.
Thereafter beginning from the left he poured drinks for the other
gods, dipping up from the mixing bowl the sweet nectar.
But among the blessed immortals uncontrollable laughter
went up as they saw Hephaistos bustling about the palace.

Thus thereafter the whole day long until the sun went under
they feasted, nor was anyone's hunger denied a fair portion,
nor denied the beautifully wrought lyre in the hands of Apollo
nor the antiphonal sweet sound of the Muses singing.

Afterwards when the light of the flaming sun went under
they went away each one to sleep in his home where
for each one the far-renowned strong-handed Hephaisto
had built a house by means of his craftsmanship and cunning.
Zeus the Olympian and lord of the lightning went to
his own bed, where always he lay when sweet sleep came on him.
Going up to the bed he slept and Hera of the gold throne beside him.

Max Weber

(1864-1920)

THE PROTESTANT ETHIC AND THE SPIRIT OF CAPITALISM

(1905)

Max Weber was from a wealthy middle class family of textile manufacturers in Erfurt (in central Germany), but grew up in Berlin, the Prussian capital of the newly unified Germany, where his father was a lawyer and a member of the new national legislature. Weber's mother, from a pietistic Lutheran family, showed strong humanitarian interests. A severe childhood illness isolated Weber in his youth and enabled him to indulge a voracious appetite for knowledge and study. At the university, however, he assumed the more usual extroverted mold of many nineteenth century German students. He also studied intensely in the fields of law and economics, for him a fruitful combination. Torn between his love of study and his desire to be an active man of the world, Weber at first trained for a career as lawyer or judge, but finally became more and more involved with teaching and research, which culminated in an enormous study of Prussian agricultural labor and an appointment as professor at Freiburg University. Then, after accepting a new offer at prestigious Heidelberg University, Weber at age 33 suffered a complete mental collapse which left him unable to work for more than four years. After this period he eased back into teaching responsibilities, but finally money from an inheritance enabled him to leave the university and spend his full time in intensive research and writing during the final thirteen years of his life. In 1893, Weber married Marianne Schnitger, who became a prominent German author, feminist, and political leader.

Weber's research and knowledge were exceedingly wide-ranging. He wrote extensively in the field of sociology of religion, dealing in depth with Confucianism and Hinduism. He tried to show the inter-relationship between religion and social structure, revealing the unintended effects of religious belief upon social and economic life (much as he does in the excerpts below for Protestant beliefs). His final, unfinished work was a massive study of economy and society, an investigation of sociological concepts using historical evidence to clarify the explanatory role of these concepts and to make them into more precise tools of analysis. Weber's analyses have provided fertile ground for debate among later sociologists, and he remains one of the giants of the discipline.

A central interest of Weber's study of society was the role of religion in shaping people's economic activities throughout the world. Weber believed that the development of economic rationalism, specifically capitalism, in Western European society made it fundamentally different from all other cultures. For him capitalism was more a "spirit" than an economic system; it was a set of attitudes which led capitalists to accumulate wealth for reinvestment and further accumulation, rather than consuming it for personal pleasure, status, or display. Weber argued that the growth of these attitudes went hand in hand with religious attitudes that are observable in certain forms of Christianity, especially among early modern Calvinists in Great Britain, but that could be partly traced back to medieval monasticism. Calvinists practiced an "innerworldly asceticism"; like medieval monks they denied themselves the worldly enjoyments associated with economic consumption, but—unlike the monks—they did not withdraw from the world into a monastery. For them, work in a secular occupation could be a religious "calling," and they devoted themselves to work with a religious fervor. They believed (contrary to Calvin himself) that economic success was a sign of God's favor, so they accumulated vast quantities of wealth; but instead of spending it, they reinvested it, thus becoming even wealthier. The ironic result was that ascetic religious attitudes led to unprecedented material prosperity.

SOURCE

Weber, Max. *Gesammelte Aufsätze zur Religionssoziologie*. Vol. 1. Tübingen: J.C.B. Mohr (Paul Siebeck), 1922. Pp. 1-4, 30-32, 116, 162, 190-192, 202-206.

Selections from: *The Protestant Ethic and The Spirit of Capitalism* (translated by Phillip Stump)

Pp. 1-4

An offspring of the world of modern European civilization will unavoidably and rightly consider problems in world history by asking what chain of events has led to the fact that precisely in the West, and only here, cultural forms appeared which nevertheless (or at least we so imagine) developed in the direction of universal meaning and validity. [Weber gives numerous examples, such as modern science, the bureaucratic, parliamentary state, etc.] And it is also thus with the most fateful power of modern life—capitalism.

"Drive for economic gain," "desire for profit,"—for monetary profit, the highest possible monetary profit—in itself has nothing to do with capitalism. This struggle was found and is still found among waiters, doctors, cabdrivers, artists, prostitutes, corruptible officials, soldiers, thieves, crusaders, gamblers, and beggars—one could say "in all sorts and conditions of men," in all epochs and lands of the earth. It is in the kindergarten of the history of civilization that people give up this naïve definition of capitalism once and for all. Unlimited greed for profit is not in the slightest degree similar to capitalism, much less to the "spirit" of capitalism. Capitalism can in fact be identical to the restraint of this greed, at least to the rational moderation of this irrational drive. But, to be sure, capitalism is identical to the drive for profit, in the continuous, rational capitalistic firm: drive for ever-renewed profit, for maximization of profit. . . .

Pp. 30-32

In the title of this study the somewhat pretentious sounding term "spirit of capitalism" is used. What is to be understood by this term? . . .

If an object can be found at all for which the use of this term "spirit of capitalism" has any meaning, it can only be something "historically unique," i.e., a complex of connections in historical reality that we can synthesize conceptually into a whole from the viewpoint of its meaning for culture. . . .

If we succeed in identifying this object which we seek to analyze and explain historically, it cannot be a conceptual definition that we are dealing with, but, at least initially, a provisional demonstration of what we mean here by the "spirit" of capitalism. Such a demonstration is in fact essential to the subject of our investigation, and we rely for this purpose on a document which reveals this "spirit," which contains in nearly classic purity the demonstration of what matters most here, and nevertheless offers the advantage that it is detached from all direct connection with the religious, therefore—for our theme—"free from presuppositions":

> Remember that time is money. He that
> can earn ten shillings a day by his labor, and
> goes abroad, or sits idle one half of that day,

though he spend but sixpence during his diversion or idleness, ought not to reckon that the only expense; he has really spent or thrown away five shillings besides.

Remember that credit is money. If a man lets his money lie in my hands after it is due, he gives me the interest, or so much as I can make of it during that time. This amounts to a considerable sum where a man has a good and large credit, and makes good use of it.

Remember that money is of a prolific generating nature. Money can beget money, and its offspring can beget more, and so on. Five shillings turned is six: turned again is seven and three pence; an so on until it becomes one hundred pounds. The more there is of it, the more it produces every turning, so that the profits rise quicker and quicker. He that kills a breeding sow, destroys all her offspring to the thousandth generation. He that murders a crown, destroys all it might have produced, even scores of pounds.

Remember that six pounds a year is but a groat a day. For this little sum (which may be daily wasted in time or expense unperceived) a man of credit may on his own security have the constant possession and use of one hundred pounds. So much in stock briskly turned by an industrious man, produces great advantage.

Remember this saying, *That the good Paymaster is Lord of another Man's Purse.* He that is known to pay punctually and exactly to the time he promises, may at any time, and on any occasion, raise all of the money his friends can spare. This is sometimes of great use:

therefore never keep borrowed money an hour beyond the time you promised, lest a disappointment shuts up your friends purse forever.

The most trifling actions that affect a man's credit, are to be regarded. The sound of your hammer at five in the morning or nine at night, heard by a creditor, makes him easy six months longer. But if he sees you at a billiard table, or hears your voice in a tavern, when you should be at work, he sends for his money the next day.

It shows, besides, that you are mindful of what you owe; it makes you appear a careful as well as an honest man; and that still increases your credit.

Beware of thinking all your own that you possess, and of living accordingly. It is a mistake that many people who have credit fall into. To prevent this, keep an exact account for some time of both your expenses and your incomes. If you take the pains at first to mention particulars, it will have this good effect; you will discover how wonderfully small trifling expenses mount up to large sums, and will discern what might have been, and may for the future be saved. . . .

For six pounds a year you may have the use of one hundred pounds, provided you are a man of known prudence and honesty. He that spends a groat a day idly spends idly above six pounds a year, which is the price for the use of one hundred pounds. He that wastes idly a groat's worth of his time per day, one day with another, wastes the privilege of using one hundred pounds each day. He that idly loses five shillings' worth of time loses five shillings, and might as prudently throw five shillings into the sea. He that loses five shillings not only loses that sum, but all the advantage that might be made by turning it in dealing, which by the time that a young man becomes old will amount to a considerable sum of money.

It is Benjamin Franklin who preaches to us in these sentences.

P. 116

Christian asceticism doubtless contains highly diverse elements, both in their outer form and their inner meaning. By the time of the Middle Ages in the West it had already taken on a rational character in its highest manifestation, and in many aspects it showed this rational character even in antiquity. On this rational character rests the meaning of the wider importance of the Western monastic lifestyle, as opposed to Eastern monasticism (not the entirety of Eastern monasticism, but its general ideal type). It was already there in principle in the Benedictine Rule, still more so in the Cluniacs, and even more in the Cistercians, and most decisively finally in the Jesuits, freed from mindless rejection of the world and self-torture. It had turned into a systematically structured method of living one's life rationally with the goal of conquering the state of nature, of freeing the monk from the power of irrational urges and dependency on the world and on nature, of subjecting him to the supremacy of systematic volition, subordinating his actions to constant self-control and consideration of their ethical significance. Thus its goal—objectively—was to train the monk to be a worker in the service of God's kingdom and in this way in turn—subjectively—to insure the salvation of his soul. This—active self-mastery was, like the goal of St. Ignatius's Exercises and the highest forms of rational monastic virtues in general, also the decisive practical model of life for Puritanism. . . .

P. 162

We have now to pursue the Puritanical idea of "calling" in its impact on economic life, after having sought in the preceding sketch to develop its religious foundation. In spite of all the deviations in detail and the varieties in the stress placed on the most relevant perspectives in the various religious communities, this idea of calling proved to be present and active in all of them. But to recapitulate, the decisive factor in our consideration was always the conception of the religious "state of grace" which recurs in all the denominations. This is precisely a state (*status*) which separates the individual from the depravity of nature, from "the world." But the possession of it—no matter how it is attained according to the dogmatic teaching of each denomination—could not be guaranteed through any magical-sacramental means, or through unburdening in the confessional, or through individual acts of piety, but only through confirmation in a specifically constructed way of living that is unequivocally different from the life-style of "natural man." The consequence for individuals was the impulse toward methodical control of this state of grace in their way of life and thus toward their permeation by asceticism. But this ascetic lifestyle meant precisely, as we have observed, a rational reshaping, oriented on God's will, of one's entire existence. And this asceticism was not a supererogatory good work, but an accomplishment expected of everyone who wanted to be sure of one's salvation. This special life of holiness, required by religion and distinct from "natural" life, no longer took place apart from the world in monastic communities—this is the decisive point—but within the world and its structures. This rationalizing of one's conduct within the world with a view towards eternity was the effect of the conception of calling in ascetic Protestantism.

Christian asceticism, at first fleeing from the world into solitude, had already gone outside the cloister; by renouncing the world it mastered the world ecclesiastically. But in doing so, it had relinquished to the everyday life of the world all its naturally simple character. Now asceticism entered the market of life, slammed the doors of the monastery and undertook to permeate the worldly, everyday life with its method; to transform it to a rational life—in this world, but not of this world or for this world. Our study will attempt to demonstrate its success.

Pp. 190-192:

The innerworldly Protestant asceticism—as we can perhaps sum up what we so far have said—thus worked with full force against the uninhibited enjoyment of possessions; it throttled consumption, especially of luxury goods. At the same time, in its psychological effect, it freed the acquisition of wealth from the restraints of traditionalist morality, breaking the shackles on the pursuit of profit, in that it not only legalized it, but viewed it (as shown above) as directly willed by God. As explicitly declared by not only the Puritans, but also by Barclay, the greatest apologist for Quaker belief, the struggle against lust and the attachment to material goods was not a struggle against rational acquisition, but against irrational use of possessions. Such irrational use lay primarily in the love of the outward forms of luxury, a love tainted with idolatry, but which suggested itself so readily to the feudal sensibility, instead of the rational and utilitarian use of these possessions for the life goals of the individual and society as willed by God. Barclay and the Puritans did not want to force mortification on those with property, but rather to force them to use their property for necessary and practically useful things. The concept of comfort encompasses in a characteristic manner the range of ethically admissible uses, and it is naturally no accident that we observe the development of the lifestyle that is bound up with this concept first and most clearly among exactly the most consistent representatives of this entire view of life: the Quakers. They prefer the well-worn refinement of sober simplicity to the tinsel and pretense of chivalric pomp, built as it is on an unreliable economic basis; they contrast this pomp with the ideal and reliable comfort of the bourgeois "home."

In the production of wealth in private enterprise, asceticism opposes injustice as well as unbridled greed; for these are what it condemns as "covetousness," "Mammon," etc.—the pursuit of wealth with the final goal of being rich. For possessions as such were a temptation. But here asceticism was the power that always "wills the good and creates the 'bad'"—the bad in the sense that it is property and a temptation. For this asceticism (along with the Old Testament and completely analogous to the ethical valuation of "good works") considered the striving for wealth as a goal to be the height of the bad, but the achievement of wealth as fruit of labor in one's calling to be the blessing of God. But even more importantly, the religious value placed on indefatigable, constant, systematic, secular work in one's vocation as simply the highest means of asceticism and at the same time the most certain and visible confirmation of the regenerated man and the genuineness of his faith had indeed to be the most powerful possible impetus for the expansion of that view of life that we have depicted as the "spirit" of capitalism. And if we then combine this restriction of consumption with this liberation of acquisitiveness, the external result is obvious: Capital formation through ascetic compulsion towards thrift.

Pp. 202-206:

One of the intrinsic components of the modern capitalist spirit, and not only of it, but also of all modern civilization—

the rational conduct of life on the basis of the idea of "calling"—was born, as this study has sought to demonstrate, out of the spirit of Christian asceticism. If you read once more the tract of Benjamin Franklin, cited at the beginning of this essay, you will see that the essential elements we have described there as the "spirit of capitalism" are indeed those that we projected to be the content of Puritan work asceticism, but without the religious foundation that had already died off in Franklin's view. The idea that modern vocations carry an ascetic stamp is indeed not new. That the restriction of people to specialized occupations and the renunciation of Faustian universality which this implies in today's world are absolutely essential to profitable business, that therefore "deed" and "resignation" inevitably depend on each other—this ascetic motif of the bourgeois life-style (if we can indeed call it style and not lack of style) was what Goethe wanted to teach us at the peak of his life's wisdom, when he wrote of Faust's years of travel and his final years. For him this realization meant a resigned farewell to a time of full and beautiful humanity, which can no more repeat itself in the unfolding of our civilization than could the full bloom of Athens in the ancient world. The Puritans *wanted to* work—we *must* do so. For asceticism was brought out of the monk's cell into the life of work and began to dominate the innerworldly morality; and in doing so it contributed to building that mighty cosmos of modern mechanical, machine-driven production, bound to technical and economic prerequisites, that today determines with overwhelming force the lifestyle of every person born into this mechanized world, not just those who actually work the machines, and will probably determine it until the last barrel of fossil fuel is burned. In Baxter's view, concern for worldly goods should lie on the shoulders of the saints only as a cloak, which one can throw off at any time. But fate has made the cloak into a casing hard as steel. Because asceticism undertook to reshape the world and extend its power into the world, the external goods of this world gained an increasing, and ultimately an inescapable, power over humanity as never before in history. Today asceticism's spirit has vanished from this casing, whether permanently who can say? At any rate victorious capitalism no longer needs its support since it rests on a mechanical foundation. Even the rosy countenance of its smiling heir, the Enlightenment, has finally paled, and the idea of duty to one's vocation haunts our lives like a ghost of earlier religious doctrine.

Ruth Benedict

1887-1948

PATTERNS OF CULTURE

1934

Ruth Benedict was one of the great anthropologists of the last century, achieving international recognition for her studies of American Indian and Japanese cultures. Born in 1887 in New York City, at the age of two she experienced the death of her father, a prominent homeopathic surgeon. Benedict was raised by her mother, a Vassar graduate and daughter of a prosperous New York farming family. Like her mother, Benedict attended Vassar College, from which she graduated Phi Beta Kappa in English literature; upon graduation she moved to Southern California and taught English at a girls' school. Then she met and fell in love with Stanley Benedict, a New York biochemist. After their marriage, they lived together in New York, where she worked as social worker. She began attending a new school in Manhattan known as the School for Social Research. The influence of two prominent anthropologists there led her to Franz Boas, director of the anthropology department at Columbia University and pioneer of the formal study of anthropology in the U.S.

Benedict earned her doctorate at Columbia and then taught there until her death, training other excellent anthropologists, including Margaret Mead. For many years Columbia denied her the recognition she deserved, offering her only annual appointments and not selecting her to succeed Boas. However, *Patterns of Culture*, published in 1934, became a classic, and after she published an important anthropological portrait of Japanese culture (*The Chrysanthemum and the Sword*) in 1947, she was showered with success. The U.S. government awarded her a grant as project director for a massive research project, she was elected president of the American Anthropological Association, and at long last Columbia awarded her a full professorship. Sadly, she had little time to enjoy these belated honors for she died a year later of a massive heart attack.

Patterns of Culture begins and ends with theoretical considerations about culture and anthropology. The central part of the book applies the theory to the description of three very different cultures: two Native American nations (the Zuñi of the Southwest U.S., the Kwakiutl of the Pacific Northwest) and the Dobu people of New Guinea. The excerpts below are from the theoretical portions of the book and the description of the Zuñi, which she contrasts with the Kwakiutl, a tribe that gained its livelihood through fishing the very rich waters of the Northern Pacific. The Kwakiutl and Zuñi were engaged in a constant competition with each other for honor and wealth, the signs of which were both material (stores of fish oil, blankets and sheets of copper) and spiritual (honorific names, titles, and privileges). At great feasts called *potlatches*, powerful leaders of the nation would flaunt their wealth by munificence and conspicuous consumption, thus shaming their rivals. By contrast, the Zuñi sought social harmony, and for them, correct ceremonial observances were the major focus of their lives.

SOURCE

Benedict, Ruth. 1934. *Patterns of Culture.* Second Edition.
Cambridge: The Riverside Press. 1959.

Selections from:
>Chapter 3: The Integration of Culture
>(excerpted 45-49)
>Chapter 4: The Pueblos of New Mexico
>(excerpted 57-62, 67-70, 73-79)
>Chapter 7: The Nature of Society (excerpted
>223, 226-230, 232-233, 244-250)

CHAPTER III

THE INTEGRATION OF CULTURE

THE diversity of cultures can be endlessly documented.
A field of human behaviour may be ignored in some societies
until it barely exists; it may even be in some cases unimagined.
Or it may almost monopolize the whole organized behaviour
of the society, and the most alien situations be manipulated
only in its terms. Traits having no intrinsic relation one with
the other, and historically independent, merge and become
inextricable, providing the occasion for behaviour that has
no counterpart in regions that do not make these
identifications. It is a corollary of this that standards, no
matter in what aspect of behaviour, range in different
cultures from the positive to the negative pole. We might
suppose that in the matter of taking life all peoples would
agree in condemnation. On the contrary, in a matter of
homicide, it may be held that one is blameless if diplomatic
relations have been severed between neighboring countries,
or that one kills by custom his first two children, or that a
husband has right of life and death over his wife, or that it is
the duty of the child to kill his parents before they are old.

It may be that those are killed who steal a fowl, or who cut their upper teeth first, or who are born on a Wednesday. Among some peoples a person suffers torments at having caused an accidental death; among others it is a matter of no consequence. Suicide also may be a light matter, the recourse of anyone who has suffered some slight rebuff, an act that occurs constantly in a tribe. It may be the highest and noblest act a wise man can perform. The very tale of it, on the other hand, may be a matter for incredulous mirth, and the act itself impossible to conceive as a human possibility. Or it may be a crime punishable by law, or regarded as a sin against the gods.

The diversity of custom in the world is not, however, a matter which we can only helplessly chronicle. Self-torture here, head-hunting there, prenuptial chastity in one tribe and adolescent licence in another, are not a list of unrelated facts, each of them to be greeted with surprise wherever it is found or wherever it is absent. The tabus on killing oneself or another, similarly, though they relate to no absolute standard, are not therefore fortuitous. The significance of cultural behaviour is not exhausted when we have clearly understood that it is local and man-made and hugely variable. It tends also to be integrated. A culture, like an individual, is a more or less consistent pattern of thought and action. Within each culture there come into being characteristic purposes not necessarily shared by other types of society. In obedience to these purposes, each people further and further consolidates its experience, and in proportion to the urgency of these drives the heterogeneous items of behaviour take more and more congruous shape. Taken up by a well-integrated culture, the most ill-assorted acts become characteristic of its peculiar goals, often by the most unlikely metamorphoses. The form that these acts take we can understand only by understanding first the emotional and intellectual mainsprings of that society.

Such patterning of culture cannot be ignored as if it were an unimportant detail. The whole, as modern science is insisting in many fields, is not merely the sum of all its parts, but the result of a unique arrangement and interrelation of the parts that has brought about a new entity. Gunpowder is not merely the sum of sulphur and charcoal and saltpeter, and no amount of knowledge even of all three of its elements in all the forms they take in the natural world will demonstrate the nature of gunpowder. New potentialities have come into being in the resulting compound that were not present in its elements, and its mode of behaviour is indefinitely changed from that of any of its elements in other combinations.

Cultures, likewise, are more than the sum of their traits. We may know all about the distribution of a tribe's form of marriage, ritual dances, and puberty initiations, and yet understand nothing of the culture as a whole which has used these elements to its own purpose. This purpose selects from among the possible traits in the surrounding regions those which it can use, and discards those which it cannot. Other traits it recasts into conformity with its demands. The process of course need never be conscious during its whole course, but to overlook it in the study of the patternings of human behaviour is to renounce the possibility of intelligent interpretation.

This integration of cultures is not in the least mystical. It is the same process by which a style in art comes into being and persists. Gothic architecture, beginning in what was hardly more than a preference for altitude and light, became, by the operation of some canon of taste that developed within its technique, the unique and homogeneous art of the thirteenth century. It discarded elements that were incongruous, modified others to its purposes, and invented others that accorded with its taste.

When we describe the process historically, we inevitably use animistic forms of expression as if there were choice and purpose in the growth of this great art-form. But this is due to the difficulty in our language-forms. There was no conscious choice, and no purpose. What was at first no more than a slight bias in local forms and techniques expressed itself more and more forcibly, integrated itself in more and more definite standards, and eventuated in Gothic art.

What has happened in the great art-styles happens also in cultures as a whole. All the miscellaneous behaviour directed toward getting a living, mating, warring, and worshipping the gods, is made over into consistent patterns in accordance with unconscious canons of choice that develop within the culture. Some cultures, like some periods of art, fail of such integration, and about many others we know too little to understand the motives that actuate them. But cultures at every level of complexity, even the simplest, have achieved it. Such cultures are more or less successful attainments of integrated behaviour, and the marvel is that there can be so many of these possible configurations.

Anthropological work has been overwhelmingly devoted to the analysis of culture traits, however, rather than to the study of cultures as articulated wholes. This has been due in great measure to the nature of earlier ethnological descriptions. The classical anthropologists did not write out of first-hand knowledge of primitive people. They were armchair students who had at their disposal the anecdotes of travellers and missionaries and the formal and schematic accounts of the early ethnologists. It was possible to trace from these details the distribution of the custom of knocking out teeth, or of divination by entrails, but it was not possible to see how these traits were embedded in different tribes in characteristic configurations that gave form and meaning to the procedures.

Studies of culture like *The Golden Bough* and the usual comparative ethnological volumes are analytical discussions of traits and ignore all the aspects of cultural integration. Mating or death practices are illustrated by bits of behaviour selected indiscriminately from the most different cultures, and the discussion builds up a kind of mechanical Frankenstein's monster with a right eye from Fiji, a left from Europe, one leg from Tierra del Fuego, and one from Tahiti, and all the fingers and toes from still different regions. Such a figure corresponds to no reality in the past or present, and the fundamental difficulty is the same as if, let us say, psychiatry ended with a catalogue of the symbols of which psychopathic individuals make use, and ignored the study of patterns of symptomatic behaviour—schizophrenia, hysteria, and manic-depressive disorders—into which they are built. . . .

CHAPTER IV

THE PUEBLOS OF NEW MEXICO

THE Pueblo Indians of the Southwest are one of the most widely known primitive peoples in Western civilization. They live in the midst of America, within easy reach of any transcontinental traveller. And they are living after the old native fashion. Their culture has not disintegrated like that of the Indian communities outside of Arizona and New Mexico. Month by month and year by year, the old dances of the gods are danced in their stone villages, life follows essentially the old routines, and what they have taken from our civilization they have remodelled and subordinated to their own attitudes.

They have a romantic history. All through that part of America which they still inhabit are found the homes of their cultural ancestors, the cliff-dwellings and great planned valley cities of the golden age of the Pueblos. Their unbelievably numerous cities were built in the twelfth and thirteenth centuries, but we can follow their history much further back to its simple beginnings in one room stone houses to each of which an underground ceremonial chamber was attached.

These early Pueblo people, however, were not the first who had taken this Southwest desert for their home. An earlier people, the Basket-makers, had lived there so long before that we cannot calculate the period of their occupancy, and they were supplanted, and perhaps largely exterminated, by the early Pueblo people.

The Pueblo culture flourished greatly after it had settled upon its arid plateau. It had brought with it the bow and arrow, a knowledge of stone architecture, and a diversified agriculture. Why it chose for the site of its greatest development the inhospitable, almost waterless valley of the San Juan, which flows into the Colorado River from the north, no one ventures to explain. It seems one of the most forbidding regions in the whole of what is now the United States, yet it was here that there grew up the greatest Indian cities north of Mexico. These were of two kinds, and they seem to have been built by the same civilization at the same period: the cliff-dwellings, and the semicircular valley citadels. The cliff-dwellings dug into the sheer face of the precipice, or built on a ledge hundreds of feet from the valley floor, are some of the most romantic habitations of mankind. We cannot guess what the circumstances were that led to the construction of these homes, far from the cornfields and far from any water-supply, which must have been serious if they were planned as fortifications, but some of the ruins enduringly challenge our admiration of ingenuity and beauty. One thing is never omitted in them, no matter how solid the rock ledge upon which the pueblo is built: the underground ceremonial chamber, the kiva, is hewed out to accommodate a man upright, and is large enough to serve as a gathering-room. It is entered by a ladder through a hatchway.

The other type of dwelling was a prototype of the modern planned city: a semicircular sweep of wall that rose three stories at the fortified exterior and was terraced inward as it approached the underground kivas that clustered in the embrace of the great masonry arms. Some of these great valley cities of this type have not only the small kivas, but one great additional temple similarly sunk into the earth and of the most finished and perfect masonry.

The peak of Pueblo civilization had been reached and passed before the Spanish adventurers came searching for cities of gold. It seems likely that the Navajo-Apache tribes from the north cut off the supplies of water from the cities of these ancient peoples and overcame them. When the Spanish came, they had already abandoned their cliff-dwellings and great semicircular cities and had settled along the Rio Grande in villages they still occupy. Toward the west there were also Acoma, Zuñi, and Hopi, the great western Pueblos.

Pueblo culture, therefore, has a long homogeneous history behind it, and we have special need of this knowledge of it because the cultural life of these peoples is so at variance with that of the rest of North America. Unfortunately archeology cannot go further and tell us how it came about that here in this small region of America a culture gradually differentiated itself from all those that surrounded it and came always more and more drastically to express a consistent and particular attitude toward existence.

We cannot understand the Pueblo configuration of culture without a certain acquaintance with their customs and modes of living. Before we discuss their cultural goals, we must set before ourselves briefly the framework of their society.

The Zuñi are a ceremonious people, a people who value sobriety and inoffensiveness above all other virtues. Their interest is centred upon their rich and complex ceremonial life. Their cults of the masked gods, of healing, of the sun, of the sacred fetishes, of war, of the dead, are formal and established bodies of ritual with priestly officials and calendric observances. No field of activity competes with ritual for foremost place in their attention. Probably most grown men among the western Pueblos give to it the greater part of their waking life. It requires the memorizing of an amount of word-perfect ritual that our less trained minds find staggering, and the performance of neatly dovetailed ceremonies that are charted by the calendar and complexly interlock all the different cults and the governing body in endless formal procedure.

The ceremonial life not only demands their time; it preoccupies their attention. Not only those who are responsible for the ritual and those who take part in it, but all the people of the pueblo, women and families who 'have nothing,' that is, that have no ritual possessions, centre their daily conversation about it. While it is in progress, they stand all day as spectators. If a priest is ill, or if no rain comes during his retreat, village gossip runs over and over his ceremonial missteps and the implications of his failure. Did the priest of the masked gods give offence to some supernatural being? Did he break his retreat by going home to his wife before the days were up? These are the subjects of talk in the village for a fortnight. If an impersonator wears a new feather on his mask, it eclipses all talk of sheep or gardens or marriage or divorce.

This preoccupation with detail is logical enough. Zuñi religious practices are believed to be supernaturally powerful in their own right. At every step of the way, if the procedure is correct, the costume of the masked god traditional to the last detail, the offerings unimpeachable, the words of the hours-long prayers letter-perfect, the effect will follow according to man's desires. One has only, in the phrase they have always on their tongues, to 'know how.' According to all the tenets of their religion, it is a major matter if one of the eagle feathers of a mask has been taken from the shoulder of the bird instead of from the breast. Every detail has magical efficacy.

Zuñi places great reliance upon imitative magic. In the priests' retreats for rain they roll round stones across the floor to produce thunder, water is sprinkled to cause the rain, a bowl of water is placed upon the altar that the springs may be full, suds are beaten up from a native plant that clouds may pile in the heavens, tobacco smoke is blown out that the gods 'may not withhold their misty breath.' In the masked-god dances mortals clothe themselves with the 'flesh' of the supernaturals, that is, their paint and their masks, and by this means the gods are constrained to grant their blessings. Even the observances that are less obviously in the realm of magic partake in Zuñi thought of the same mechanistic efficacy. One of the obligations that rest upon every priest or official during the time when he is actively participating in religious observances is that of feeling no anger. But anger is not tabu in order to facilitate communication with a righteous god who can only be approached by those with a clean heart. It is rather a sign of concentration upon supernatural affairs, a state of mind that constrains the supernaturals and makes it impossible for them to withhold their share of the bargain. It has magical efficacy.

Their prayers also are formulas, the effectiveness of which comes from their faithful rendition. The amount of traditional prayer forms of this sort in Zuñi can hardly be exaggerated. Typically they describe in ritualistic language the whole course of the reciter's ceremonial obligations leading up to the present culmination of the ceremony. They itemize the appointment of the impersonator, the gathering of willow shoots for prayer-sticks, the binding of the bird feathers to them with cotton string, the painting of the sticks, the offering to the gods of the finished plume wands, the visits to sacred springs, the periods of retreat. No less than the original religious act, the recital must be meticulously correct.

> Seeking yonder along the river courses
> The ones who are our fathers,
> Male willow, Female willow,
> Four times cutting the straight young shoots,

To my house
I brought my road.
This day
With my warm human hands
I took hold of them.
I gave my prayer-sticks human form.
With the striped cloud tail
Of the one who is my grandfather,
The male turkey,
With eagle's thin cloud tail,
With the striped cloud wings
And massed cloud tails
Of all the birds of summer,
With these four times I gave my prayer-sticks
    human form.
With the flesh of the one who is my mother,
Cotton woman,
Even a poorly made cotton thread,
Four times encircling them and tying it about
    their bodies,
I gave my prayer-sticks human form.
With the flesh of the one who is our mother,
Black paint woman,
Four times covering them with flesh,
I gave my prayer-sticks human form: . . .

The heads of the major priesthoods, with the chief priest of the sun cult and the two chief priests of the war cult, constitute the ruling body, the council, of Zuñi. Zuñi is a theocracy to the last implication. Since priests are holy men and must never during the prosecution of their duties feel anger, nothing is brought before them about which there will not be unanimous agreement. They initiate the great ceremonial events of the Zuñi calendar, they make ritual appointments, and they give judgment in cases of witchcraft.

To our sense of what a governing body should be, they are without jurisdiction and without authority.

If the priesthoods stand on the level of greatest sanctity, the cult of the masked gods is most popular. It has first claim in Zuñi affection, and it flourishes today like the green bay tree.

There are two kinds of masked gods: the masked gods proper, the kachinas; and the kachina priests. These kachina priests are the chiefs of the supernatural world and are themselves impersonated with masks by Zuñi dancers. Their sanctity in Zuñi eyes makes it necessary that their cult should be quite separate from that of the dancing gods proper. The dancing gods are happy and comradely supernaturals who live at the bottom of a lake far off in the empty desert south of Zuñi. There they are always dancing. But they like best to return to Zuñi to dance. To impersonate them, therefore, is to give them the pleasure they most desire. A man, when he puts on the mask of the god, becomes for the time being the supernatural himself. He has no longer human speech, but only the cry which is peculiar to that god. He is tabu, and must assume all the obligations of anyone who is for the time being sacred. He not only dances, but he observes an esoteric retreat before the dance, and plants prayer-sticks and observes continence.

There are more than a hundred different masked gods of the Zuñi pantheon, and many of these are dance groups that come in sets, thirty or forty of a kind. Others come in sets of six, coloured for the six directions—for Zuñi counts up and down as cardinal points. Each of these gods has individual details of costuming, an individual mask, an individual place in the hierarchy of the gods, myths that recount his doings, and ceremonies during which he is expected.

The dances of the masked gods are administered and carried out by a tribal society of all adult males. Women too may be initiated 'to save their lives,' but it is not customary.

They are not excluded because of any tabu, but membership for a woman is not customary, and there are today only three women members. As far back as tradition reaches there seem not to have been many more at any one time. The men's tribal society is organized in six groups, each with its kiva or ceremonial chamber. Each kiva has its officials, its dances that belong to it, and its own roll of members.

Membership in one or the other of these kivas follows from the choice of a boy's ceremonial father at birth, but there is no initiation till the child is between five and nine years old. It is his first attainment of ceremonial status. This initiation, as Dr. Bunzel points out, does not teach him esoteric mysteries; it establishes a bond with supernatural forces. It makes him strong, and, as they say, valuable. The 'scare kachinas,' the punitive masked gods, come for the initiation, and they whip the children with their yucca whips. It is a rite of exorcism, 'to take off the bad happenings,' and to make future events propitious. In Zuñi whipping is never used as a corrective of children. The fact that white parents use it in punishment is a matter for unending amazement. In the initiation children are supposed to be very frightened, and they are not shamed if they cry aloud. It makes the rite the more valuable.

Later, traditionally when the boy is about fourteen and old enough to be responsible, he is whipped again by even stronger masked gods. It is at this initiation that the kachina mask is put upon his head, and it is revealed to him that the dancers, instead of being the supernaturals from the Sacred Lake, are in reality his neighbours and his relatives. After the final whipping, the four tallest boys are made to stand face to face with the scare kachinas who have whipped them. The priests lift the masks from their heads and place them upon the heads of the boys. It is the great revelation. The boys are terrified. The yucca whips are taken from the hands of the scare kachinas and put in the hands of the boys who face them, now with the masks upon their heads. They are commanded to whip the kachinas. It is their first object lesson in the truth that they, as mortals, must exercise all the functions which the uninitiated ascribe to the supernaturals themselves. The boys whip them, four times on the right arm, four on the left, four times on the right leg, four on the left. Afterward the kachinas are whipped in turn in the same way by all the boys, and the priests tell them the long myth of the boy who let fall the secret that the kachinas were merely impersonations and was killed by the masked gods. They cut his head from his body and kicked it all the way to the Sacred Lake. His body they left lying in the plaza. The boys must never, never tell. They are now members of the cult and may impersonate the masked gods. . . .

No other aspect of existence seriously competes in Zuñi interest with the dances and the religious observances. Domestic affairs like marriage and divorce are casually and individually arranged. Zuñi is a strongly socialized culture and not much interested in those things that are matters for the individual to attend to. Marriage is arranged almost without courtship. Traditionally girls had few opportunities for speaking to a boy alone, but in the evening when all the girls carried the water-jars on their heads to the spring for water, a boy might waylay one and ask for a drink. If she liked him she gave it to him. He might ask her also to make him a throwing stick for the rabbit hunt, and give her afterwards the rabbits he had killed. Boys and girls were supposed to have no other meetings, and certainly there are many Zuñi women today who were married with no more preliminary sex experience than this.

When the boy decides to ask her father for the girl, he goes to her house. As in every Zuñi visit, he first tastes the food that is set before him, and the father says to him as he must say to every visitor, 'Perhaps you came for something.' The boy answers, 'Yes, I came thinking of your daughter.' The father calls his daughter, saying, 'I cannot speak for her. Let her say.' If she is willing, the mother goes into the next room and makes up the pallet and they retire together. Next day she washes his hair. After four days she dresses in her best clothes and carries a large basket of fine corn flour to his mother's house as a present. There are no further formalities and little social interest is aroused in the affair.

If they are not happy together, and think of separating, especially if they have no children that have lived, the wife will make a point of going to serve at the ceremonial feasts. When she has a tête-à-tête with some eligible man they will arrange a meeting. In Zuñi it is never thought to be difficult for a woman to acquire a new husband. There are fewer women than men, and it is more dignified for a man to live with a wife than to remain in his mother's house. Men are perennially willing. When the woman is satisfied that she will not be left husbandless, she gathers together her husband's possessions and places them on the doorsill, in olden times on the roof by the hatchway. There are not many: his extra pair of moccasins, his dance skirt and sash, if he has them, his box of precious feathers for prayer-sticks, his paint-pots for prayer-sticks and for refurbishing masks. All his more important ceremonial possessions he has never brought from his mother's house. When he comes home in the evening he sees the little bundle, picks it up and cries, and returns with it to his mother's house. He and his family weep and are regarded as unfortunate. But the rearrangement of living-quarters is the subject of only fleeting gossip. There is rarely an interplay of deep feeling. Husbands and wives abide by the rules, and these rules hardly provide for violent emotions, either of jealousy or of revenge, or of an attachment that refuses to accept dismissal.

In spite of the casual nature of marriage and divorce, a very large proportion of Zuñi marriages endure through the greater part of a lifetime. Bickering is not liked, and most marriages are peaceful. The permanence of Zuñi marriages is the more striking because marriage, instead of being the social form behind which all the forces of tradition are massed, as in our culture, cuts directly across the most strongly institutionalized social bond in Zuñi.

This is the matrilineal family, which is ceremonially united in its ownership and care of the sacred fetishes. To the women of the household, the grandmother and her sisters, her daughters and their daughters, belong the house and the corn that is stored in it. No matter what may happen to marriages, the women of the household remain with the house for life. They present a solid front. They care for and feed the sacred objects that belong to them. They keep their secrets together. Their husbands are outsiders, and it is their brothers, married now into the houses of other clans, who are united with the household in all affairs of moment. It is they who return for all the retreats when the sacred objects of the house are set out before the altar. It is they, not the women, who learn the word-perfect ritual of their sacred bundle and perpetuate it. A man goes always, for all important occasions, to his mother's house, which, when she dies, becomes his sister's house, and if his marriage breaks up, he returns to the same stronghold.

This blood-relationship group, rooted in the ownership of the house, united in the care of sacred objects, is the important group in Zuñi. It has permanence and important common concerns. But it is not the economically functioning group. Each married son, each married brother, spends his labour upon the corn which will fill his wife's storeroom. Only when his mother's or sister's house lacks male labour does he care for the cornfield of his blood relationship group. The economic group is the household that lives together, the old grandmother and her husband, her daughters and their husbands. These husbands count in the economic group, though in the ceremonial group they are outsiders.

For women there is no conflict. They have no allegiance of any kind to their husbands' groups. But for all men there is double allegiance. They are husbands in one group and brothers in another. Certainly in the more important families, in those which care for permanent fetishes, a man's allegiance as brother has more social weight than his allegiance as husband. In all families a man's position derives, not, as with us, from his position as breadwinner, but from his role in relation to the sacred objects of the household. The husband, with no such relationship to the ceremonial possessions of his wife's house to trade upon, only gradually attains to position in the household as his children grow to maturity. It is as their father, not as provider or as their mother's husband, that he finally attains some authority in the household where he may have lived for twenty years.

Economic affairs are always as comparatively unimportant in Zuñi as they are in determining the family alignments. Like all the Pueblos, and perhaps in greater degree than the rest, Zuñi is rich. It has gardens and peach orchards and sheep and silver and turquoise. These are important to a man when they make it possible for him to have a mask made for himself, or to pay for the learning of ritual, or to entertain the tribal masked gods at the Shalako. For this last he must build a new house for the gods to bless at housewarming. All that year he must feed the cult members who build for him, he must provide the great beams for the rafters, he must entertain the whole tribe at the final ceremony. There are endless responsibilities he must assume. For this purpose he will plant heavily the year before and increase his herd. He will receive help from his clan group, all of which he must return in kind. Riches used in this way are of course indispensable to a man of prestige, but neither he nor anyone else is concerned with the reckoning of possessions, but with the ceremonial rôle which he has taken. A 'valuable' family, in native parlance, is always a family which owns permanent fetishes, and a man of importance is one who has undertaken many ceremonial rôles.

All the traditional arrangements tend to make wealth play as small a part as possible in the performance of ritual prerogatives. Ceremonial objects, even though they are recognized personal property and attained by the expenditure of money and effort, are free to the use of anyone who can employ them. There are many sacred things too dangerous to be handled except by those who have qualified, but the tabus are not property tabus. Hunting fetishes are owned in the hunters' society, but anyone who is going hunting may take them for his use. He will have to assume the usual responsibilities for using holy things; he will have to plant prayer-sticks and be continent and benevolent for four days. But he pays nothing, and those who possess the fetishes as private property have no monopoly of their supernatural powers. Similarly a man who has no mask borrows one freely and is not thought of as a beggar or a suppliant.

Besides this unusual discontinuity between vested interests and the ownership of ceremonial objects in Zuñi, other more common arrangements make wealth of comparative unimportance. Membership in a clan with numerous ceremonial prerogatives outweighs wealth, and a poor man may be sought repeatedly for ritual offices because he is of the required lineage. Most ceremonial participation, in addition, is the responsibility of a group of people. An individual acts in assuming ritual posts as he does in all other affairs of life, as a member of a group. He may be a comparatively poor man, but the household or the kiva acting through him provides the ceremonial necessaries. The group gains always from this participation because of the great blessing that accrues to it, and the property owned by a self-respecting individual is not the count on which he is admitted to or denied ceremonial rôles.

The Pueblos are a ceremonious people. But that is not the essential fashion in which they are set off from the other peoples of North America and Mexico. It goes much deeper than any difference in degree in the amount of ritual that is current among them. The Aztec civilization of Mexico was as ritualistic as the Pueblo, and even the Plains Indians with their sun dance and their men's societies, their tobacco orders and their war rituals, had a rich ceremonialism.

The basic contrast between the Pueblos and the other cultures of North America is the contrast that is named and described by Nietzsche in his studies of Greek tragedy. He discusses two diametrically opposed ways of arriving at the values of existence. The Dionysian pursues them through 'the annihilation of the ordinary bounds and limits of existence'; he seeks to attain in his most valued moments escape from the boundaries imposed upon him by his five senses, to break through into another order of experience. The desire of the Dionysian, in personal experience or in ritual, is to press through it toward a certain psychological state, to achieve excess. The closest analogy to the emotions he seeks is drunkenness, and he values the illuminations of frenzy. With Blake, he believes 'the path of excess leads to the palace of wisdom.' The Apollonian distrusts all this, and has often little idea of the nature of such experiences. He finds means to outlaw them from his conscious life. He 'knows but one law, measure in the Hellenic sense.' He keeps the middle of the road, stays within the known map, does not meddle with disruptive psychological states. In Nietzsche's fine phrase, even in the exaltation of the dance he 'remains what he is, and retains his civic name.'

The Southwest Pueblos are Apollonian. Not all of Nietzsche's discussion of the contrast between Apollonian and Dionysian applies to the contrast between the Pueblos and the surrounding peoples. The fragments I have quoted are faithful descriptions, but there were refinements of the types in Greece that do not occur among the Indians of the Southwest, and among these latter, again, there are refinements that did not occur in Greece. It is with no thought of equating the civilization of Greece with that of aboriginal America that I use, in describing the cultural configurations of the latter, terms borrowed from the culture of Greece. I use them because they are categories that bring clearly to the fore the major qualities that differentiate Pueblo culture from those of other American Indians, not because all the attitudes that are found in Greece are found also in aboriginal America. . . .

CHAPTER VII

THE NATURE OF SOCIETY

THE three cultures of Zuñi, of Dobu, and of the Kwakiutl are not merely heterogeneous assortments of acts and beliefs. They have each certain goals toward which their behaviour is directed and which their institutions further. They differ from one another not only because one trait is present here and absent there, and because another trait is found in two regions in two different forms. They differ still more because they are oriented as wholes in different directions. They are travelling along different roads in pursuit of different ends, and these ends and these means in one society cannot be judged in terms of those of another society, because essentially they are incommensurable.

All cultures, of course, have not shaped their thousand items of behaviour to a balanced and rhythmic pattern. Like certain individuals, certain social orders do not subordinate activities to a ruling motivation. They scatter. If at one moment they seem to be pursuing certain ends, at another they are off on some tangent apparently inconsistent with all that has gone before, which gives no clue to activity that will come after. . . .

An intimate and understanding study of a genuinely disoriented culture would be of extraordinary interest. Probably the nature of the specific conflicts or of the facile hospitality to new influences would prove more important than any blanket characterizations of 'lack of integration,' but what such characterizations would be we cannot guess. Probably in even the most disoriented cultures it would be necessary to take account of accommodations that tend to rule out disharmonious elements and establish selected elements more securely. The process might even be the more apparent for the diversity of material upon which it operated. Some of the best available examples of the conflict of disharmonious elements are from the past history of tribes that have achieved integration. The Kwakiutl have not always boasted the consistent civilization which we have described. Before they settled on the coast and on Vancouver Island, they shared in general the culture of the Salish people to the south. They still keep myths and village organization and relationship terminology that link them with these people. But the Salish tribes are individualists. Hereditary privileges are at a minimum. Every man has, according to his ability, practically the same opportunity as any other man. His importance depends on his skill in hunting, or his luck in gambling, or his success in manipulating his supernatural claims as a doctor or diviner. There could hardly be a greater contrast than with the social order of the Northwest Coast.

Even this extreme contrast, however, did not militate against Kwakiutl acceptance of the alien pattern. They came to regard as private property even names, myths, house-posts, guardian spirits, and the right to be initiated into certain societies. But the adjustment that was necessary is still apparent in their institutions, and it is conspicuous at just those points where the two social orders were at odds; that is, in the mechanisms of the social organization. For though the Kwakiutl adopted the whole Northwest Coast system of prerogatives and potlatches, they did not similarly adopt the rigid matrilineal clans of the northern tribes which provided a fixed framework within which the privileges descended. The individual in the northern tribes fitted automatically into the title of nobility to which he had a right by birth. The individual among the Kwakiutl, as we have seen, spent his life bargaining for these titles, and could lay claim to any one that had been held in any branch of his family. The

Kwakiutl adopted the whole system of prerogatives, but they left to the individual a free play in the game of prestige which contrasted with the caste system of the northern tribes, and retained the old customs of the south that the Kwakiutl had brought with them to the coast.

Certain very definite cultural traits of the Kwakiutl are the reflections of specific conflicts between the old and the new configurations. With the new emphasis on property, inheritance rules assumed a new importance. The interior Salish tribes were loosely organized in families and villages, and most property was destroyed at death. The rigid matrilineal clan system of the northern tribes, as we have seen, did not gain acceptance among the Kwakiutl, but they compromised by stressing the right of the son-in-law to claim privileges from his wife's father, these privileges to be held in trust for his children. The inheritance, therefore, passed matrilineally, but it skipped a generation, as it were. In every alternate generation the prerogatives were not exercised but merely held in trust. As we have seen, all these privileges were manipulated according to the conventional potlatch techniques. It was an unusual adjustment and one which was clearly a compromise between two incompatible social orders. We have described in an earlier chapter how thoroughly they solved the problem of bringing two antagonistic social orders into harmony.

Integration, therefore, may take place in the face of fundamental conflicts. The cases of cultural disorientation may well be less than appear at the present time. There is always the possibility that the description of the culture is disoriented rather than the culture itself. Then again, the nature of the integration may be merely outside our experience and difficult to perceive. When these difficulties have been removed, the former by better fieldwork, the latter by more acute analysis, the importance of the integration of cultures may be even clearer than it is today. Nevertheless it is important to recognize the fact that not all cultures are by any means the homogeneous structures we have described for Zuñi and the Kwakiutl. It would be absurd to cut every culture down to the Procrustean bed of some catchword characterization. The danger of lopping off important facts that do not illustrate the main proposition is grave enough even at best. It is indefensible to set out upon an operation that mutilates the subject and erects additional obstacles against our eventual understanding of it.

Facile generalizations about the integration of culture are most dangerous in field-work. When one is mastering the language and all the idiosyncrasies of behaviour of an esoteric culture, preoccupation with its configuration may well be an obstacle to a genuine understanding. The field-worker must be faithfully objective. He must chronicle all the relevant behaviour, taking care not to select according to any challenging hypothesis the facts that will fit a thesis. None of the peoples we have discussed in this volume were studied in the field with any preconception of a consistent type of behaviour which that culture illustrated. The ethnology was set down as it came, with no attempt to make it self-consistent. The total pictures are therefore much more convincing to the student. In theoretical discussions of culture, also, generalizations about the integration of culture will be empty in proportion as they are dogmatic and universalized. We need detailed information about contrasting limits of behaviour and the motivations that are dynamic in one society and not in another. We do not need a plank of configuration written into the platform of an ethnological school. On the other hand, the contrasted goods which different cultures pursue, the different intentions which are at the basis of their institutions, are essential to the understanding both of different social orders and of individual psychology.

The relation of cultural integration to studies of Western civilization and hence to sociological theory is easily misunderstood. Our own society is often pictured as an extreme example of lack of integration. Its huge complexity and rapid changes from generation to generation make inevitable a lack of harmony between its elements that does not occur in simpler societies. The lack of integration is exaggerated and misinterpreted, however, in most studies because of a simple technical error. Primitive society is integrated in geographical units. Western civilization, however, is stratified, and different social groups of the same time and place live by quite different standards and are actuated by different motivations.

The effort to apply the anthropological culture area in modern sociology can only be fruitful to a very limited degree because different ways of living are today not primarily a matter of spatial distribution. There is a tendency among sociologists to waste time over the 'culture area concept.' There is properly no such 'concept.' When traits group themselves geographically, they must be handled geographically. When they do not, it is idle to make a principle out of what is at best a loose empirical category. In our civilization there is, in the anthropological sense, a uniform cosmopolitan culture that can be found in any part of the globe, but there is likewise unprecedented divergence between the labouring class and the Four Hundred, between those groups whose life centres in the church and those whose life centres on the race-track. The comparative freedom of choice in modern society makes possible important voluntary groups which stand for as different principles as the Rotary Clubs and Greenwich Village. The nature of the cultural processes is not changed with these modern conditions, but the unit in which they can be studied is no longer the local group. . . .

In all studies of social custom, the crux of the matter is that the behaviour under consideration must pass through the needle's eye of social acceptance, and only history in its widest sense can give an account of these social acceptances and rejections. It is not merely psychology that is in question, it is also history, and history is by no means a set of facts that can be discovered by introspection. Therefore those explanations of custom which derive our economic scheme from human competitiveness, modern war from human combativeness, and all the rest of the ready explanations that we meet in every magazine and modern volume, have for the anthropologist a hollow ring. Rivers was one of the first to phrase the issue vigorously. He pointed out that instead of trying to understand the blood feud from vengeance, it was necessary rather to understand vengeance from the institution of the blood feud. In the same way it is necessary to study jealousy from its conditioning by local sexual regulations and property institutions.

The difficulty with naïve interpretations of culture in terms of individual behaviour is not that these interpretations are those of psychology, but that they ignore history and the historical process of acceptance or rejection of traits. Any configurational interpretation of cultures also is an exposition in terms of individual psychology, but it depends upon history as well as upon psychology. It holds that Dionysian behaviour is stressed in the institutions of certain cultures because it is a permanent possibility in individual psychology, but that it is stressed in certain cultures and not in others because of historical events that have in one place fostered its development and in others have ruled it out. At different points in the interpretation of cultural forms, both history and psychology are necessary; one cannot make the one do the service of the other. . . .

The significant sociological unit, from this point of view, therefore, is not the institution but the cultural configuration. The studies of the family, of primitive economics, or of moral ideas need to be broken up into studies that emphasize the different configurations that in instance after instance have dominated these traits. The peculiar nature of Kwakiutl life can never be clear in a discussion which singles out the family for discussion and derives Kwakiutl behaviour at marriage from the marriage situation. Similarly, marriage in our own civilization is a situation which can never be made clear as a mere variant on mating and domesticity. Without the clue that in our civilization at large man's paramount aim is to amass private possessions and multiply occasions of display, the modern position of the wife and the modern emotions of jealousy are alike unintelligible. Our attitudes toward our children are equally evidences of this same cultural goal. Our children are not individuals whose rights and tastes are casually respected from infancy, as they are in some primitive societies, but special responsibilities, like our possessions, to which we succumb or in which we glory, as the case may be. They are fundamentally extensions of our own egos and give a special opportunity for the display of authority. The pattern is not inherent in the parent-children situation, as we so glibly assume. It is impressed upon the situation by the major drives of our culture, and it is only one of the occasions in which we follow our traditional obsessions.

As we become increasingly culture-conscious, we shall be able to isolate the tiny core that is generic in a situation and the vast accretions that are local and cultural and man-made. The fact that these accretions are not inevitable consequences of the situation as such does not make them easier to change or less important in our behaviour. Indeed they are probably harder to change than we have realized. Detailed changes in the mother's nursery behaviour, for instance, may well be inadequate to save a neurotic child when he is trapped in a repugnant situation which is reinforced by every contact he makes and which will extend past his mother to his school and his business and his wife. The whole course of life which is presented to him emphasizes rivalry and ownership. Probably the child's way out lies through luck or detachment. In any case, the solution of the problem might well place less emphasis upon the difficulties inherent in the parent-child situation and more upon the forms taken in Western behaviour by ego-extension and the exploiting of personal relations.

The problem of social value is intimately involved in the fact of the different patternings of cultures. Discussions of social value have usually been content to characterize certain human traits as desirable and to indicate a social goal that would involve these virtues. Certainly, it is said, exploitation of others in personal relations and overweening claims of the ego are bad whereas absorption in group activities is good; a temper is good that seeks satisfaction neither in sadism nor in masochism and is willing to live and let live. A social order, however, which like Zuñi standardizes this 'good' is far from Utopian. It manifests likewise the defects of its virtues. It has no place, for instance, for dispositions we are accustomed to value highly, such as force of will or personal initiative or the disposition to take up arms against a sea of troubles. It is incorrigibly mild. The group activity that fills existence in Zuñi is out of touch with human life—with birth, love, death, success, failure, and prestige. A ritual pageant serves their purpose and minimizes more human interests. The freedom from any forms of social exploitation or of social sadism appears on the other side of the coin as endless ceremonialism not designed to serve major ends of human existence. It is the old inescapable fact that every upper has its lower, every right side its left.

The complexity of the problem of social values is exceptionally clear in Kwakiutl culture. The chief motive that the institutions of the Kwakiutl rely upon and which they share in great measure with modern society is the motive of rivalry. Rivalry is a struggle that is not centred upon the real objects of the activity but upon outdoing a competitor. The attention is no longer directed toward providing adequately for a family or toward owning goods that can be utilized or enjoyed, but toward outdistancing one's neighbours and owning more than anyone else. Everything else is lost sight of in the one great aim of victory. Rivalry does not, like competition, keep its eyes upon the original activity; whether making a basket or selling shoes, it creates an artificial situation: the game of showing that one can win out over others.

Rivalry is notoriously wasteful. It ranks low in the scale of human values. It is a tyranny from which, once it is encouraged in any culture, no man may free himself. The wish for superiority is gargantuan; it can never be satisfied. The contest goes on forever. The more goods the community accumulates, the greater the counters with which men play, but the game is as far from being won as it was when the stakes were small. In Kwakiutl institutions, such rivalry reaches its final absurdity in equating investment with wholesale destruction of goods. They contest for superiority chiefly in accumulation of goods, but often also, and without a consciousness of the contrast, in breaking in pieces their highest units of value, their coppers, and in making bonfires of their house-planks, their blankets and canoes. The social waste is obvious. It is just as obvious in the obsessive rivalry of *Middletown* where houses are built and clothing bought and entertainments attended that each family may prove that it has not been left out of the game.

It is an unattractive picture. In Kwakiutl life the rivalry is carried out in such a way that all success must be built upon the ruin of rivals; in *Middletown* in such a way that individual choices and direct satisfactions are reduced to a minimum and conformity is sought beyond all other human gratifications. In both cases it is clear that wealth is not sought and valued for its direct satisfaction of human needs but as a series of counters in the game of rivalry. If the will to victory were eliminated from the economic life, as it is in Zuñi, distribution and consumption of wealth would follow quite different 'laws.'

Nevertheless, as we can see in Kwakiutl society and in the rugged individualism of American pioneer life, the pursuit of victory can give vigor and zest to human existence. Kwakiutl life is rich and forceful in its own terms. Its chosen goal has its appropriate virtues, and social values in Kwakiutl civilization are even more inextricably mixed than they are in Zuñi. Whatever the social orientation, a society which exemplifies it vigorously will develop certain virtues that are natural to the goals it has chosen, and it is most unlikely that even the best society will be able to stress in one social order all the virtues we prize in human life. Utopia cannot be achieved as a final and perfect structure within which human life will reach a faultless flowering. Utopias of this sort should be recognized as pure day-dreaming. Real improvements in the social order depend upon more modest and more difficult discriminations. It is possible to scrutinize different institutions and cast up their cost in terms of social capital, in terms of the less desirable behaviour traits they stimulate, and in terms of human suffering and frustration. If any society wishes to pay that cost for its chosen and congenial traits, certain values will develop within this pattern, however 'bad' it may be. But the risk is great, and the social order may not be able to pay the price. It may break down beneath them with all the consequent wanton waste of revolution and economic and emotional disaster. In modern society this problem is the most pressing this generation has to face, and those who are obsessed with it too often imagine that an economic reorganization will give the world a Utopia out of their day-dreams, forgetting that no social order can separate its virtues from the defects of its virtues. There is no royal road to a real Utopia.

There is, however, one difficult exercise to which we may accustom ourselves as we become increasingly culture-conscious. We may train ourselves to pass judgment upon the dominant traits of our own civilization. It is difficult enough for anyone brought up under their power to recognize them. It is still more difficult to discount, upon necessity, our predilection for them. They are as familiar as an old loved homestead. Any world in which they do not appear seems to us cheerless and untenable. Yet it is these very traits which by the operation of a fundamental cultural process are most often carried to extremes. They overreach themselves, and more than any other traits they are likely to get out of hand. Just at the very point where there is greatest likelihood of the need of criticism, we are bound to be least critical. Revision comes, but it comes by way of revolution or of breakdown. The possibility of orderly progress is shut off because the generation in question could not make any appraisal of its overgrown institutions. It could not cast them up in terms of profit and loss because it had lost its power to look at them objectively. The situation had to reach a breaking-point before relief was possible.

Appraisal of our own dominant traits has so far waited till the trait in question was no longer a living issue. Religion was not objectively discussed till it was no longer the cultural trait to which our civilization was most deeply committed. Now for the first time the comparative study of religions is free to pursue any point at issue. It is not yet possible to discuss capitalism in the same way, and during wartime, warfare and the problems of international relations are similarly tabu. Yet the dominant traits of our civilization need special scrutiny. We need to realize that they are compulsive, not in proportion as they are basic and essential in human behaviour, but rather in the degree to which they are local and overgrown in our own culture. The one way of life which the Dobuan regards as basic in human nature is one that is fundamentally treacherous and safeguarded with morbid fears. The Kwakiutl similarly cannot see life except as a series of rivalry situations, wherein success is measured by the humiliation of one's fellows. Their belief is based on the importance of these modes of life in their civilizations. But the importance of an institution in a culture gives no direct indication of its usefulness or its inevitability. The argument is suspect, and any cultural control which we may be able to exercise will depend upon the degree to which we can evaluate objectively the favoured and passionately fostered traits of our Western civilization.

DOMINIQUE ZAHAN

(1915-1991)

THE RELIGION, SPIRITUALITY, AND THOUGHT OF TRADITIONAL AFRICA

(1970)

Dominique Zahan (1915-1991) was born in Romania, where he lived until the 1940s, when he moved to France. There he taught many years at the University of Strasbourg and became professor of African ethnology and sociology at the University of Paris V (Sorbonne). He has written several highly acclaimed studies of African religion. In the course of his field studies he lived for long periods among the Bambara people of West Africa; he also worked in the French colonial administration in Niger from 1948 to 1958 as chief of the section on immigration, responsible for dealing with the human problems created by the African colonization of the Central Niger Delta.

The excerpt below is drawn from a work originally published in 1970 as a preliminary effort to arrive at a synthesis on African religion, tentative though any such effort must still be. In it Zahan concluded that "the essence of African spirituality lies in the feeling man has of being at once image, model, and integral part of the world in whose cyclical life he senses himself deeply and necessarily engaged."

SOURCE

Zahan, Dominique. 1970. *The Religion, Spirituality, and Thought of Traditional Africa* [*Religion, spiritualité, et pensée africaines*]. Trans. Kate Ezra Martin and Lawrence M. Martin. Chicago: University of Chicago Press, 1979. 36-52.

Selections from: Chapter 3: Life, Death, and Time (36-52)

CHAPTER 3

LIFE, DEATH, AND TIME

"To be born, to live, and to die,
that is to change form."
Diderot, *Le rêve de d'Alembert*

In Africa the problem of life and death constitutes the basis for religious feeling and is the unconscious foundation of philosophical reflection. Life and death are both "given" to man by the creator; they are the fundamental terms of existence and are so closely linked that one cannot be conceived without the other. Death, however, enjoys the incontestable advantage over life in that it is necessary, for it was not inevitable that life be given, but as soon as it appeared death had to follow. It is fair to say that death seems to be the unavoidable consequence of life.

Almost all African myths of the origin of death (long analyzed and classified by Western scholarship) deal with this dialectic. Their themes reveal the great variety of motifs called upon by their users to "justify" the appearance of death in the world of men. However, this diversity allows certain main strands to be detected as soon as we look through the meshes of the narrative. Some of these myths are simple, repetitive signifiers of the human condition. Others are presented as superficially plausible lines of argument linking man's immortality to a certain requirement which he cannot satisfy because it implies the negation of one of the essential aspects of that same human condition.

A considerable number of these accounts relate to what certain authors have called the "message that failed."[1] According to this theme, the divinity decides to send man two messages, one of mortality, the other of immortality. The first to reach its destination will determine man's destiny once and for all. In most cases God entrusts the message of immortality to a slow animal, while a fast animal is delegated to carry the message of mortality. A Thonga myth on this subject can be considered typical.

When the first human beings emerged from the marsh of reeds, the chief of this marsh sent the Chameleon (Lumpfana) to them, with this message: "Men will die, but they will rise again." The Chameleon started walking slowly, according to his habit. Then the big lizard with the blue head, the Galagala, was sent to tell men: "You will die and you will rot." Galagala started with his swift gait and soon passed Lumpfana. He delivered his message, and when Lumpfana arrived with his errand, men said to him: "You are too late. We have already accepted another message." This is why men are subject to death.[2]

---

[1] See H. Baumann, *Schöpfung und Urzeit der Menschen im Mythos der Afrikanischen Völker* (Berlin: Dietrich Reimer, 1936), p. 268; and H. Abrahamsson, *The Origin of Death*, Studia Ethnographica Upsaliensia, vol. 3 (Uppsala: Almquist and Wiksells, 1951), p. 4. For the synthesis presented here we refer with few exceptions to the myths cited by the latter author.

[2] H. A. Junod, *The Life of a South African Tribe*, 2d ed. (London: Macmillan, 1927), 2:350-51.

Myths of this type have a wide distribution throughout Africa and even elsewhere. Among the Bantu peoples, where they are most in evidence, one of the two messengers is generally the chameleon, either in the role of the herald of immortality or as the one charged with informing man of his mortality. He is set against a wide range of animals carrying the opposite message. Sometimes the chameleon and his antagonists are replaced by other animals, or the message leaves the world of men in the form of a request addressed to God, or it happens that we find only a single message instead of two.

The diversity in the forms of these accounts need not conceal their meaning, which is easily revealed by applying the methods of communications theory. These myths possess three fundamental postulates, the first two of which are discernible at the narrative level, while the third must be inferred from those preceding. These postulates are: (1) the distinction between the world of men and the world of God; (2) the existence, between these two worlds, of a "space" which alters the message, a sort of "black box" which "explains" the difference between the message when it "enters" and "leaves"; and (3) the inversion of the relationship between "speed" and "slowness" on one hand, and between life and death on the other, in passing from the world of God into the world of men.

It is important to note first that the myths of the "failed message" do not confuse the celestial world with the terrestrial one. In accounts of this type there is never cohabitation between God and men; the raison d'être of the message is opposed to this. Certain of the myths are so definite on this subject that they take care to clearly specify this postulate. An Ashanti story recounts that long ago men had familiar dealings with God, who gave them everything they needed. One day, the women, annoyed by the divine presence, compelled God to withdraw, which he did, leaving the world to the power of the spirits. Some time later the Invisible sent men a goat with this message: "There is something which is called death (*owu*). One day it will kill some of you. But, even if you die, you will not be completely lost; you will come to join me in the sky." The goat dawdled along the way in order to eat. Seeing this, God sent a second messenger, a sheep, to carry the same message. This animal, however, altered the contents of the message to mean mortality and, arriving first among men, communicated it to them. Afterwards, when the goat presented himself and transmitted the words of God, no one believed him. Men had already accepted the sheep's message.[3]

We must also consider the "black box," the space between the two worlds which relays the message. It "contains" the factors which alter the message and the information it carries. These include: the bush (which in the preceding myth offers food to the goat and slows him down), the grass (which in a Kratchi account "captures" the medicine of immortality intended for men and benefits from it in their place),[4] and the termites (which according to a Tikar legend become the food for the frog who carries the message of life, thus delaying him in his mission).[5] The "black box" essentially accounts for the lead taken by the message of mortality over that of life. Indeed, as we will see later, it furnishes on the narrative level the justification for the semantic change in the ideas of speed and slowness.

These two concepts do not possess the same significance in the world of God as in the world of men. In the former,

---

[3]   See Edmond Perregaux, "Chez les Achanti," *Bulletin de la Société Neuchâtelosise de Géographie,* 17 (1906):198, as cited by Abrahamsson, *Origin of Death, p.* 5.

[4]   See A. W. Cardinall, *Tales Told in Togoland* (London: Oxford University Press, 1931), pp. 27ff., as cited by Abrhamsson, *Origin of Death,* p. 6.

[5]   See J. Sieber, "Aus dem sozialen Leben der Nord-Tikar," *Zeitschrift für Ethnologie,* 67 (1936):273ff., as cited by Abrahamsson, *Origin of Death,* p. 9.

speed connotes death, while slowness is tied to life. When the dead are "agitated" they constitute the Invisible's greatest menace towards men; in this sense their "activity" is synonymous with irritation and wrath. Similarly, when the sky kills it does so by means of a thunderbolt, and with the celerity of lightning. The dead must exist in slow time, for them "life" is equivalent to calm, rest, and peace. The living, by contrast, only merit their status by virtue of activity. Movement, speed, exertion, and zeal are the surest indices of their vitality. Inactivity, sleep, and torpor bring them closer to death and the inertia of the corpse.

We can now see that having left the "sky," each of the two heralds sees himself entrusted with the message which conforms to his behavior: the fast animal brings the message of death, the slow animal "conveys" life. According to human "logic," however, to receive "speed" is to have life, while to welcome "slowness" is to accept death. In addition, the swift messenger arrives in the terrestrial world first not only because he is more diligent but because, according to men, he signifies life. In sum, death introduces itself among the living under cover of the idea of speed, which signifies "life" from the human point of view and death according to the "logic" of the sky.

The "black box" and the messengers play the role of mediator between the celestial and terrestrial worlds. They allow the changeover from one signification to the other in the ideas signified by life and death (see fig. 1).

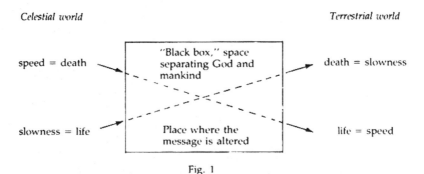

Celestial world   Terrestrial world

speed = death   "Black box," space   death = slowness
                       separating God and
                       mankind

slowness = life   Place where the   life = speed
                       message is altered

Fig. 1

The "black box" in particular assures the proper functioning of each of the worlds according to its specific modality. Without this mediating space human beings would pass without transition from their own "life-speed" to the "death-speed" of the sky, and the notion of speed would overlay the confusion of life and death.

This eventuality is not at all theoretical, since sometimes the sky sends death to men without the consideration shown in the myths which concern us here. Thus those struck by lightning, who enjoy a unique status throughout Africa precisely because they constitute points of immediate impact between the sky and the earth, pass from life to death without, so to speak, changing their "manner" of existing: they remain in a rapid time and yet belong totally to the sky.[6] The practices concerning lightning follow the same idea: the spot touched by this unmediated irruption of the sky becomes "sky" and must be withdrawn from ownership by men.[7]

It is interesting to note the way in which the peoples who have "failed-message" myths treat the two messengers. Aversion to both is practically universal. The chameleon in particular is held in disfavor by almost all the Bantu peoples and by others as well. This dislike for the slow animal is doubly justified, first because on the mythical level he let himself be overtaken by his teammate, the messenger of death, and second because in the human world slowness is associated with death.[8] The way in which the chameleon is "punished"

---

[6] In African societies the "altar" of people struck by lightning is usually not permitted in the same place as the "altars" of normal dead people. In Buganda and Burundi a woman who has survived being struck by lightning legally belongs to the sovereign, who is considered to be of celestial origin.

[7] The "cult" of thunder stones is explained in the same way.

[8] Except in cases where the slow animal also enjoys great longevity, such as the tortoise. In this case slowness—death is overshadowed by slowness—long life.

for its slowness by those who "hate" it is also significant. The Thonga, Zulu, Venda, Xhosa, Lamba, Acholi, Nyanja, Ngoni, and Mushikongo tribes force its mouth open and then throw in a pinch of tobacco, which causes the animal to die while its color changes first from green to orange and then from orange to black. This practice undoubtedly has the aim of showing the relation between the chameleon and lightning in terms of death: one kills by its slowness, the other by its speed; one is "slowness-death," the other is "speed-death." Even better, the chameleon may be considered a being permanently struck by lightning, like the albinos of the Baronga, who are called "lightning-ember" because they are thought to have been "burnt (*hisa*) by lightning in their mother's womb before their birth."[9] The bringing together of lightning, the person struck by lightning, and the chameleon is further justified when one realizes that this animal is used by "magicians" as if it were a piece of a tree struck by lightning in order to discover thieves. "It is used by certain magicians to discover thieves. They smear a chameleon with a drug which makes it turn white and then let it go: 'Then the thief, wherever he may be, also turns white, and if he does not confess his theft, he dies.'"[10]

Thus, insofar as it mediates between the sky and the earth regarding the "origin" of death, the chameleon is in an exceptional position. It is both "slowness," like "life" in the world above, and the celestial "cause" of human death, like lightning. In other words, the chameleon is the "incarnation" of the two contradictory ideas, life and death, united in one and the same being.

It is now easy to establish that the "failed-message" accounts of the origin of death are devoid of etiological intentionality concerning their apparent theme. Instead it can be said that they emphatically affirm the distinction

---

9   H. A. Junod, *Life of a South African Tribe*, 2:437n.

10   Ibid., 2:339.

between the world of God and that of men, the existence of a "no-man's-land" (the "black box") between these two worlds, and the mortal nature of man and the immortality of God. This manner of "speaking" about death is not without interest. It indicates the concern for locating the problem of human existence according to coordinates which are certainly open to question, but which conform to the culture and philosophy of men who cannot conceive of life and death without reference to the intervention of the "sky."

This same concern is reflected in another group of myths which fully accentuate the human condition. The stories of this category can be validly grouped into various referential sectors corresponding to essential life processes.

The ability to reproduce which man shares with the animal and vegetable world and which, at the same time, distinguishes him from the inorganic world, is most appropriate for allowing us to understand the origin of death. There is nothing more striking than the succession of beings endowed with life issuing from a single founder in which the offspring replace one another over the course of time. In a certain way isn't death linked to this very ability to reproduce? If life regenerates in order to preserve itself, it is fair to think that death is hidden within the act of life like a "portion" of the living person. Furthermore, to suppress the reproduction of the living would be equivalent to confusing the organic world with the inorganic world.

A Nupe myth on this subject recounts that in the beginning God created tortoises, men, and stones, and, with the exception of the stones, he made them both male and female and provided them with life. However, none of the species reproduced. One day the tortoise wanted to have descendants and asked this of God, whose response was that he had granted life to the tortoise and to men but had not given them permission to have children. At this time, the story adds, men did not die; when they became old they were automatically rejuvenated. The tortoise renewed his appeal and God warned him against the danger of death, which would result from a positive response on his part. But the tortoise took no notice and pressed his request. He was joined by men, who had decided to have children even at the risk of death, while the stones refused to join in with them. Thus God granted tortoises and men the ability to have a posterity, and death entered the world, but the stones remained unaffected.[11]

No less essential to life is sleep, which periodically plunges the living person into a state of unconsciousness which men in all times and places have likened to death. If the similarities between the two phenomena recall their "necessary" connection, then the absence of one will provoke the disappearance of the other and give rise to the idea of immortality. From this isn't it perfectly logical for mythical thought to establish just as "necessary" a connection between immortality and the state of wakefulness?

At the beginning of creation, states a Bassa myth, men were immortal. At this time there were no animosities or disputes, and animals were respected as brothers by men, who in return were done no harm by the animals. *Lolomb*, the divinity who never slept, enjoined men to stay awake at all times or else death would make its appearance in the world. But men could not resist sleeping and for this reason death began its work.[12]

Other accounts emphasize the need for food and relate death to the consumption of the nourishment essential for life. In the Congo basin, where bananas constitute man's basic source of food, it is natural that this fruit be chosen as the significant element in the narrative. Among the BaSonge,

---

[11] L. Frobenius, *Atlantis*, vol. 23 (Jena: E. Diedrerichs, 1924), p. 227, as cited by Abrahamsson, *Origin of Death*, p. 68.

[12] Georg Haessig, *Unter den Urwaldstämmen in Kamerun* (Stuttgart and Basel: Evangelischer Missionsverlag, 1933), p. 98.

the creator Fidi Mukullu made all things including man. He also planted banana trees. When the bananas were ripe he sent the sun to harvest them. The sun brought back a full basket to Fidi Mukullu, who asked him if he had eaten any. The sun answered no, and the creator decided to put his response to a test. He made the sun go down into a hole dug in the earth, then asked him when he wanted to get out. The sun answered, "Tomorrow morning, early." "If you did not lie," the creator told him, "you will get out early tomorrow morning." The next day the sun appeared at the desired moment, confirming his honesty. Next the moon was ordered to gather God's bananas and was put to the same test. She also got out successfully. Then came man's turn to perform the same task. However, on his way to the creator he ate a portion of the bananas and denied doing so. Put to the same test as the heavenly bodies, man said he wanted to leave the hole at the end of five days. But he never got out. Fidi Mukullu said "Man lied. That is why man will die and will never reappear."[13]

Aversion to the dead body and decay constitutes another of life's distinctive traits. Contact with organic matter in the state of decomposition, especially when it is the mortal remains of a fellow man, is a serious menace to the living being. Even in those societies which practice "desiccation" of the corpse, man eventually separates himself from anyone, no matter how beloved. Myths in the category of "premature burial" seem to ignore this requirement and associate the immortality of man with the nonburial of the corpse.

Among the Kongo, Nzambi created man and woman. The woman gave birth to a child. The creator forbade the parents from burying it in the event that it died; they were told to simply put the child in a corner of the hut and cover it up with wood, because after three days the child would come

[13] L. Frobenius, *Atlantis*, vol. 12 (Jena: E. Diederichs, 1928), p. 140, as cited by Abrahamsson, *Origin of Death*, p. 52.

124

back to life. The parents did not believe the words of God and when the child died they placed it in the earth. Then Nzambi declared: "I told you not to bury the child and you have buried it. For this reason all your descendants will be subject to the same malady; they will die because you violated my prohibition."[14]

This second category of myths about the origin of death is noticeably different from that of the "failed message." In the latter case we witnessed a complex "discourse" based, it could be said, on a veritable "theory" of information. But here the story is simpler and more direct. It takes the form of a line of argument whose conclusion consists of an option which conforms to the present human condition concerning one of the essential characteristics of life. Indeed, each of the myths in this category forces man to choose between mortality and immortality. But while the first alternative (mortality) expresses the present condition of man, the second (immortality) leads to its negation.

It is evident that the keystone of this line of argument, the human condition, is characterized among other things by reproduction, sleep, nourishment, and aversion to decay.[15] If mythical thought establishes a connection between death and each of these characteristics taken separately, it is because such a link exists beforehand between them and man's nature. Moreover, immortality is opposed to man's nature in the same way that the negative aspect of the essential characteristics of the human condition is opposed to their positive aspect. The result is that man

---

[14] J. van Wing, "Etudes Bakongo: Religion et Magie," Mémoires de l'Institut Royal Colonial Belge, vol. 9, no. 1, p. 25, as cited by Abrahamsson, *Origin of Death*, p. 98.

[15] We have only enumerated those aspects discussed above. The myths of the origin of death take into consideration other aspects, such as activity, health, the distinction between men and animals and between men and plants, and time.

"opts" for mortality because it conforms to his condition. In no way can he "opt" for immortality without automatically rejecting his very nature (see fig. 2).

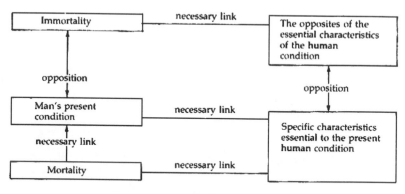

Fig. 2

Beyond this, what is interesting in the myths of this category, other than the type of reasoning for which they have a predilection, are the specific aspects according to which the human condition is grasped. These most often relate to the functions judged to be vital: sexuality, strength-regenerating rest, food, hygiene, and so on. But there are others which are concerned with, for example, knowledge or the emotional state which death causes among the living. Serer and Korongo myths deal with the first of these elements. In the beginning, say the Serer, men did not die. The first being to experience death was a dog. He was buried in a termite hill at the foot of a baobab tree, and, as no one had ever before seen a dead creature, this was a great event. While the women danced, the dog was wrapped in a cloth and gunshots were fired. When God (*Koh*) saw all that men were doing for the corpse of a dog he became angry, and from that moment on death became the lot of men as well.[16] The Korongo story chooses a tree trunk as the object to be

---

[16]   C. Tastevin, *Etudes Missionnaires, 2:85,* as cited by Abrahamsson, *Origin of Death*, p. 100.

buried. In the beginning of things, it is said, men did not die and their number seemed to be increasing indefinitely. In their happiness men began to perform mock burials and carried in procession tree trunks which they later buried with great ceremony. When God saw this he was irritated and sent sickness and death into the world to punish men for their mockery.[17]

It is easy to establish the structure of these two narratives in terms of what was said earlier. The present human condition is linked to the distinction between men and animals (Serer myth) and between men and trees (Korongo myth) in that men are buried but animals and trees are not. Thus death is found to be associated with an element which confirms this distinction, while immortality ("impossible" to realize) goes together with the confusion of men with animals or men with trees. Both of these stories emphasize the aspects of intelligence and the mind which are given the highest value by the two cultures involved: the ability to distinguish and classify, oppose and associate things in order to avoid confusion.

The emotional state resulting from death is the object of a Bena Kanioka myth. A hunter named Kassongo was visiting the village of Mauesse without permission during the dry season, a period marked by death and the desiccation of the celestial beings. One day Mauesse reprimanded the hunter and at the same time gave him a package. Shortly thereafter Kassongo's son died. Kassongo, not understanding what had happened (since at this time men enjoyed eternal life), returned to Mauesse's village to find out. He was given to understand that the package received by him contained the punishment for his transgression and he was advised to return to his home, place his dead son on a mat, and cry. Kassongo did what Mauesse prescribed. All the people assembled around the corpse and began to dance while they

---

[17]   S. F. Nadel, *The Nuba* (London: Oxford University Press, 1947), p. 268, as cited by Abrahamsson, *Origin of Death*, p. 101.

lamented. Meanwhile, Mauesse sent his dog to see if the humans were eating and laughing instead of crying. The dog returned to his master and said, "First, I saw men lamenting. Then I saw them eating, then I saw them lamenting. After that I saw men playing and laughing." Mauesse then pronounced his sentence: "Since men cannot even be sad, they must all learn to die."[18]

The structure of this myth is similar to that of the preceding stories. The present human condition involves complex funerary rites whose execution does not exclude, and in fact requires, feasting, drinking, exaltation, and even a certain gaiety. Thus, in order to avoid death, the men of the myth would have had to confine themselves to tears and lamentation. This requirement for immortality contradicts man's nature and thus becomes "unacceptable."

As can be seen, all these myths—like the "failed-message" stories—are not intended, despite their appearances, to inform us of the origin of death. Rather, by means of the problem which they set out to resolve, they make known their possessor's conception of the human condition. Life (the original "immortality") constitutes the fundamental principle of man's nature, from which all others derive. It can only be grasped by endowing it with all the attributes opposite to those which characterize mortality. This goes without saying since, on the one hand, death is the opposite of life, while on the other death furnishes men with an experience far more realistic and convincing than life.

Life also has priority in terms of time, since it precedes death. As a result of this intellectual requirement (which is so evident in the myths), these stories constitute the human being's first attempt to apprehend himself diachronically. They are man's attempts to find the elements of his own history, or even rough outlines for the first history of human

---

[18] Frobenius, *Atlantis*, vol. 12, p. 174, as cited by Abrahamsson, *Origin of Death*, pp. 100-101.

destiny. This means that death and the myths of its origin lead the mind directly toward the problem of social time, of time lived and of duration.

For the African, time is inconceivable without generations as its framework. The succession of human beings issuing one from another offers to African thought the ideal basis for establishing the three fundamental correlative stages of duration: past, present, and future. However, contrary to what we might expect, a succession of individuals linked by ties of birth appears on the ideal axis of time facing not the future but the past. The human being goes backward in time: he is oriented toward the world of the ancestors, toward those who no longer belong to the world of the living, while he turns his back on what is to come, the future. Future and past are thus determined in relation to the two major sides of the human body, the back and the front. Between them, the flanks, containing the ribs, are analogous to the present, connecting the two extremes.

From the point of view of the generations, the woman is equivalent to the rib because in bringing children into the world she assures the link between successive generations, between ascendants and descendants, between the past and the future. For this reason the woman remains the most engaging image of the present.

Within the lineage the past and the future are represented by the head of the family and his son. Between the two of them, the mother, carrying their descendants on her back, is extra-generational. As the present she belongs to both at once. She is above all a mediator, since the child perched on her hips is none other than an ancestor returned to the world of men through her. Thus everything occurs as if woman were the crossroad where future and past, death and life intersect. She results from ambiguity, from that which is at once tomb and resurrection, decay and vitality. But she incarnates the junction, the beginning and the end of the cycle of human existence. It is within the entrails of woman that we should locate the *ouroboros* as a symbol of rebirth. The mythical theme of the woman giving birth to a snake thus acquires its full meaning.[19]

Within this context the limits between life and death do not really exist. Life is born from death and death, in turn, is the prolongation of life.

Many so-called barbaric and savage customs may be explained in the light of these brief remarks. Take, for example, the alleged indifference if not cruelty towards the elderly, who are often abandoned to their fate. Certain Bushman tribes do not burden themselves on their difficult travels through the desert with old people who are helpless or hard to transport. Instead they build them a small enclosure of brush wood and abandon them there with, if possible, a small provision of wood, food, and water. If the rest of the community finds game and water quickly they send someone back with new provisions for the old people left behind. If not, they avoid even returning to visit those they deserted, knowing that the old ones would not be able to prolong their existence for very long and that soon the hyenas would not allow them to survive.[20] The Hottentots treat the elderly of their communities in a similar way. According to Kolb, when an aged Hottentot reaches extremely bad physical condition, his oldest son, or a close relative, asks the residents of the kraal for authorization to unburden himself of such a load and to deliver the old person from his misery. Since this permission is never refused, a bull or several sheep are killed for a feast and then, on the

[19] One of the many examples of this theme can be found in R. P. Eugene Hurel, *La Poésie chez les Primitifs, ou Contes, Fables, Récits et Proverbes du Rwanda (Lac Kivu)*, Bibliothèque-Congo (Brussels: Goemaere, 1922), pp.41-48.

[20] I. Schapera, *The Khoisan Peoples of South Africa* (London: Routledge and Kegan Paul, 1930), p. 162.

appointed day, the old person is placed on a carrier bull and escorted to a small hut constructed for this purpose at some distance from the kraal. He is abandoned there with only a small amount of food. The old person soon dies of starvation or is devoured by wild animals.[21]

These and other such customs encountered in Africa have often provoked the indignation of researchers, who have denounced them as cruel and inhuman. But these denunciations have constituted a rather quick judgment without accomplishing beforehand the necessary unraveling of the intricacies which order these practices. We must add that it is essentially the indifference to death and the contempt for life which cause astonishment. Bowdich reports that during his voyage to Kumasi he found himself one day in a village where the chief, accused of committing a serious offense, was awaiting execution. "He conversed cheerfully with us," recounts the explorer, "congratulated himself on seeing white men before he died, and spread his cloth over his leg with an emotion of dignity rather than shame; his head arrived in Coomassie the day after we had."[22] Winwood-Reade relates the story of an Akropon woman who had been stripped before the sacrifice, then clubbed unconscious but not killed. He writes,

> She recovered her senses and found herself lying upon the ground surrounded by dead bodies. She rose, went into town, where the elders were seated in council, and told them that she had been to the land of the Dead and had been sent back because she was naked.

---

[21] P. Kolb, *Reise zum Vorgebirge der Guten Hoffnung*, ed. Paul Germann (Liepzig: F. A. Brockhaus, 1926), as cited by Schapera, *Khoisan Peoples, p. 359.*

[22] T. E. Bowdich, *A Mission from Cape Coast Castle to Ashantee* (London: J. Murray, 1819), as cited by R. S. Rattray, *Religion and Art in Ashanti* (London: Oxford University Press, 1927), p. 106.

The elders must dress her finely and kill her over again. This was accordingly done.[23]

Almost everywhere in Africa the royal burial ceremonies of the past were accompanied by numerous human sacrifices, of which many were voluntary. "It is said," reports le Hérissé, "that for the kings of Dahomey those wives [of the deceased chief] not designated to be sacrificed would ask for it as a favor."[24] And R. S. Rattray adds, concerning the Ashanti,

Among the scores killed at royal funerals were some of the highest of the land—high court officials, relatives and wives of the dead monarch, who, no longer having any desire to live once "the great tree had fallen," compelled their relatives to slay them by swearing the great oath that they must do so, thus not leaving them any option except to carry out their wishes.[25]

Innumerable cases like these could be cited, and others from different areas could be added. Think, for example, of the impressive custom of ritually putting kings to death, and of the ease with which in the past human beings were sacrificed (particularly certain types such as albinos). Africa was undoubtedly a land stained red with human blood. All these deeds denote a religious "confusion" on the part of Africans between life and death, or rather an astonishing sense of life which in their eyes could only be fully realized if interrupted by momentary stopping points. Instead of diminishing and weakening life, these moments of rest give

---

[23] Winwood-Reade, *The Story of the Ashanti Campaign*, as cited by Rattray, *Religion and Art in Ashanti*, pp. 106-7.

[24] A. le Hérissé, *L'Ancien Royaume du Dahomey* (Paris: Larose, 1911), p. 180, n.1.

[25] Rattray, *Religion and Art in Ashanti*, p. 107.

it a new vigor each time, to the extent that life continues reinforced and renewed after each ordeal.

This conception of life and death, and implicitly of time, has extensions in other areas. Being oriented towards the past, the African finds the justification and meaning of his actions not in the future but in time already elapsed. His reasoning is thus "regressive": "I do this because my forefathers did it. And they did it because our ancestor did it." The profound and necessary connection between present activity and the past thus appears. The aim is to trace the present from the past and thereby justify it. This line of thought reveals on one hand the role played by tradition in African culture and, on the other, the meaning which is given to action.

This single word "tradition," when applied to African "customs" and beliefs, too often makes us think of some simplistic system of habits and routines according to which, turning against progress, Africans content themselves with the inability to grasp the new. However nothing of the kind is included in the notion of tradition as it should be understood to explain African religious behavior.

For Africans, tradition is above all the collective experience of the community. It constitutes the totality of all that successive generations have accumulated since the dawn of time, both in spiritual and practical life. It is the sum total of the wisdom held by a society at a given moment of its existence. If we admit that the ancestors do not constitute a closed community, but that they are seen as an assembly which is perpetually increasing and incessantly evolving, then we must recognize that tradition too is not at all static. In the same way that the past augments the "group" of those whom it keeps in its den, the living enrich their spiritual holdings owing to the experiences of the dead. Thus tradition is like the continual reappearance of buds from the protective scales at the tip of the supporting branch.

Tradition for Africans is, then, a means of communication between the dead and the living, as it represents the "word" of the ancestors. It belongs to a vast network of communications between the two worlds which embodies "prayer," offerings, sacrifices, and myths. In this relationship tradition possesses a real originality. At times it is direct, that is, it precludes any intermediary between man and the beyond. The living "feel" the wills and prescriptions of the ancestors; they divine them by a kind of intuition which does not seem to be based on any consciously perceived sign. In this sense tradition is a sort of tacit agreement between the past and the present. This is why in all good faith many Africans justify their religious behavior by invoking the similar comportment of their ancestors. At other times tradition is indirect, and in this case the human being perceives more or less clearly the reasons for his religious actions. By means of perception he seizes upon one or more indices (accidents, disasters, and so on) which justify both his conduct and the religious act which he performs. To an observer located outside the "system" this is particularly striking in medicine and the treatment of diseases according to traditional methods and remedies.

Whether in the form of one or the other of these two types of communication, tradition as the "word" of the dead remains the most vital means of assuring the link between the dead and the living. Owing to this "speech," which is transmitted through the ages, the presence of the ancestors among men is assured at each instant. By conforming to the legacy of the dead, the living in turn recognize their authority and avoid "dangerous" undertakings. Presence on the one hand and submission on the other, this is the very object of the exchanges between two worlds whose reciprocal permeability is never contested by any African. On the contrary, the African lives with the idea of a perpetual osmosis between the two interfacing realities. Yet one can see that it is the world of the living which occupies the unfavorable position in this exchange. It exists at the expense of the other, which is proof enough of its imperfection. From this fact spring the sad laments of the living, who wish to abandon the earth and "rise" to the sky. Take for example a funeral chant of the BaSotho, as reported by E. Casalis:

> We stayed outside,
> We stayed for the sorrow,
> We stayed for the tears.
> Oh, if there were a place in heaven for me!
> That I would have wings to fly there!
> If a strong cord came down from the sky,
> I would tie myself to it, I would climb up above,
> I would go to live there.[26]

H. Callaway[27] and H. A. Junod,[28] respectively, cite almost identical threnodies from the Zulu and the Thonga which demonstrate that this theme is quite widespread among the Bantu peoples of southeast Africa.

But it is not simply because the world of the ancestors is automatically associated with ideas of repose, tranquility, and peace that it appears as the quintessence of perfection. It is "magnificent" above all because of the prestigious character of its inhabitants. Not just anyone can become an ancestor. The society of the living "directs" towards this "paradise" only those dead who satisfy certain well-defined conditions.

Proceeding to the analysis of the notion of ancestor in African societies, we notice that it constitutes the crossroads of many ideas concerning the individual, society, time, and the divinity. In each society the notion of ancestor is formulated in relation to certain key ideas and according to a dialectic of thought which puts into play the law of oppositions and contrasts.

---

[26] Casalis, *Les Bassoutos* (Paris: Société des Missions Evangéliques, 1933), p.304. A Christian influence in this threnody is not ruled out.

[27] See H. Callaway, *The Religious System of the Amazulu* (London: Folk-Lore Society, 1884).

[28] Junod, *Life of a South African Tribe*, 2:430.

The ancestor is, first of all, a man who has reached a great age and who has acquired along with longevity a profound experience of people and things. He is thus distinguished from people less advanced in age and whose credulity and inexperience in life classify them with children or youths; the latter are usually not given elaborate funerals and are never the focus of a "cult." Second, an individual who dies from a "dishonorable" disease is definitively struck from the list of ancestors. Thus it is impossible for a man dying from, say, leprosy to become an ancestor. There exist in Africa several specific illnesses which are incompatible with the esteem, radiance, and glory of the dead.[29] It seems that the dead can only be honored by the living if they have ended their lives in conformity with the rules of society. An accidental death also constitutes a humiliation and a stigma, and its consequences in the hereafter are inauspicious for gaining a "halo." A mortal accident breaks in some way the natural and regular progression of things; it constitutes a distressing event which is striking because of the suddenness with which it shatters order by brutally destroying the continuum of time. In addition, physical and psychic integrity represents a fundamental condition for aspiring to the rank of ancestor. All those who are abnormal, all those who deviate from the usual type of person in a society, are automatically excluded from the category of "illustrious" dead. Thus the deformed and mentally ill can never figure among the "chosen." The same ostracism applies to perjurers and any individual who does not enjoy moral integrity. It should be said here that, for the African, moral integrity is of prime importance; he places it before all else in the mastery of the self and, in particular, in the mastery of one's speech. Finally, the ancestor in Africa is always and everywhere an "organic" member of the

---

[29] It would seem that the opposition between these illnesses and the "glorious" state of the ancestors is among many peoples based on the impossibility of burying the dead according to the normal practices.

community of the living; he is one of the links in the chain. Thus the stranger even if he is adopted and integrated into a given society, cannot pretend to the title of ancestor there, since he is forever a juxtaposed component. The stranger lacks participation and communion with the life of the group in its spatial and temporal continuity.

Considered closely, the body of norms which govern the elaboration and preservation of the notion of ancestor seems to rest on two key ideas: (1) the purity of a type of man, conceived by the group as a social and religious model to which individuals must conform in order to avoid their destruction; and (2) the concern for the continuity and identity of the group over time and despite the vicissitudes of existence. In this regard it is interesting to note that the characteristics of the ancestor—wisdom, physical and moral integrity, passage through life without deviating from its normal course, and communal identification with the society to which one belongs—all constitute attributes involving the idea of completion. And ideally, if they are extended to their highest degree, we arrive at the supreme ideal, superhuman perfection, the divinity. We can thus understand that according to African thought God is often located at the farthest extension of the idea of ancestor, the latter sometimes envisioned as the eponymous hero of the group, sometimes as the intermediary between the divinity and men.

Whatever the circumstances, the ancestor can only fully play his role in the spiritual life of the society of the living if he withdraws from it to a certain extent. This separation is sometimes more symbolic than real. Among the Bantu of southeast Africa solitary old people are assimilated in anticipation with those from their age-set who have disappeared, that is, the ancestors.[30] Normally, however, wise men do not enjoy this status until after their death, and

---

[30] See J. Roumeguère-Eberhardt, *Penseé et société africaines* (Paris and the Hague: Mouton, 1963), p. 31.

particularly not until after their clear separation from the society of the living has been marked by second burial ceremonies (the lifting of mourning) or by alterations to their tombs.

Even if in principle all dead people who have satisfied the social and religious requirements discussed above can be considered as ancestors, in reality few of them are invoked as such by their descendants. From the total number of the "chosen" each society seems to distinguish a "useful" portion, arranged at various points in the series of generations, who alone are advantageously put to the service of the living. The remainder become blurred in the memory of the living and constitute the refuse of the hereafter, whose memory is recalled without precise reference particularly during new-year rites. Thus, in the same way that some people join the lot of the useless dead at the time of their departure for the hereafter, so the ancestors themselves become partially unusable through the weakness of the living.

We see from this brief analysis of the notion of ancestor that men are doubly indebted to their "glorious" dead. On one hand they owe them their knowledge and wisdom as well as the guarantee of authenticity with respect to tradition, while on the other they are indebted to them for their intervention and mediation on the level of spiritual life strictly speaking. This explains the considerable hold which so-called "ancestor-worship" has on the African soul.

But the relation between the past, present, and future also generates the meaning which the African attributes to his own action. As we have seen before, this action is rooted not in the future but in the past. Action is also synonymous with realization, which is why it is opposed to speech, which has neither form nor measure and which, once spoken, takes off and dissolves in the air. By contrast, action is what man does, what supports him when he undertakes a new effort. And yet one cannot be understood without the other. Speech and action are like two aspects of the same reality, which, in the eyes of Africans, constitutes the full realization of man himself. The balanced dosage of word and act expresses the perfection and completion of the human being.

Still, it is the past which gives measure and volume to this completion, on the condition that man relies on the experience and wisdom of the generations which preceded him, that he agrees to be subject to the authority of the ancestors and tradition, and that he accepts their example as the stimulus and norm of his behavior.

In this aspect of African thinking we are witness to a total reversal of our usual conceptions of the ideal and of progress. For the African the ideal takes the form of an exemplary past which is realized in the present. The supreme ideal for him is the indefinite repetition of the normative past, enriched at each realization by the acquisitions furnished by the present. The ideal does not constitute a model or standard tied to the future but rather an ensemble of values ascribed to the past.

It is easy to see that under these conditions the African, living according to tradition, sees progress above all as the realization by a given generation of stages which others have reached before it. It is always the present generation which is at the point of progress, but this generation is in some way unconscious of the acquisitions which it makes and which will form the first step for the next generation in its own climb to the past. Any religious or social innovation is thus less profitable to its authors than to those who come after them. Like the ideal, progress too is intimately linked to the past.

But the reference to the past is a human reference, because, of all the moments of time, only the past carries traces of human action. It is the only truly humanized period. This explains the profound relation which exists in the eyes of Africans between the idea of progress and the moral achievement of man.

OLAUDAH EQUIANO

(1745-1797)

THE INTERESTING NARRATIVE OF THE LIFE OF OLAUDAH EQUIANO OR GUSTAVUS VASSA, THE AFRICAN

(1789)

Equiano's *Life* is the first of a great series of slave narratives and probably influenced the slave narrative of Frederick Douglass (see LCSR, Vol. 2). In the excerpt below Equiano tells of his birth and happy early life as a son of an Ibo chief in the Essaka region of what is today Nigeria, West Africa.[1] Then, when he was eleven, he and his sister were captured

---

[1] Recently Vincent Carretta has called into question Equiano's African birth, noting that his baptismal record and naval muster state that he was born in South Carolina. However, these documents must have been based on Equiano's own statements, and many scholars believe he had reason to conceal the truth about his African birth during his precarious early life as a slave and newly freed slave. The strong accuracy of the rest of his autobiography suggests that its account is to be preferred over the earlier documents. See Vincent Carretta, "Olaudah Equiano or Gustavus Vassa? New Light on an Eighteenth-century Question of Identity," *Slavery and Abolition*, 20:3 (December 1999), 96-105.

by slave traders, and after spending time with several African masters, he was sent across the Atlantic (the excerpt below describes the infamous "middle passage") and sold to a Captain Pascal of the Royal Navy.

He fought on Pascal's flagship during the Seven Years' War. Even though he had earned enough to buy his freedom, Pascal resold him, confiscating the money. Pascal had renamed him Gustavus Vassa, but Equiano hated the name and assumed his original name after buying his freedom. This he finally gained in 1766 after working several years for his new master, a Pennsylvania Quaker, who trained him in the skilled craft of gauger.

After this, he continued to sail widely in the Atlantic and Mediterranean and even on an Arctic expedition; he worked in many occupations, including navigator, cook, and shipping clerk. A decisive event was his conversion; he became a fervent Christian and trained to become a missionary in both Central America and Africa, but these plans were thwarted.

The inhuman treatment of the slaves he had observed led him to become a leading abolitionist in Britain. The publication of his autobiography in 1789 greatly contributed to the British abolitionist movement, and Equiano went on numerous lecture tours to promote the book, which was reprinted eight times in his lifetime and another sixteen before 1900.

Equiano married an Englishwoman, Susanna Cullen, and they had two daughters. The daughter who survived him inherited a substantial fortune accumulated from the earnings of his book.

SOURCE

Equiano, Olaudah. The Interesting Narrative of the Life of Olaudah Equiano, or Gustavus Vassa, the African: Written by himself. Leeds: James Nichols, 1814.

Selections from:
>Chapter I (excerpted 3-13)
>Chapter II (excerpted 20-22, 26-29, 31-38)

CHAPTER I

. . . II. That part of Africa, known by the name of Guinea, to which the trade for slaves is carried on, extends along the coast above 3,400 miles, from Senegal to Angola, and includes a variety of kingdoms. Of these the most considerable is the kingdom of Benin, both as to extent and wealth, the richness and cultivation of the soil, the power of its king, and the number and warlike disposition of the inhabitants. It is situated nearly under the line, and extends along the coast about 170 miles, but runs back into the interior of Africa to a distance hitherto, I believe, unexplored by any traveller; and seems only terminated at length by the empire of Abyssinia, near 1,500 miles from its beginning. This kingdom is divided into many provinces or districts; in one of the most remote and fertile of which, named Essaka, situated in a charming fruitful vale, I was born. The distance of this province from the capital of Benin and the sea coast must be very considerable: for I had never heard of white men or Europeans, nor of the sea: and our subjection to the king of Benin was little more than nominal. Every transaction of the government, as far as my slender observation extended, was conducted by the chiefs or elders of the place. The manners and government of a people who have little commerce with other countries, are generally very simple; and the history of what passes in one family or village may serve as a specimen of nation. My father was one of those elders or chiefs of whom I have spoken, and was stiled Embrenche; a term, as I remember, importing the highest distinction, and signifying in our language "a mark of grandeur." This mark is conferred on the person entitled to it, by cutting the skin across at the top of the forehead, and drawing it down to the eye brows; and applying a warm hand to it, while in this situation, and rubbing it until it shrinks up into a thick wale across the lower part of the forehead. Most of the judges and senators were thus marked; my father had long borne this badge: I had seen it conferred on one of my brothers, and I was also destined to receive it by my parents. Those Embrenche, or chief men, decided disputes, and punished crimes; for which purpose they always assembled together. The proceedings were generally short; and in most cases the law of retaliation prevailed. I remember a man was brought before my father, and the other judges, for kidnapping a boy; and, although he was the son of a chief, or senator, he was condemned to make recompense by a man or woman slave. Adultery, however, was sometimes punished by slavery or death; a punishment which I believe is inflicted on it throughout most of the nations of Africa; so sacred among them is the honour of the marriage bed, and so jealous are they of the fidelity of their wives. Of this I recollect an instance;—A woman was convicted, before the judges, of adultery, and delivered over, as the custom was, to her husband to be punished. Accordingly he determined to put her to death; but it being found, just before her execution, that she had an infant at her breast; and no woman being prevailed on to perform the part of a nurse, she was spared on account of the child. The men, however, do not preserve the same constancy to their wives, which they expect from them; for they indulge in a plurality, though seldom in more than two. Their mode of marriage is this:— Both parties are usually betrothed when young by their parents, though I have known the males betroth themselves. On this occasion a feast is prepared, and the bride and bridegroom stand up in the midst of all their friends, who are assembled for the purpose, while he declares she is thenceforth to be looked upon as his wife, and that no person is to pay any addresses to her. This is also immediately proclaimed in the vicinity, on which the bride retires from the assembly. Some time after she is brought home to her husband, and then another feast is made, to which the relations of both parties are invited. Her parents then deliver her to the bridegroom, accompanied with a number of blessings, and at the same time they tie round her waist a cotton string of the thickness of a goose-quill, which none but married women are permitted to wear. She is now considered as completely his wife; and at this time the dowry is given to the new married pair, which generally consists of *portions of land, slaves and cattle, household goods, and implements of husbandry.* These are offered by the friends of both parties: besides which the parents of the bride-groom present gifts to those of the bride, whose property she is looked upon before marriage; but after it she is esteemed the sole property of her husband. The ceremony being now ended, the festival begins, which is celebrated with bonfires, and loud acclamations of joy, accompanied with music and dancing.

III. We are almost a nation of dancers, musicians, and poets. Every great event, such as a triumphant return from battle, or other cause of public rejoicing, is celebrated in public dances, which are accompanied with songs and music suited to the occasion. The assembly is separated into four divisions, which dance either apart or in succession, and each with a character peculiar to itself. The first division contains the married men, who in their dances frequently exhibit feats of arms, and the representation of a battle. To these succeed the married women, who dance in the second division. The young men occupy the third; and the maidens the fourth. Each represents some interesting scene of real life, such as a great achievement, domestic employment, a pathetic story, or some rural sport. And as the subject is generally founded on some recent event, it is therefore ever new. This gives our dances a spirit and variety which I have scarcely seen elsewhere. We have many musical instruments, particularly drums of different kinds, a piece of music which resembles a guitar, and another much like a sticcado. These last are chiefly used by betrothed virgins, who play on them on all grand festivals.

As our manners are simple, our luxuries are few. The dress of both sexes is nearly the same. It generally consists of a long piece of calico or muslin, wrapped loosely round the body, somewhat in the form of a Highland plaid. This is usually dyed blue, which is our favourite colour. It is extracted from a berry, and is brighter and richer than any I have seen in Europe. Besides this, our women of distinction wear golden ornaments; which they dispose with some profusion on their arms and legs. When our women are not employed with the men in tillage, their usual occupation is spinning and weaving cotton, which they afterwards dye, and make into garments. They also manufacture earthen vessels, of which we have many kinds; among the rest tobacco pipes, made after the same fashion, and used in the same manner, as those in Turkey.

Our manner of living is entirely plain; for as yet the natives are unacquainted with those refinements in cookery which debauch the taste. Bullocks, goats, and poultry, supply the greatest part of their food. These constitute likewise the principal wealth of the country, and the chief articles of its commerce. The flesh is usually stewed in a pan; to make it savory we sometimes use also pepper, and other spices, and we have salt made of wood ashes. Our vegetables are mostly plantains, eadas, yams, beans, and Indian corn. The head of the family usually eats alone; his wives and slaves have also their separate tables. Before we taste food we always wash our hands: indeed our cleanliness on all occasions is extreme; but on this it is an indispensable ceremony. After washing, libation is made, by pouring out a small portion of the drink on the floor, and by tossing a small quantity of the food in a certain place, for the spirits of departed relations, which the natives suppose to preside over their conduct, and to guard them from evil. They are totally unacquainted with strong or spirituous liquors; and their principal beverage is palm wine. This is got from a tree of that name by tapping it at the top, and fastening a large gourd to it; and sometimes one tree will yield three or four gallons in a night. When just drawn it is of a most delicious sweetness; but in a few days it acquires a spirituous flavour: though I never saw any one intoxicated by it. The same tree also produces nuts and oil. Our principal luxury is in perfumes; one sort of these is an odoriferous wood of delicious fragrance: the other a kind of earth; a small portion of which thrown into the fire diffuses a most powerful odour. We beat this wood into powder, and mix it with palm oil; with which both men and women perfume themselves.

IV. In our buildings we study convenience rather than ornament. Each master of a family has a large square piece of ground, surrounded with a moat or fence, or enclosed with a wall made of red earth tempered: which, when dry, is as hard as brick. Within this are his houses to accommodate his family and slaves; which, if numerous, frequently cause these tenements to present the appearance of a village. In the middle stands the principal building, appropriated to the sole use of the master, and consisting of two apartments; in one of which he sits in the day with his family, the other is left apart for the reception of his friends. He has besides these a distinct apartment in which he sleeps, together with his male children. On each side are the apartments of his wives, who have also their separate day and night houses. The habitations of the slaves and their families are distributed throughout the rest of the enclosure. These houses never exceed one story in height: they are always built of wood, or stakes driven into the ground, crossed with wattles, and neatly plastered within and without. The roof is thatched with reeds. Our day-houses are left open at the sides; but those in which we sleep are always covered, and plastered in the inside with a composition mixed with cowdung, to keep off the different insects, which annoy us during the night. The walls and floors also of these are generally covered with mats. Our beds consist of a platform, raised three or four feet from the ground, on which are laid skins, and different parts of a spungy tree called plantain. Our covering is calico, or muslin, the same as our dress. The usual seats are a few logs of wood; but we have benches, which are generally perfumed, to accommodate strangers: these compose the greater part of our household furniture. Houses so constructed and furnished require but little skill to erect them. Every man is a sufficient architect for the purpose. The whole neighbourhood afford their unanimous assistance in building them, and in return receive, and expect no other recompense than a feast.

As we live in a country where nature is prodigal of her favours, our wants are few and easily supplied; of course we have few manufactures. They consist for the most part of calicoes, earthenware, ornaments, and instruments of war and husbandry. But these make no part of our commerce, the principal articles of which, as I have observed, are provisions. In such a state money is of little use; however we have some small pieces of coin, if I may call them such. They are made something like an anchor; but I do not remember either their value or denomination. We have also markets, at which I have been frequently with my mother. These are sometimes visited by stout mahogany-coloured men from the south-west of us: we call them Oye-Eboe, which term signifies "red men living at a distance." They generally bring us fire-arms, gunpowder, hats, beads, and dried fish. The last we esteemed a great rarity, as our waters were only brooks and springs. These articles they barter with us for odoriferous woods and earth, and our salt of wood ashes. They always carry slaves through our land; but the strictest account is exacted of their manner of procuring them, before they are suffered to pass. Sometimes, indeed, we sold slaves to them, but they were only prisoners of war, or such among us as had been convicted of kidnapping, or adultery, and some other crimes, which we esteemed heinous. This practice of kidnapping induces me to think, that, notwithstanding all our strictness, their principal business among us was to trepan our people. I remember, too, they carried great sacks along with them, which not long after, I had an opportunity of fatally seeing applied to that infamous purpose.

V. Our land is uncommonly rich and fruitful, and produces all kinds of vegetables in great abundance. We have plenty of Indian corn, and vast quantities of cotton and tobacco. Pine-apples grow without culture; they are about the size of the largest sugar-loaf, and finely flavoured. We have also spices of different kinds, particularly pepper; and a variety of delicious fruits which I have never seen in Europe; together with gums of various kinds, and honey in abundance. All our industry is exerted to improve those blessings of nature. Agriculture is our chief employment; and every one, even to children and women, is engaged in it. Thus we are habituated to labour from our earliest years. Every one contributes something to the common stock: and as we are unacquainted with idleness, we have no beggars. The benefits of such a mode of living are obvious.—The West India planters prefer the slaves of Benin or Eboe, to those of any other part of Guinea, for their hardiness, intelligence, integrity, and zeal.—Those benefits are felt by us in the general healthiness of the people, and in their vigour and activity; I might have added, too, in their comeliness. Deformity is indeed unknown amongst us, I mean that of shape. Numbers of the natives of Eboe, now in London, might be brought in support of this assertion: for, in regard to complexion, ideas of beauty are wholly relative. I remember while in Africa to have seen three negro children, who were tawny, and another quite white, who were universally regarded as deformed by myself and the natives in general, as far as related to their complexions. Our women, too, were in my eyes at least uncommonly graceful, alert, and modest to a degree of bashfulness; nor do I remember to have ever heard of an instance of incontinence amongst them before marriage. They are also remarkably cheerful. Indeed cheerfulness and affability are two of the leading characteristics of our nation.

Our tillage is exercised in a large plain or common, some hours walk from our dwellings, and all the neighbours resort thither in a body. They use no beasts of husbandry; and their only instruments are hoes, axes, shovels, and beaks, or pointed iron to dig with. Sometimes we are visited by locusts, which come in large clouds, so as to darken the air, and destroy our harvest. This, however, happens rarely, but when it does, a famine is produced by it. I remember an instance or two of this happening. This common is often the theatre of war; and therefore, when our people go out to till their land, they not only go in a body, but generally take their arms with them for fear of a surprise: and when they apprehend an invasion, they guard the avenues to their dwellings by striking sticks into the ground, which are so sharp at one end as to pierce the foot, and are generally dipped in poison. From what I can recollect of these battles, they appear to have been irruptions of one little state or district into another, to obtain prisoners or booty. Perhaps they were incited to this by those traders, who brought amongst us the European goods which I mentioned. Such a mode of obtaining slaves in Africa is common; and I believe more are procured this way, and by kidnapping, than in any other. When a trader wants slaves, he applies to a chief for them, and tempts him with his wares. It is not extraordinary, if on this occasion he yields to the temptation with as little firmness, and accepts the price of his fellow-creature's liberty with as little reluctance as the enlightened merchant. Accordingly he falls on his neighbours, and a desperate battle ensues. If he prevails and takes prisoners, he gratifies his avarice by selling them; but if his party be vanquished, and he falls into the hands of the enemy, he is put to death: for, as he has been known to foment their quarrels, it is thought dangerous to let him survive, and no ransom can save him, though all other prisoners may be redeemed. We have fire-arms, bows and arrows, broad two-edged swords and javelins, also shields which will cover a man from head to foot. All are taught the use of these weapons; even our women are warriors, and march boldly out to fight along with the men. Our whole district is a kind of militia: on a certain signal given, such as the firing of a gun at night, they all rise in arms and rush upon their enemy. It is perhaps, something remarkable, that when our people march to the field, a red flag or banner is borne before them. I was once a witness to a battle on our common. We had been all at work in it one day, as usual, when our people were suddenly attacked. I climbed a tree at some distance, from which I beheld the fight. There were many women, as well as men, on both sides; among others my mother was there, and armed with a broad sword. After fighting for a considerable time with great fury, when many had been killed, our people obtained the victory, and took their enemy's chief prisoner. He was carried off in great triumph, and though he offered a large ransom for his life, he was put to death. A virgin of note among our enemies had been slain in the battle, and her arm was exposed in our market-place, where our trophies were always exhibited. The spoils were divided according to the merit of the warriors. Those prisoners which were not sold or redeemed we kept as slaves: but how different was their condition from that of the slaves in the West Indies! With us they do no more work than other members of the community, than even their masters; their food, clothing, and lodging, were nearly the same as theirs, except that they were not permitted to eat with those who were free-born; and there was scarcely any other difference between them, than a superior degree of importance, which the head of a family possesses in our state, and that authority which, as such, he exercises over every part of his household. Some of these slaves have even slaves under them, as their own property, and for their own use.

VI. As to religion, the natives believe that there is one Creator of all things, and that he lives in the sun, and is girded round with a belt that he may never eat or drink; but, according to some, he smokes a pipe, which is our own favourite luxury. They believe he governs events, especially our deaths or captivity; but, as for the doctrine of eternity, I do not remember to have ever heard of it: some, however, believe in the transmigration of souls in a certain degree.— Those spirits, which are not transmigrated, such as their dear friends or relations, they believe always attend them, and guard them from the bad spirits, or their foes. For this reason they always before eating, as I have observed, put some small portion of the meat, and pour some of the drink, on the ground for them; and they often make oblations of the blood of beasts, or fowls at their graves. I was very fond of my mother, and was almost constantly with her. When she went to make these oblations at her mother's tomb, which was a kind of small solitary thatched house, I sometimes attended her. There she made her libations, and spent most of the night in cries and lamentations. I have been often extremely terrified on these occasions. The loneliness of the place, the darkness of the night, and the ceremony of libation, naturally awful and gloomy, were heightened by my mother's lamentations; and these, concurring with the doleful cries of birds, by which these places were frequented, gave an inexpressible terror to the scene. . . .

CHAPTER II

I. . . . I have already acquainted the reader with the time and place of my birth. My father, besides many slaves, had a numerous family, of which seven lived to grow up, including myself and a sister, who was the only daughter. As I was the youngest of the sons, I became, of course, the greatest favourite with my mother, and was always with her, and she used to take particular pains to form my mind. I was trained up from my earliest years in the art of war; my daily exercise was shooting and throwing javelins; and my mother adorned me with emblems, after the manner of our greatest warriors. In this way I grew up till I was turned the age of eleven, when an end was put to my happiness in the following manner:—When the grown people in the neighbourhood were gone far in the fields to labour, the children generally assembled together in some of the neighbours' premises to play; and some of us often used to get up into a tree to look out for any assailant, or kidnapper, that might come upon us. For they sometimes took those opportunities of our parents' absence to attack and carry off as many as they could seize. One day, as I was watching at the top of a tree in our yard, I saw one of those people come into the yard of our next neighbour but one, to kidnap, there being many stout young people in it. Immediately on this I gave the alarm of the rogue, and he was surrounded by the stoutest of them, who entangled him with cords, so that he could not escape till some of the grown people came and secured him.

II. But alas! ere long it was my fate to be thus attacked, and to be carried off, when none of the grown people were nigh. One day, when all our people were gone out to their work as usual, and only I and my sister were left to mind the house, two men and a woman got over our walls, and in a moment seized us both; and without giving us time to cry out, or to make resistance, they stopped our mouths, and ran off with us into the nearest wood. Here they tied our hands, and continued to carry us as far as they could, till night came on, when we reached a small house, where the robbers halted for refreshment and spent the night. We were then unbound, but were unable to take any food; and being quite overpowered by fatigue and grief, our only relief was some sleep, which allayed our misfortune for a short time. The next morning we left the house, and continued travelling all the day. For a long time we had kept the woods, but at last we came into a road which I believed I knew. I had now some hopes of being delivered; for we had advanced but a little way before I discovered some people at a distance, on which I began to cry out for their assistance; but my cries had no other effect than to make them tie me faster and stop my mouth; they then put me into a large sack. They also stopped my sister's mouth, and tied her hands; and in this manner we proceeded till we were out of sight of these people.

When we went to rest the following night, they offered us some victuals; but we refused it; and the only comfort we had was in being in one another's arms all that night, and bathing each other with our tears. But alas! we were soon deprived of even the small comfort of weeping together. The next day proved one of greater sorrow than I had yet experienced; for my sister and I were then separated, while we lay clasped in each other's arms. It was in vain that we besought them not to part us; she was torn from me, and immediately carried away, while I was left in a state of distraction not to be described. I cried and grieved continually; and for several days I did not eat any thing but what they forced into my mouth. . . .

[Equiano tells about his experiences in Africa after his capture.]

IV. . . . From the time I left my own nation I always found somebody that understood me till I came to the sea coast. The languages of different nations did not totally differ, nor were they so copious as those of the Europeans, particularly the English. They were therefore easily learned; and, while I was journeying thus through Africa, I acquired two or three different tongues. In this manner I had been travelling for a considerable time, when one evening, to my great surprise, whom should I see brought to the house where I was, but my dear sister? As soon as she saw me she gave a loud shriek, and ran into my arms. I was quite overpowered: neither of us could speak; but, for a considerable time, clung to each other in mutual embraces, unable to do any thing but weep.

Our meeting affected all who saw us; and indeed I must acknowledge, in honour of those sable destroyers of human rights, that I never met with any ill treatment, or saw any offered to their slaves, except tying them, when necessary, to keep them from running away.

When these people knew we were brother and sister, they indulged us to be together; and the man, to whom I supposed we belonged, lay with us, he in the middle, while she and I held one another by the hands across his breast all night; and thus for a while we forgot our misfortunes in the joy of being together. But even this small comfort was soon to have an end, for scarcely had the fatal morning appeared, when she was again torn from me for ever! I was now more miserable, if possible, than before. The small relief which her presence gave me from pain was gone, and the wretchedness of my situation was redoubled by my anxiety after her fate, and my apprehensions lest her sufferings should be greater than mine, when I could not be with her to alleviate them.

Yes, dear partner of all my childish sports! Sharer of my joys and sorrows; happy should I have ever esteemed myself to encounter every misery for you, and to procure your freedom by the sacrifice of my own! Though you were early forced from my arms, your image has been always rivetted in my heart, from which neither time nor fortune has been able to remove it: so that, while the thoughts of your sufferings have damped my prosperity, they have mingled with adversity and increased its bitterness. To that Heaven, which protects the weak from the strong, I commit the care of your innocence and virtues, if they have not already received their full reward, and if your youth and delicacy have not long since fallen victims to the violence of the African trader, the pestilential stench of a Guinea ship, the seasoning in the European colonies, or the lash and lust of a brutal and unrelenting overseer.

I did not long remain after my sister. I was again sold, and carried through a number of places, till, after travelling a considerable time, I came to a town called Tinmah, in the most beautiful country I had yet seen in Africa. It was extremely rich, and there were many rivulets which flowed through it, and supplied a large pond in the centre of the town, where the people washed. Here I first saw and tasted cocoa nuts, which I thought superior to any nuts I had ever tasted before; and the trees which were loaded, were also interspersed among the houses, which had commodious shades adjoining, and were in the same manner as ours, the insides being neatly plastered and whitewashed. Here I also saw and tasted, for the first time, sugar-cane. Their money consisted of little white shells, the size of the finger nail. I was sold here for one hundred and seventy-two of these, by a merchant who lived at this place. I had been about two or three days at his house, when a wealthy widow, a neighbour of his came there one evening, and brought with her an only son, a young gentleman about my own age and size. Here they saw me; and, having taken a fancy to me, I was bought of the merchant, and went home with them. Her house and premises were situated close to one of those rivulets I have mentioned, and were the finest I ever saw in Africa: they were very extensive, and she had a number of slaves to attend her. The next day I was washed and perfumed, and when meal-time came, I was led into the presence of my mistress, and ate and drank before her with her son. This filled me with astonishment; and I could scarcely avoid expressing my surprise that the young gentleman should suffer me, who was bound, to eat with him who was free; and not only so, but that he would not at any time either eat or drink till I had taken first, because I was the eldest, which was agreeable to our custom. Indeed every thing here, and their treatment of me, made me forget that I was a slave. The language of these people resembled ours so nearly, that we understood each other perfectly. They had also the very same customs as we. There were likewise slaves daily to attend us, while my young master and I, with other boys, sported with our darts, and bows and arrows, as I had been used to do at home. In this resemblance to my former happy state, I passed about two months; and I now began to think I was to be adopted into the family, and was beginning to be reconciled to my situation, and to forget by degrees my misfortunes, when all at once the delusion vanished; for, without the least previous knowledge, one morning early, while my dear master and companion was still asleep, I was wakened out of my reverie to fresh sorrow, and hurried away even amongst the uncircumcised.

Thus, at the very moment I dreamed of the greatest happiness, I found myself most miserable; and it seemed as if fortune wished to give me this taste of joy, only to render the reverse more poignant. The change I now experienced was as painful as it was sudden and unexpected. It was a change indeed from a state of bliss to a scene which is inexpressible by me, as it discovered to me an element I had never before beheld, and of which till then had no idea; and wherein such instances of hardship and cruelty continually occurred, as I can never reflect on but with horror. . . .

V. [Equiano describes the African peoples whom he encountered along the coast.] . . . The first object which saluted my eyes when I arrived on the coast was the sea, and a slave ship, which was then riding at anchor, and waiting for its cargo. These filled me with astonishment, that was soon converted into terror, which I am yet at a loss to describe, and much more the then feelings of my mind when I was carried on board. I was immediately handled and tossed up to see if I were sound, by some of the crew; and I was now persuaded that I had got into a world of bad spirits, and that they were going to kill me. Their complexions too, differing so much from ours, their long hair, and the language they spoke, which was very different from any I had ever heard united to confirm me in this belief. Indeed such were the horrors of my views and fears at the moment, that if ten thousand worlds had been my own, I would have freely parted with them all to have exchanged my condition with that of the meanest slave in my own country. When I looked round the ship too, and saw a large furnace or copper boiling, and a multitude of black people, of every description chained together, every one of their countenances expressing dejection and sorrow, I no longer doubted of my fate; and, quite overpowered with horror and anguish, I fell motionless on the deck, and fainted. When I recovered a little I found some black people about me, who I believed were some of those who brought me on board, and had been receiving their pay: they talked to me in order to cheer me, but all in vain. I asked them if we were not to be eaten by those white men with horrible looks, red faces, and long hair. They told me I was not: and one of the crew brought me a small portion of spirituous liquor in a wine glass; but, being afraid of him, I would not take it out of his hand. One of the blacks therefore took it from him and gave it to me, and I took a little down my palate, which, instead of reviving me, as they thought it would, threw me into the greatest consternation at the strange feeling it produced, having never tasted any such liquor before.

Soon after this the blacks who brought me on board went off, and left me abandoned to despair. I now saw myself deprived of all chance of returning to my native country, or even the least glimpse of gaining the shore, which I now considered as friendly; and I even wished for my former slavery, in preference to my present situation, which was filled with horrors of every kind, still heightened by my ignorance of what I was to undergo. I was not long suffered to indulge my grief; I was soon put down under the decks, and there I received such a salutation in my nostrils as I had never experienced in my life: so that, with the loathsomeness of the stench, and with my crying together, I became so sick and low that I was not able to eat, nor had I the least desire to taste any thing. I now wished for the last friend, death, to relieve me; but soon, to my grief, two of the white men offered me eatables; and, on my refusing to eat, one of them held me fast by the hands, and laid me across, I think, the windlass, and tied my feet, while the other flogged me severely. I had never experienced any thing of this kind before, and although, not being used to the water, I naturally feared that element the first time I saw it, yet nevertheless, could I have got over the nettings, I would have jumped over the side, but I could not; and besides, the crew used to watch us very closely who were not chained down to the decks, lest we should leap into the water. I have seen some of these poor African prisoners most severely cut for attempting to do so, and hourly whipped for not eating. This indeed was often the case with myself. In a little time after, amongst the poor chained men, I found some of my own nation, which in a small degree gave ease to my mind. I inquired of these what was to be done with us. They gave me to understand we were to be carried to these white people's country to work for them. I then was a little revived, and thought if it were no worse than working, my situation was not so desperate. But still I feared I should be put to death, the white people looked and acted, as I thought, in so savage a manner; for I had never seen among any people such instances of brutal cruelty; and this not only shewn towards us blacks, but also to some of the whites, themselves. One white man in particular I saw, when we were permitted to be on deck, flogged so unmercifully with a large rope near the foremast, that he died in consequence of it; and they tossed him over the side as they would have done a brute. This made me fear these people the more; and I expected nothing less than to be treated in the same manner. . . .

. . . The stench of the hold while we were on the coast was so intolerably loathsome, that it was dangerous to remain there for any time, and some of us had been permitted to stay on the deck for the fresh air; but now that the whole ship's cargo were confined together, it became absolutely pestilential. The closeness of the place, and the heat of the climate, added to the number in the ship, which was so crowded that each had scarcely room to turn himself, almost suffocated us. This produced copious perspirations, so that the air soon became unfit for respiration, from a variety of loathsome smells, and brought on a sickness among the slaves, of which many died, thus falling victims to the improvident avarice, as I may call it, of their purchasers. This deplorable situation was again aggravated by the galling of the chains, now become insupportable; and the filth of the necessary tubs, into which the children often fell, and were almost suffocated. The shrieks of the women, and the groans of the dying, rendered it a scene of horror almost inconceivable. Happily, perhaps for myself, I was soon reduced so low here that it was thought necessary to keep me almost continually on deck; and from my extreme youth, I was not put in fetters. In this situation I expected every hour to share the fate of my companions, some of whom were almost daily brought upon deck at the point of death, and I began to hope that death would soon put an end to my miseries. Often did I think many of the inhabitants of the deep much more happy than myself; I envied them the freedom they enjoyed, and as often wished I could change my condition for theirs. Every circumstance I met with served only to render my state more painful, and heighten my apprehensions and my opinion of the cruelty of the whites. One day they had taken a number of fishes; and when they had killed and satisfied themselves with as many as they thought fit, to our astonishment who were on the deck, rather than give any of them to us to eat, as we expected, they tossed the remaining fish into the sea again, although we begged and prayed for some as well as we could, but in vain; and some of my countrymen, being pressed by hunger, took an opportunity, when they thought no one saw them, of trying to get a little privately; but were discovered, and the attempt procured them some very severe floggings.

One day, when we had a smooth sea and moderate wind, two of my wearied countrymen who were chained together, (I was near them at the time) preferring death to such a life of misery, somehow made through the nettings and jumped into the sea: immediately another quite dejected fellow, who on account of his illness was suffered to be out of irons, also followed their example; and I believe many more would very soon have done the same, if they had not been prevented by the ship's crew, who were instantly alarmed. Those of us that were the most active were in a moment put down under the deck; and there was such a noise and confusion amongst the people of the ship as I never heard before, to stop her, and get the boat out to go after the slaves. However, two of the wretches were drowned; but they got the other, and afterwards flogged him unmercifully, for thus attempting to prefer death to slavery. In this manner we continued to undergo more hardships than I can now relate, hardships which are inseparable from this accursed trade. Many a time we were near suffocation from the want of fresh air, being deprived thereof for days together. This, and the stench of the necessary tubs, carried off many. . . .

[The ship arrives in Barbadoes.] Many merchants and planters now came on board, though it was in the evening. They put us in separate parcels, and examined us attentively. They also made us jump, and pointed to the land, signifying we were to go there. We thought by this we should be eaten by these ugly men, as they appeared to us; and, when soon after we were all put down under the deck again, there was much dread and trembling among us, and nothing but bitter cries to be heard all the night from these apprehensions, insomuch that at last the white people got some old slaves from the land to pacify us. They told us we were not to be eaten, but to work, and were soon to go on land, where we should see many of our country people. This report eased us much, and sure enough, soon after we were landed, there came to us Africans of all languages.

We were conducted immediately to the merchant's yard, where we were all pent up together like so many sheep in a fold, without regard to sex or age. As every object was new to me, every thing I saw filled me with surprise. What struck me first was that the houses were built with bricks with stories, and in every other respect different from those in Africa: but I was still more astonished on seeing people on horseback. I did not know what this could mean; and indeed I thought these people full of nothing but magical arts. While I was in this astonishment one of my fellow prisoners spoke to a countryman of his about the horses, who said they were the same kind they had in their country. I understood them, though they were from a distant part of Africa, and I thought it odd I had not seen any horses there; but afterwards, when I came to converse with different Africans, I found they had many horses amongst them, and much larger than those I then saw.

We were not many days in the merchants' custody before we were sold after their usual manner, which is this:—On a signal given, such as the beat of a drum, the buyers rush at once into the yard where the slaves are confined, and make choice of that parcel they like best. The noise and clamour with which this is attended, and the eagerness visible in the countenances of the buyers, serve not a little to increase the apprehensions of the terrified Africans, who may well be supposed to consider them the ministers of that destruction to which they think themselves devoted. In this manner, without scruple, are relations and friends separated, most of them never to see each other again. I remember in the vessel in which I was brought over, in the man's apartment, there were several brothers, who, in the sale, were sold in different lots; and it was very moving on this occasion to see and hear their cries at parting. O, ye nominal Christians! might not an African ask you, "learned you this from your God, who says unto you, Do unto all men as you would men should do unto you? Is it not enough that we are torn from our country and friends, to toil for your luxury and lust of gain? Must every tender feeling be likewise sacrificed to your avarice? Are the dearest friends and relations, now rendered more dear by their separation from the rest of their kindred, still to be parted from each other, and thus prevented from cheering the gloom of slavery, with the small comfort of being together, and mingling their sufferings and sorrows? Why are parents to lose their children, brothers their sisters, or husbands their wives? Surely this is a new refinement in cruelty, which, while it has no advantage to atone for it, thus aggravates distress, and adds fresh horrors even to the wretchedness of slavery."

MARY WOLLSTONECRAFT

(1759-1797)

A VINDICATION OF THE RIGHTS OF WOMAN

(1792)

Mary Wollstonecraft's mother, Elizabeth Dickson, was from a well-off family in Ireland; she married Edward Wollstonecraft, a London weaver, who squandered the fortune amassed by his father in urban real estate investment. Not only did Edward impoverish his family through his abortive efforts to become a country gentleman, but he tormented them through his drunkenness and the battering of his wife, from which Mary strove to defend her mother. Mary (1759-1797) was the second of seven children, the first daughter.

Against her parents' wishes, Mary sought employment outside the home at 19, and at 25, with her two younger sisters and her best friend, Fanny Blood, she founded a school for girls. Two years earlier she had rescued one of these younger sisters from an abusive marriage; public opinion regarded this as an abduction and censured her severely for it. Fanny Blood had been a powerful influence on Mary Wollstonecraft, helping her to develop her self-education and her sense of independence. Though she suffered from tuberculosis, Blood decided to marry and have a child, despite the dangers of a pregnancy for her health. Wollstonecraft joined her in Lisbon where she had to witness her friend's death in childbirth.

Soon after this the school they had founded failed; however, Wollstonecraft had formed some very significant relationships with the families of a number of the students. These families were part of a circle of radical Dissenters which included Joseph Priestley, Richard Price, and Sarah Burgh. They encouraged the publication of her first work, *Thoughts on the Education of Daughters.* Wollstonecraft then took a position as governess for the children of a wealthy Anglo-Irish family in Ireland, Lord and Lady Kingsborough. The patronizing attitudes of these parents fueled Wollstonecraft's dislike for the hereditary English nobility, but she won the full and lasting friendship of the children, especially the eldest daughter, prior to her dismissal after only nine months of service.

Upon returning to England she was employed as a writer by Joseph Johnson, the editor of a new journal, the *Analytical Review*, which became an organ for the Dissenting views of the circle she had met earlier. Wollstonecraft increasingly shared the views of these radicals who questioned the social inequality and injustice in England and who challenged the staid complacency of the established Anglican Church. She also applied these ideas to her criticism of the subjection of women. Her employment as a teacher, governess, and writer had enabled Wollstonecraft to remain independent and self-supporting in an age when this was very difficult; she wrote from experience and authority, exposing the sexism even of liberal Enlightenment thinkers like Rousseau. In addition to these major works, Wollstonecraft also published a history of the French Revolution, many articles, two novels, and a number of letters and short stories.

After her marriage to William Godwin, a member of her circle of friends and fellow authors, Wollstonecraft gave birth to a daughter, but died as a result of complications of childbirth, as had her best friend, Fanny. The daughter survived, and later became a famous writer herself, Mary Wollstonecraft Shelley. Excerpts from her novel, *Frankenstein,* are included in another volume of the *Lynchburg College Symposium Readings.*

SOURCE

Wollstonecraft, Mary. 1792. *Vindication of the Rights of Woman: with Strictures on Political and Moral Subjects.* New York: The Humboldt Publishing Company, 1891.

Selections from:

> Introduction to the First Edition (excerpted 23-25)
> Chapter II (excerpted 38-44)
> Chapter III (excerpted 58-60, 61-66)
> Chapter IV (excerpted 68, 69-72, 73-74, 75-77)

INTRODUCTION

TO THE FIRST EDITION

After considering the historic page, and viewing the living world with anxious solicitude, the most melancholy emotions of sorrowful indignation have depressed my spirits, and I have sighed when obliged to confess that either nature has made a great difference between man and man, or that the civilization which has hitherto taken place in the world has been very partial. I have turned over various books written on the subject of education, and patiently observed the conduct of parents and the management of schools; but what has been the result?—a profound conviction that the neglected education of my fellow-creatures is the grand source of the misery I deplore; and that women, in particular, are rendered weak and wretched by a variety of concurring causes, originating from one hasty conclusion. The conduct and manners of women, in fact, evidently prove that their minds are not in a healthy state; for, like the flowers which are planted in too rich a soil, strength and usefulness are sacrificed to beauty; and the flaunting leaves, after having pleased a fastidious eye, fade, disregarded, on the stalk, long before the season when they ought to have arrived at maturity. One cause of this barren blooming I attribute to a false system of education, gathered from the books written on this subject by men who, considering females rather as women than human creatures, have been more anxious to make them alluring mistresses than affectionate wives and rational mothers; and the understanding of the sex has been so bubbled by this specious homage, that the civilized women of the present century, with a few exceptions, are only anxious to inspire love, when they ought to cherish a nobler ambition, and, by their abilities and virtues, exact respect.

In a treatise, therefore, on female rights and manners, the works which have been particularly written for their improvement must not be overlooked; especially when it is asserted, in direct terms, that the minds of women are enfeebled by false refinement; that the books of instruction, written by men of genius, have had the same tendency as more frivolous productions; and that, in the true style of Mahometanism, they are treated as a kind of subordinate beings, and not as a part of the human species, when improvable reason is allowed to be the dignified distinction which raises men above the brute creation, and puts a natural sceptre in a feeble hand.

Yet, because I am a woman, I would not lead my readers to suppose that I mean violently to agitate the contested question respecting the equality or inferiority of the sex; but as the subject lies in my way, and I cannot pass it over without subjecting the main tendency of my reasoning to misconstruction, I shall stop a moment to deliver, in few words, my opinion. In the government of the physical world it is observable that the female in point of strength is, in general, inferior to the male. This is the law of Nature; and it does not appear to be suspended or abrogated in favor of woman. A degree of physical superiority cannot, therefore, be denied—and it is a noble prerogative! But not content with this natural pre-eminence, men endeavor to sink us still lower, merely to render us alluring objects for a moment; and women, intoxicated by the adoration which men, under the influence of their senses, pay them, do not seek to obtain a durable interest in their hearts, or to become the friends of the fellow-creatures who find amusement in their society.

I am aware of an obvious inference—from every quarter have I heard exclamations against masculine women; but where are they to be found? If by this appellation men mean to inveigh against their ardor in hunting, shooting, and gaming, I shall most cordially join in the cry; but if it be against the imitation of manly virtues, or, more properly speaking, the attainment of those talents and virtues, the exercise of which ennobles the human character, and which raise females in the scale of animal being, when they are comprehensively termed mankind, all those who view them with a philosophic eye must, I should think, wish with me that they may every day grow more and more masculine.

This discussion naturally divides the subject. I shall first consider women in the grand light of human creatures, who, in common with men, are placed on this earth to unfold their faculties; and afterwards I shall more particularly point out their peculiar designation.

I wish also to steer clear of an error which many respectable writers have fallen into; for the instruction which has hitherto been addressed to women, has rather been applicable to *ladies*, if the little indirect advice that is scattered through "Sandford and Merton" be excepted; but, addressing my sex in a firmer tone, I pay particular attention to those in the middle class, because they appear to be in the most natural state. Perhaps the seeds of false refinement, immorality, and vanity have ever been shed by the great. Weak, artificial beings, raised above the common wants and affections of their race, in a premature, unnatural manner, undermine the very foundation of virtue, and spread corruption through the whole mass of society! As a class of mankind they have the strongest claim to pity; the education of the rich tends to render them vain and helpless, and the unfolding mind is not strengthened by the practice of those duties which dignify the human character. They only live to amuse themselves, and by the same law which in Nature invariably produces certain effects, they soon only afford barren amusement.

But as I purpose taking a separate view of the different ranks of society, and of the moral character of women in each, this hint is for the present sufficient; and I have only alluded to the subject because it appears to me to be the very essence of an introduction to give a cursory account of the contents of the work it introduces.

My own sex, I hope, will excuse me if I treat them like rational creatures, instead of flattering their *fascinating* graces, and viewing them as if they were in a state of perpetual childhood, unable to stand alone. I earnestly wish to point out in what true dignity and human happiness consists; I wish to persuade women to endeavor to acquire strength, both of mind and body, and to convince them that the soft phrases, "susceptibility of heart," "delicacy of sentiment," and "refinement of taste," are almost synonymous with epithets of weakness, and that those beings who are only the objects of pity and that kind of love which has been termed its sister, will soon become objects of contempt.

Dismissing, then, those pretty feminine phrases, which the men condescendingly use to soften our slavish dependence, and despising that weak elegancy of mind, exquisite sensibility, and sweet docility of manners supposed to be the sexual characteristics of the weaker vessel, I wish to show that elegance is inferior to virtue, that the first object of laudable ambition is to obtain a character as a human being, regardless of the distinction of sex; and that secondary views should be brought to this simple touchstone.

This is a rough sketch of my plan: [In Chapter One, Wollstonecraft considers general principles of society, arguing for human equality of opportunity. She argues against the existence of privileged classes such as nobility, royalty, military, and clergy, whose powers are not based on their virtue.]

CHAPTER II

... **[Women, like men, become virtuous by the exercise of their reason.]** Consequently the most perfect education, in my opinion, is such an exercise of the understanding as is best calculated to strengthen the body and form the heart—or, in other words, to enable the individual to attain such habits of virtue as will render it independent. In fact, it is a farce to call any being virtuous whose virtues do not result from the exercise of its own reason. This was [J-J.] Rousseau's opinion respecting men: I extend it to women, and confidently assert that they have been drawn out of their sphere by false refinement, and not by an endeavor to acquire masculine qualities. Still the regal homage which they receive is so intoxicating, that till the manners of the times are changed, and formed on more reasonable principles, it may be impossible to convince them that the illegitimate power which they obtain by degrading themselves, is a curse, and that they must return to Nature and equality if they wish to secure the placid satisfaction that unsophisticated affections impart. But for this epoch we must wait—wait, perhaps, till kings and nobles, enlightened by reason, and preferring the real dignity of man to childish state, throw off their gaudy hereditary trappings; and if then women do not resign the arbitrary power of beauty, they will prove that they have *less* mind than man.

I may be accused of arrogance; still I must declare what I firmly believe, that all the writers who have written on the subject of female education and manners, from Rousseau to Dr. Gregory, have contributed to render women more artificial, weak characters, than they would otherwise have been, and, consequently, more useless members of society. I might have expressed this conviction in a lower key; but I am afraid it would have been the whine of affectation, and not the faithful expression of my feelings, of the clear result which experience and reflection have led me to draw. When I come to that division of the subject, I shall advert to the passages that I more particularly disapprove of in the works of the authors I have just alluded to; but it is first necessary to observe, that my objection extends to the whole purport of those books, which tend, in my opinion, to degrade one half of the human species, and render women pleasing at the expense of every solid virtue.

Though, to reason on Rousseau's ground, if man did attain a degree of perfection of mind when his body arrived at maturity, it might be proper, in order to make a man and his wife *one*, that she should rely entirely on his understanding; and the graceful ivy, clasping the oak that supported it, would form a whole in which strength and beauty would be equally conspicuous. But, alas! husbands, as well as their helpmates, are often only overgrown children;—nay, thanks to early debauchery, scarcely men in their outward form—and if the blind lead the blind, one need not come from heaven to tell us the consequence. . . .

[Wollstonecraft continues with a lengthy description of the many ways the corrupt society of her day enslaved women including a "disorderly education" for women as compared to men.]

. . . Strengthen the female mind by enlarging it, and there will be an end to blind obedience; but, as blind obedience is ever fought for by power, tyrants and sensualists are in the right when they endeavor to keep women in the dark, because the former only want slaves, and the latter a plaything. The sensualist, indeed, has been the most dangerous of tyrants, and women have been duped by their lovers, as princes by their ministers, while dreaming that they reigned over them.

I now principally allude to Rousseau, for his character of *Sophia* is undoubtedly, a captivating one, though it appears to me grossly unnatural; however, it is not the superstructure, but the foundation, of her character, the principles on which her education was built, that I mean to attack; nay, warmly as I admire the genius of that able writer, whose opinions I shall often have occasion to cite, indignation always takes place of admiration, and the rigid frown of insulted virtue effaces the smile of complacency, which his eloquent periods are wont to raise, when I read his voluptuous reveries. Is this the man who, in his ardor for virtue, would banish all the soft arts of peace, and almost carry us back to Spartan discipline? Is this the man who delights to paint the useful struggles of passion, the triumphs of good dispositions, and the heroic flights which carry the glowing soul out of itself? How are these mighty sentiments lowered when he describes the pretty foot and enticing airs of his little favorite! But, for the present, I waive the subject, and, instead of severely reprehending the transient effusions of overweening sensibility, I shall only observe, that whoever has cast a benevolent eye on society must often have been gratified by the sight of humble, mutual love, not dignified by sentiment nor strengthened by a union in intellectual pursuits. The domestic trifles of the day have afforded matters for cheerful converse, and innocent caresses have softened toils which did not require great exercise of mind or stretch of thought: yet, has not the sight of this moderate felicity excited more tenderness than respect?—an emotion similar to what we feel when children are playing, or animals sporting;—whilst the contemplation of the noble struggles of suffering merit has raised admiration, and carried our thoughts to that world where sensation will give place to reason.

Women are, therefore, to be considered either as moral beings, or so weak that they must be entirely subjected to the superior faculties of men.

Let us examine this question. Rousseau declares that a woman should never, for a moment, feel herself independent; that she should be governed by fear to exercise her *natural* cunning, and made a coquettish slave in order to render her a more alluring object of desire, a *sweeter* companion to man, whenever he chooses to relax himself. He carries the arguments, which he pretends to draw from the indications of Nature, still further, and insinuates that truth and fortitude, the corner-stones of all human virtue, should be cultivated with certain restrictions, because, with respect to the female character, obedience is the grand lesson which ought to be impressed with unrelenting rigor.

What nonsense! When will a great man arise with sufficient strength of mind to puff away the fumes which pride and sensuality have thus spread over the subject? If women are by nature inferior to men, their virtues must be the same in quality, if not in degree, or virtue is a relative idea; consequently, their conduct should be founded on the same principles, and have the same aim.

Connected with man as daughters, wives and mothers, their moral character may be estimated by their manner of fulfilling those simple duties; but the end, the grand end, of their exertions should be to unfold their own faculties, and acquire the dignity of conscious virtue. They may try to render their road pleasant; but ought never to forget, in common with man, that life yields not the felicity which can satisfy an immortal soul. I do not mean to insinuate that either sex should be so lost in abstract reflections, or distant views, as to forget the affections and duties that lie before them, and are, in truth, the means appointed to produce the fruit of life; on the contrary, I would warmly recommend them, even while I assert, that they afford most satisfaction when they are considered in their true, sober light.

Probably, the prevailing opinion, that woman was created for man may have taken its rise from Moses'[s]poetical story; yet, as very few, it is presumed, have bestowed any serious thought on the subject, ever supposed that Eve was, literally speaking, one of Adam's ribs, the deduction must be allowed to fall to the ground; or only be so far admitted as it proves that man, from the remotest antiquity, found it convenient to exert his strength to subjugate his companion; and his invention to show that she ought to have her neck bent under the yoke, because the whole creation was only created for his convenience or pleasure.

Let it not be concluded that I wish to invert the order of things; I have already granted that, from the constitution of their bodies, men seem to be designed by Providence to attain a greater degree of virtue. I speak collectively of the whole sex; but I see not the shadow of a reason to conclude that their virtues should differ in respect to their nature. In fact how can they, if virtue has only one eternal standard? I must, therefore, if I reason consequentially, as strenuously maintain that they have the same simple direction, as that there is a God. . . .

CHAPTER III

[Wollestonecraft argues against Rousseau's and Gregory's assertions that women should be educated to please men and to be dependent on men. Instead, women should be educated to develop their own reason and virtue, and to develop these by the same means as men, since reason and virtue are the same by nature in men and women] . . . But, supposing a woman, trained up to obedience, be married to a sensible man, who directs her judgment without making her feel the servility of her subjection, to act with as much propriety by this reflected light as can be expected when reason is taken at second-hand; yet she cannot ensure the life of her protector—he may die and leave her with a large family.

A double duty devolves on her—to educate them in the character of both father and mother; to form their principles and secure their property. But, alas! she has never thought, much less acted, for herself. She has only learned to please men, to depend gracefully on them; yet, encumbered with children, how is she to obtain another protector—a husband to supply the place of reason? A rational man—for we are not treading on romantic ground—though he may think her a pleasing, docile creature, will not choose to marry a *family* for love when the world contains many more pretty creatures. What is then to become of her? She either falls an easy prey to some mean fortune-hunter, who defrauds her children of their paternal inheritance, and renders her miserable; or becomes the victim of discontent and blind indulgence. Unable to educate her sons, or impress them with respect—for it is not a play on words to assert that people are never respected, though filling an important station, who are not respectable—she pines under the anguish of unavailing, impotent regret. The serpent's tooth enters into her very soul, and the vices of licentious youth bring her with sorrow, if not with poverty also, to the grave.

This is not an overcharged picture; on the contrary, it is a very possible case, and something similar must have fallen under every attentive eye.

I have, however, taken it for granted that she was well-disposed, though experience shows, that the blind may as easily be led into a ditch as along the beaten road. But supposing (no very improbable conjecture) that a being only taught to please must still find her happiness in pleasing; what an example of folly, not to say vice, will she be to her innocent daughters! The mother will be lost in the coquette, and, instead of making friends of her daughters, view them with eyes askance, for they are rivals—rivals more cruel than any other, because they invite a comparison, and drive her from the throne of beauty, who has never thought of a seat on the bench of reason.

It does not require a lively pencil, or the discriminating outline of a caricature, to sketch the domestic miseries and petty vices which such a mistress of a family diffuses. Still, she only acts as a woman ought to act brought up according to Rousseau's system. She can never be reproached for being masculine, or turning out of her sphere; nay, she may observe another of his grand rules, and, cautiously preserving her reputation free from spot, be reckoned a good kind of woman. Yet in what respect can she be termed good? She abstains, it is true, without any great struggle, from committing gross crimes; but how does she fulfil her duties? Duties!—in truth she has enough to think of to adorn her body and nurse a weak constitution.

With respect to religion, she never presumed to judge for herself; but conformed, as a dependent creature should, to the ceremonies of the Church which she was brought up in, piously believing that wiser heads than her own have settled that business—and not to doubt is her point of perfection. She therefore pays her tithe of mint and cumin, and thanks her God that she is not as other women are. These are the blessed effects of a good education!—these are the virtues of man's help-mate!

I must relieve myself by drawing a different picture.

Let fancy now present a woman with a tolerable understanding—for I do not wish to leave the line of mediocrity—whose constitution, strengthened by exercise, has allowed her body to acquire its full vigor; her mind, at the same time, gradually expanding itself to comprehend the moral duties of life, and in what human virtue and dignity consist.

Formed thus by the discharge of the relative duties of her station, she marries from affection, without losing sight of prudence; and, looking beyond matrimonial felicity, she secures her husband's respect before it is necessary to exert mean arts to please him and feed a dying flame, which Nature doomed to expire when the object became familiar, when friendship and forbearance take place of a more ardent affection. This is the natural death of love, and domestic peace is not destroyed by struggles to prevent its extinction. I also suppose the husband to be virtuous; or she is still more in want of independent principles.

Fate, however, breaks this tie. She is left a widow, perhaps, without a sufficient provision; but she is not desolate! The pang of nature is felt, but after time has softened sorrow into melancholy resignation, her heart turns to her children with redoubled fondness, and, anxious to provide for them, affection gives a sacred, heroic cast to her maternal duties. She thinks that not only the eye sees her virtuous efforts from whom all her comfort now must flow, and whose approbation is life; but her imagination, a little abstracted and exalted by grief, dwells on the fond hope that the eyes which her trembling hand closed, may still see how she subdues every wayward passion to fulfill the double duty of being the father as well as the mother of her children. Raised to heroism by her misfortunes, she represses the first faint dawning of a natural inclination, before it ripens into love, and in the bloom of life forgets her sex—forgets the pleasure of an awakening passion, which might again have been inspired and returned. She no longer thinks of pleasing, and conscious dignity prevents her from priding herself on account of the praise which her conduct demands. Her children have her love, and her brightest hopes are beyond the grave, where her imagination often strays.

I think I see her surrounded by her children, reaping the reward of her care. The intelligent eye meets hers, while health and innocence smile on their chubby cheeks, and as they grow up the cares of life are lessened by their grateful attention. She lives to see the virtues which she endeavored to plant on principles, fixed into habits, to see her children attain a strength of character sufficient to enable them to endure adversity without forgetting their mother's example.

The task of life thus fulfilled, she calmly waits for the sleep of death, and rising from the grave, may say—"Behold, Thou gavest me a talent—and here are five talents."

I wish to sum up what I have said in a few words, for I here throw down my gauntlet, and deny the existence of sexual virtues, not excepting modesty. For man and woman truth, if I understand the meaning of the word, must be the same; yet in the fanciful female character, so prettily drawn by poets and novelists, demanding the sacrifice of truth and sincerity, virtue becomes a relative idea, having no other foundation than utility, and of that utility men pretend arbitrarily to judge, shaping it to their own convenience.

Women, I allow, may have different duties to fulfill; but they are *human* duties, and the principles that should regulate the discharge of them, I sturdily maintain, must be the same.

To become respectable, the exercise of their understanding is necessary, there is no other foundation for independence of character; I mean explicitly to say that they must only bow to the authority of reason, instead of being the *modest* slaves of opinion.

In the superior ranks of life how seldom do we meet with a man of superior abilities, or even common acquirements? The reason appears to me clear; the state they are born in was an unnatural one. The human character has ever been formed by the employments the individual, or class, pursues; and, if the faculties are not sharpened by necessity, they must remain obtuse. The argument may fairly be extended to women; for, seldom occupied by serious business, the pursuit of pleasure gives that insignificancy to their character which renders the society of the *great* so insipid. The same want of firmness, produced by a similar cause, forces them both to fly from themselves to noisy pleasures and artificial passions, till vanity takes place of every social affection, and the characteristics of humanity can scarcely be discerned. Such are the blessings of civil governments, as they are at present organized, that wealth and female softness equally tend to debase mankind, and are produced by the same cause; but allowing women to be rational creatures they should be incited to acquire virtues which they may call their own, for how can a rational being be ennobled by anything that is not obtained by its *own* exertions?

CHAPTER IV

[Wollstonecraft details the causes by which women are reduced to a state of degradation. They are exalted for their beauty and delicacy rather than for their reason and strength of character.] . . . Confined then in cages like the feathered race, they have nothing to do but plume themselves, and stock with mock majesty from perch to perch. . . .

I lament that women are systematically degraded by receiving the trivial attentions which men think it manly to pay to the sex, when, in fact, they are insultingly supporting their own superiority. It is not condescension to bow to an inferior. So ludicrous, in fact, do these ceremonies appear to me that I scarcely am able to govern my muscles, when I see a man start with eager and serious solicitude to lift a handkerchief or shut a door, when the *lady* could have done it herself, had she only moved a pace or two.

A wild wish has just flown from my heart to my head, and I will not stifle it though it may excite a horse-laugh. I do earnestly wish to see the distinction of sex confounded in society, unless where love animates the behavior. For this distinction is, I am firmly persuaded, the foundation of the weakness of character ascribed to woman; is the cause why the understanding is neglected, whilst accomplishments are acquired with sedulous care; and the same cause accounts for their preferring the graceful before the heroic virtues.

Mankind, including every description, wish to be loved and respected by *something*; and the common herd will always take the nearest road to the completion of their wishes. The respect paid to wealth and beauty is the most certain and unequivocal, and, of course, will always attract the vulgar eye of common minds. Abilities and virtues are absolutely necessary to raise men from the middle rank of life into notice; and the natural consequence is notorious: the middle rank contains most virtue and abilities. Men have thus, in one station at least, an opportunity of exerting themselves with dignity, and of rising by the exertions which really improve a rational creature; but the whole female sex are, till their character is formed, in the same condition as the rich; for they are born—I now speak of a state of civilization—with certain sexual privileges, and while they are gratuitously granted them, few will ever think of works of supererogation to obtain the esteem of a small number of superior people.

When do we hear of women who, starting out of obscurity, boldly claim respect on account of their great abilities or daring virtues? Where are they to be found? "To be observed, to be attended to, to be taken notice of with sympathy, complacency, and approbation, are all the advantages which they seek." "True!" my male readers will probably exclaim; but let them, before they draw any conclusion, recollect that this was not written originally as descriptive of women, but of the rich. In Dr. Smith's [Adam Smith's] "Theory of Moral Sentiments" I have found a general character of people of rank and fortune that, in my opinion, might with the greatest propriety be applied to the female sex. I refer the sagacious reader to the whole comparison; but must be allowed to quote a passage to enforce an argument that I mean to insist on, as the one most conclusive against a sexual character. For if, excepting warriors, no great men of any denomination have ever appeared amongst the nobility, may it not be fairly inferred that their local situation swallowed up the man, and produced a character similar to that of women, who are *localized* (if I may be allowed the word) by the rank they are placed in by *courtesy?* Women, commonly called "ladies," are not to be contradicted in company, are not allowed to exert any manual strength; and from them the negative virtues only are expected (when *any* virtues are expected)—patience, docility, good-humor, and flexibility—virtues incompatible with any vigorous exertion of intellect. Besides, by living more with each other, and being seldom absolutely alone, they are more under the influence of sentiments than passions. Solitude and reflection are necessary to give to wishes the force of passions, and to enable the imagination to enlarge the object and make it the most desirable. The same may be said of the rich; they do not sufficiently deal in general ideas, collected by impassioned thinking or calm investigation, to acquire that strength of character on which great resolves are built. . . .

[**Wollstonecraft cites Adam Smith's portrayal of the behavior of nobles, who are trained from birth to lord it over others by pomp and ceremony, rather than to develop virtues like knowledge and industry, and she compares this training to that of women.**]

In the middle rank of life, to continue the comparison, men, in their youth, are prepared for professions, and marriage is not considered as the grand feature in their lives; while women, on the contrary, have no other scheme to sharpen their faculties. It is not business, extensive plans, or any of the excursive flights of ambition that engross their attention; no! their thoughts are not employed in rearing such noble structures. To rise in the world, and have the liberty of running from pleasure to pleasure, they must marry advantageously, and to this object their time is sacrificed and their persons often legally prostituted. A man, when he enters any profession, has his eye steadily fixed on some future advantage (and the mind gains great strength by having all its efforts directed to one point), and, full of his business, pleasure is considered as mere relaxation; while women seek for pleasure as the main purpose of existence. In fact, from the education which they receive from society, the love of pleasure may be said to govern them all; but does this prove that there is a sex in souls? It would be just as rational to declare that the courtiers in France, when a destructive system of despotism had formed their character, were not men, because liberty, virtue and humanity, were sacrificed to pleasure and vanity—fatal passions, which have ever domineered over the *whole* race! . . .

MARIA STEWART

(1803-1879)

AN ADDRESS, DELIVERED AT THE AFRICAN MASONIC HALL, FEB. 27, 1833

Maria W. Stewart was born to free parents in Hartford, Connecticut and orphaned at age five, after which she lived to age fifteen in a minister's house, where she worked as a bondservant. After this she hired herself out as a domestic servant, while at the same time ardently trying to educate herself. In 1826, she married a free middle-class black Bostonian, James W. Stewart, who had fought in the War of 1812 and was in the business of outfitting and provisioning fishing and whaling ships. He was considerably older than she and left her a widow after less then three years of marriage; white executors cheated her out of her inheritance through legal chicanery.

In 1830 she converted to Christianity and publicly professed her dedication to Christ. During the following three years, she became deeply involved in the struggle for equal rights for Africans. The white abolitionist leader, William Lloyd Garrison, published her tract, *Religion and the Pure Principles of Morality*, in his newspaper, *The Liberator*. Four of her speeches, including the one excerpted below, were delivered to large audiences and later also published in Garrison's newspaper. Stewart's speeches were among the most radical of her time in the explicitness of their denunciations and their demands for change. The first American to call for equal rights for black women and the first American woman to deliver public lectures, she stood remarkably alone in many ways; but she combined her message of solitary self-reliance with one of united action. In both messages she drew support from the prophetic tradition of biblical Israel, as would so many black leaders, culminating with Dr. Martin Luther King, Jr. Her writings and speeches reflect above all her deep spirituality.

After leaving Boston in 1834 she supported herself by teaching public school (one of the few respectable occupations in which a woman could then earn a living). She taught in New York, Baltimore, and finally Washington, D.C., where she was appointed matron of the Freedman's Hospital.[1] She died at the Freedman's Hospital in 1879.

SOURCE

Stewart, Maria W. 1833. "An Address Delivered at the African Masonic Hall, Boston, Feb. 27, 1833." In *Productions of Mrs. Maria W. Stewart, Presented to the First African Baptist Church & Society, of the City of Boston.* Boston: Friends of Freedom and Virtue, 1835. 63-72.

An Address,
Delivered at the African Masonic Hall
Boston, Feb. 27, 1833

African rights and liberty is a subject that ought to fire the breast of every free man of color in these United States, and excite in his bosom a lively, deep, decided and heart-felt interest. When I cast my eyes on the long list of illustrious names that are enrolled on the bright annals of fame among

---

[1] Gerda Lerner, ed., *Black Women in White America: A Documentary History* (New York: Random House, 1972), 83-84.

the whites, I turn my eyes within, and ask my thoughts, "Where are the names of *our* illustrious ones?" It must certainly have been for the want of energy on the part of the free people of color, that they have been long willing to bear the yoke of oppression. It must have been the want of ambition and force that has given the whites occasion to say, that our natural abilities are not as good, and our capacities by nature inferior to theirs. They boldly assert, that, did we possess a natural independence of soul, and feel a love for liberty within our breasts, some one of our sable race, long before this, would have testified it, notwithstanding the disadvantages under which we labor. We have made ourselves appear altogether unqualified to speak in our own defence, and are therefore looked upon as objects of pity and commiseration. We have been imposed upon, insulted and derided on every side; and now, if we complain, it is considered as the height of impertinence. We have suffered ourselves to be considered as dastards, cowards, mean, faint-hearted, wretches; and on this account (not because of our complexion) many despise us, and would gladly spurn us from their presence.

These things have fired my soul with a holy indignation, and compelled me thus to come forward, and endeavor to turn their attention to knowledge and improvement; for knowledge is power. I would ask, is it blindness of mind, or stupidity of soul, or the want of education, that has caused our men who are 60 or 70 years of age, never to let their voices be heard, nor their hands be raised in behalf of their color? Or has it been for the fear of offending the whites? If it has, O ye fearful ones, throw off your fearfulness, and come forth in the name of the Lord, and in the strength of the God of Justice, and make yourselves useful and active members in society; for they admire a noble and patriotic spirit in others; and should they not admire it in us? If you are men, convince them that you possess the spirit of men; and as your day, so shall your strength be. Have the sons of

Africa no souls? feel they no ambitious desires? shall the chains of ignorance forever confine them? shall the insipid appellation of "clever negroes," or "good creatures," any longer content them? Where can we find among ourselves the man of science, or a philosopher, or an able statesman, or a counsellor at law? Show me our fearless and brave, our noble and gallant ones. Where are our lecturers in natural history, and our critics in useful knowledge? There may be a few such men among us, but they are rare. It is true, our fathers bled and died in the revolutionary war, and others fought bravely under the command of Jackson, in defence of liberty. But where is the man that has distinguished himself in these modern days by acting wholly in the defence of African rights and liberty? There was one, although he sleeps, his memory lives.

I am sensible that there are many highly intelligent gentlemen of color in these United States, in the force of whose arguments, doubtless, I should discover my inferiority; but if they are blest with wit and talent, friends and fortune, why have they not made themselves men of eminence, by striving to take all the reproach that is cast upon the people of color, and in endeavoring to alleviate the woes of their brethren in bondage? Talk, without effort, is nothing; you are abundantly capable, gentlemen, of making yourselves men of distinction; and this gross neglect, on your part, causes my blood to boil within me. Here is the grand cause which hinders the rise and progress of people of color. It is their want of laudable ambition and requisite courage.

Individuals have been distinguished according to their genius and talents; ever since the first formation of man, and will continue to be while the world stands. The different grades rise to honor and respectability as their merits may deserve. History informs us that we sprung from one of the most learned nations of the whole earth; from the seat, if not the parent, of science; yes, poor, despised Africa was once the resort of sages and legislators of other nations, was esteemed the school for learning, and the most illustrious men in Greece flocked thither for instruction. But it was our gross sins and abominations that provoked the Almighty to frown thus heavily upon us, and give our glory unto others. Sins and prodigality have caused the downfall of nations, kings and emperors; and were it not that God in wrath remembers mercy, we might indeed despair; but a promise is left us; "Ethiopia shall again stretch forth her hands unto God."

But it is of no use for us to boast that we sprung from this learned and enlightened nation, for this day a thick mist of moral gloom hangs over millions of our race. Our condition as a people has been low for hundreds of years, and it will continue to be so, unless, by true piety and virtue, we strive to regain that which we have lost. White Americans, by their prudence, economy and exertions, have sprung up and become one of the most flourishing nations in the world, distinguished for their knowledge of the arts and sciences, for their polite literature. While our minds are vacant, and starve for want of knowledge, theirs are filled to overflowing. Most of our color have been taught to stand in fear of the white man, from their earliest infancy, to work as soon as they could walk, and to call "master," before they could scarce lisp the name of *mother*. Continual fear and laborious servitude have in some degree lessened in us that natural force and energy which belong to man; or else, in defiance of opposition, our men, before this, would have nobly and boldly contended for their rights. But give the man of color an equal opportunity with the white from the cradle to manhood, and from manhood to the grave, and you would discover the dignified statesman, the man of science, and the philosopher. But there is no such opportunity for the sons of Africa, and I fear that our powerful ones are fully determined that there never shall be. Forbid, ye Powers on high, that it should any longer be said that our men possess no force. O ye sons of Africa, when will your voices be heard in our legislative halls, in defiance of your enemies, contending for equal rights and liberty? How can you, when you reflect from what you have fallen, refrain from crying mightily unto God, to turn away from us the fierceness of his anger, and remember our transgressions against us no more forever. But a God of infinite purity will not regard the prayers of those who hold religion in one hand, and prejudice, sin and pollution in the other; he will not regard the prayers of self-righteousness and hypocrisy. Is it possible, I exclaim, that for the want of knowledge we have labored for hundreds of years to support others, and been content to receive what they chose to give us in return? Cast your eyes about, look as far as you can see; all, all is owned by the lordly white, except here and there a lowly dwelling which the man of color, midst deprivations, fraud and opposition has been scarce able to procure. Like King Solomon, who put neither nail nor hammer to the temple, yet received the praise; so also have the white Americans gained themselves a name, like the names of the great men that are in the earth, while in reality we have been their principal foundation and support. We have pursued the shadow, they have obtained the substance; we have performed the labor, they have received the profits; we have planted the vines, they have eaten the fruits of them.

I would implore our men, and especially our rising youth, to flee from the gambling board and the dance-hall; for we are poor, and have no money to throw away. I do not consider dancing as criminal in itself, but it is astonishing to me that our young men are so blind in their own interest and the future welfare of their children, as to spend their hard earnings for this frivolous amusement; for it has been carried on among us to such an unbecoming extent, that it has became [sic] absolutely disgusting. "Faithful are the wounds of a friend, but the kisses of an enemy are deceitful." Had those men among us, who have had an opportunity, turned their attention as assiduously to mental and moral improvement as they have to gambling and dancing, I might have remained quietly at home, and they stood contending in my place. These polite accomplishments will never enrol [*sic*] your names on the bright annals of fame, who admire the belle void of intellectual knowledge, or applaud the dandy that talks largely on politics, without striving to assist his fellow in the revolution, when the nerves and muscles of every other man forced him into the field of action. You have a right to rejoice, and to let your hearts cheer you in the days of your youth; yet remember that for all these things, God will bring you into judgment. Then, O ye sons of Africa, turn your mind from these perishable objects, and contend for the cause of God and the rights of man. Form yourselves into temperance societies. There are temperate men among you; then why will you any longer neglect to strive, by your example, to suppress vice in all its abhorrent forms? You have been told repeatedly of the glorious results arising from temperance, and can you bear to see the whites arising in honor and respectability, without endeavoring to grasp after that honor and respectability also?

But I forbear. Let our money, instead of being thrown away as heretofore, be appropriated for schools and seminaries of learning for our children and youth. We ought to follow the example of the whites in this respect. Nothing would raise our respectability, add to our peace and happiness, and reflect so much honor upon us, as to be ourselves the promoters of temperance, and the supporters, as far as we are able, of useful and scientific knowledge. The rays of light and knowledge have been hid from our view; we have been taught to consider ourselves as scarce superior to the brute creation; and have performed the most laborious part of American drudgery. Had we as a people received one half the early advantages the whites have received, I would defy the government of these United States to deprive us any longer of our rights.

I am informed that the agent of the colonization society has recently formed an association of young men, for the purpose of influencing those of us to go to Liberia who may feel disposed. The colonizationists are blind to their own interest, for should the nations of the earth make war with America, they would find their forces much weakened by our absence; or should we remain here, can our "brave soldiers," and "fellow-citizens," as they were termed in time of calamity, condescend to defend the rights of whites, and be again deprived of their own, or sent to Liberia in return? Or, if the colonizationists are the real friends to Africa, let them expend the money which they collect, in erecting a college to educate her injured sons in this land of gospel light and liberty; for it would be most thankfully received on our part, and convince us of the truth of their professions, and save time, expense and anxiety. Let them place before us noble objects worthy of pursuit, and see if we prove ourselves to be those unambitious negroes they term us. But ah! methinks their hearts are so frozen toward us, they had rather their money should be sunk in the ocean than to administer it to our relief; and I fear, if they dared, like Pharaoh, king of Egypt, they would order every male child among us to be drowned. But the most high God is still as able to subdue the lofty pride of these white Americans as He was the heart of that ancient rebel. They say, though we are looked upon as *things*, yet we sprang from a scientific people. Had our men the requisite force and energy they would soon convince them by their efforts both in public and private, that they were men, or things in the shape of men. Well may the colonizationists laugh us to scorn for our negligence; well may they cry, "Shame to the sons of Africa." As the burden of the Israelites was too great for Moses to bear, so also is our burden too great for our noble advocate to bear. You must feel interested, my brethren, in what he undertakes, and hold up his hands by your good works, or in spite of himself, his soul will become discouraged, and his heart will die within him; for he has, as it were, the strong bulls of Bashan to contend with.

It is of no use for us to wait any longer for a generation of well educated men to arise. We have slumbered and slept too long already; the day is far spent; the night of death approaches; and you have sound sense and good judgment sufficient to begin with, if you feel disposed to make a right use of it. Let every man of color throughout the United States, who possesses the spirit and principles of a man, sign a petition to congress, to abolish slavery in the District of Columbia, and grant you the rights and privileges of common free citizens; for if you had had faith as a grain of mustard seed, long before this the mountain of prejudice might have been removed. We are all sensible that the anti-slavery society has taken hold of the arm of our whole population, in order to raise them out of the mire. Now all we have to do is, by a spirit of virtuous ambition to strive to raise ourselves; and I am happy to have it in my power thus publicly to say that the colored inhabitants of this city, in some respects, are beginning to improve. Had the free people of color in these United States nobly and freely contended for their rights, and showed a natural genius and talent, although not so brilliant as some; had they held up, encouraged and patronized each other, nothing could have hindered us from being a thriving and flourishing people. There has been a fault among us. The reason why our distinguished men have not made themselves more influential, is because they fear that the strong current of opposition through which they must pass, would cause their downfall and prove their overthrow. And what gives rise to this opposition? Envy. And what has it amounted to? Nothing. And who are the cause of it? Our whited sepulchres, who want to be great, and don't know how; who love to be called of men 'Rabbi, Rabbi,' who put on false sanctity and humble themselves to their brethren, for the sake of acquiring the highest place in the synagogue, and the uppermost seat at the feast. You, dearly beloved, who are the genuine followers of our Lord Jesus Christ, the salt of the earth and the light of the world, are not so culpable. As I told you in the very first of my writing, I will tell you again, I am but as a drop in the bucket—as one particle of the small dust, of the earth. God, will surely raise up those among us who will plead the cause of virtue, and the pure principles of morality, more eloquently than I am able to do.

It appears to me that America has become like the great city of Babylon, for she has boasted in her heart,—'I sit a queen and am no widow, and shall see no sorrow.' She is indeed a seller of slaves and the souls of men; she has made the Africans drunk with the wine of her fornication; she has put them completely beneath her feet and she means to keep them there; her right hand supports the reins of government, and her left hand the wheel of power, and she is determined not to let go her grasp. But many powerful sons and daughters of Africa will shortly arise, who will put down vice and immorality among us, and declare by Him that sitteth upon the throne, that they will have their rights; and if refused, I am afraid they will spread horror and devastation around. I believe that the oppression of injured Africa has come up before the Majesty of Heaven; and when our cries shall have reached the ears of the Most High, it will be a tremendous day for the people of this land; for strong is the arm of the Lord God Almighty.

Life has almost lost its charms for me; death has lost its sting and the grave its terrors; and at times I have a strong desire to depart and dwell with Christ, which is far better. Let me entreat my white brethren to awake and save our sons from dissipation, and our daughters from ruin. Lend the hand of assistance to feeble merit, plead the cause of virtue among our sable race; so shall our curses upon you be turned into blessings; and though you should endeavor to drive us from these shores, still we will cling to you the more firmly; nor will we attempt to rise above you: we will presume to be called your equals only.

The unfriendly whites first drove the native American from his much loved home. Then they stole our fathers from their peaceful and quiet dwellings, and brought them hither, and made bond-men and bond-women of them and their little ones; they have obliged our brethren to labor, kept them in utter ignorance, nourished them in vice, and raised them in degradation; and now that we have enriched their soil, and filled their coffers, they say that we are not capable of becoming like white men, and that we can never rise to respectability in this country. They would drive us to a strange land. But before I go, the bayonet shall pierce me through. African rights and liberty is a subject that ought to fire the breast of every free man of color in these United States, and excite in his bosom a lively, deep, decided, and heart-felt interest.

ELIZABETH CADY STANTON

(1815-1902)

THE SOLITUDE OF SELF

(1892)

Elizabeth Cady Stanton was born into a wealthy, prominent, Presbyterian New York family. After all her brothers died young, her father, a judge, openly lamented that he had only daughters left. Elizabeth tried to excel in masculine activities, but her father's only response was to regret that she had not been born a boy. Elizabeth developed close friendships with a circle of liberal Quakers, and against her family's wishes, she married Henry Stanton, a young radical Quaker who had been deeply engaged in the anti-slavery movement.

From her early youth Stanton had been disturbed by the legal and political inequalities to which women were subjected, and in 1848 she joined with other early feminists to organize the first U.S. convention to discuss woman's rights, held in her own town of Seneca Falls. Stanton provided the guiding inspiration for the convention as well as the brilliant idea of using the *Declaration of Independence* as the model for their statement of grievances (the *Declaration of Sentiments*), and she herself proposed the most radical demand—universal woman suffrage.

Stanton strongly supported the abolitionist movement and worked tirelessly for the Union cause in the Civil War, believing that women's contributions to this effort would finally secure for them the suffrage they had so long pursued. Not only did this not occur, but the new Fourteenth and Fifteenth Amendments to the Constitution contained language that implied women did not have citizenship or voting rights (the amendments extended these rights explicitly to black *males* alone.) She loudly opposed these amendments, causing a breach between her and those struggling for racial equality.

During her entire life Stanton wrote many speeches, letters, and articles in support of woman's rights, while at the same time devoting most of her waking hours to rearing her seven children. She undertook a rigorous itinerary of speaking engagements throughout the country. Working closely with Susan B. Anthony, her lifelong colleague, she helped to found the National Woman Suffrage Association, which merged in 1890 with the more conservative American Suffrage Association to become the National American Woman Suffrage Association (NAWSA). The speech reproduced below was delivered to the House Judiciary Committee of the U.S. Congress, January 18, 1892. It was delivered another time on the occasion of her resignation as first president of the NAWSA. She had been persuaded by Susan Anthony to accept presidency of the NAWSA, and her resignation reflected in part her increasing distance from the association, which she regarded as too conservative and too exclusively devoted to suffrage rights.

Stanton died in 1902 at the age of 87, eighteen years before the demand she had first courageously enunciated found realization through the ratification of the Nineteenth Amendment to the *U.S. Constitution*, which finally gave equal voting rights to all women.

SOURCE

Stanton, Elizabeth Cady. "Solitude of Self." Address Delivered by Mrs. Stanton before the Committee of the Judiciary of the United States Congress, Monday, January 18, 1892. *The Library of Congress:American Memory.* 28 June 2005. <http://lcweb2.loc.gov/cgi-bin/query/r?ammem/ naw:@field (DOCID+@lit(rbnawsan8358div2))>.

The Solitude of Self

Mr. Chairman and gentlemen of the committee: We have been speaking before Committees of the Judiciary for the last twenty years, and we have gone over all the arguments in favor of a sixteenth amendment which are familiar to all you gentlemen; therefore, it will not be necessary that I should repeat them.

The point I wish plainly to bring before you on this occasion is the individuality of each human soul; our Protestant idea, the right of individual conscience and judgment—our republican idea, individual citizenship. In discussing the rights of woman, we are to consider, first, what belongs to her as an individual, in a world of her own, the arbiter of her own destiny, an imaginary Robinson Crusoe with her woman Friday on a solitary island. Her rights under such circumstances are to use all her faculties for her own safety and happiness.

Secondly, if we consider her as a citizen, as a member of a great nation, she must have the same rights as all other members, according to the fundamental principles of our Government.

Thirdly, viewed as a woman, an equal factor in civilization, her rights and duties are still the same—individual happiness and development.

Fourthly, it is only the incidental relations of life, such as mother, wife, sister, daughter, that may involve some special duties and training. In the usual discussion in regard to woman's sphere, such men as Herbert Spencer, Frederic Harrison, and Grant Allen uniformly subordinate her rights and duties as an individual, as a citizen, as a woman, to the necessities of these incidental relations, some of which a large class of women may never assume. In discussing the sphere of man we do not decide his rights as an individual, as a citizen, as a man by his duties as a father, a husband, a brother, or a son, relations some of which he may never fill. Moreover, he would be better fitted for these very relations, and whatever special work he might choose to do to earn his bread, by the complete development of all his faculties as an individual.

Just so with woman. The education that will fit her to discharge the duties in the largest sphere of human usefulness, will best fit her for whatever special work she may be compelled to do.

The isolation of every human soul and the necessity of self-dependence must give each individual the right to choose his own surroundings.

The strongest reason for giving woman all the opportunities for higher education, for the full development of her faculties, forces of mind and body; for giving her the most enlarged freedom of thought and action; a complete emancipation from all forms of bondage, of custom, dependence, superstition; from all the crippling influences of fear, is the solitude and personal responsibility of her own individual life. The strongest reason why we ask for woman a voice in the government under which she lives; in the religion she is asked to believe; equality in social life, where she is the chief factor; a place in the trades and professions, where she may earn her bread, is because of her birthright to self-sovereignty; because, as an individual, she must rely on herself. No matter how much women prefer to lean, to be protected and supported, nor how much men desire to have them do so, they must make the voyage of life alone, and for safety in an emergency they must know something of the laws of navigation. To guide our own craft, we must be captain, pilot, engineer; with chart and compass stand at the wheel; watch the wind and waves and know when to take in the sail, and read the signs in the firmament over all. It matters not whether the solitary voyager is man or woman. Nature having endowed them equally, leaves them to their own skill and judgment in the hour of danger, and, if not equal to the occasion, alike they perish.

To appreciate the importance of fitting every human soul for independent action, think for a moment of the immeasurable solitude of self. We come into the world alone, unlike all who have gone before us; we leave it alone under circumstances peculiar to ourselves. No mortal ever has been, nor mortal ever will be like the soul just launched on the sea of life. There can never again be just such environments as make up the infancy, youth and manhood of this one. Nature never repeats herself and the possibilities of one human soul will never be found in another. No one has ever found two blades of grass alike, and no one will ever find two human beings alike. Seeing, then, what must be the infinite diversity in human character, we can in a measure appreciate the loss to a nation when any large class of the people is uneducated and unrepresented in the government. We ask for the complete development of every individual, first, for his own benefit and happiness. In fitting out an army we give each soldier his own knapsack, arms, powder, his blanket, cup, knife, fork and spoon. We provide alike for all their individual necessities, then each man bears his own burden.

Again we ask complete individual development for the general good; for the consensus of the competent on the whole round of human interests; on all questions of national life, and here each man must bear his share of the general burden. It is sad to see how soon friendless children are left to bear their own burdens before they can analyze their feelings; before they can even tell their joys and sorrows, they are thrown on their own resources. The great lesson that nature seems to teach us at all ages is self-dependence, self-protection, self-support. What a touching instance of a child's solitude, of that hunger of the heart for love and recognition, in the case of the little girl who helped to dress a Christmas tree for the children of the family in which she served. On finding there was no present for herself, she slipped away in the darkness and spent the night in an open field sitting on a stone, and when found in the morning, was weeping as if her heart would break. No mortal will ever know the thoughts that passed through the mind of that friendless child in the long hours of that cold night, with only the silent stars to keep her company. The mention of her case in the daily papers moved many generous hearts to send her presents; but in the hours of her keenest suffering, she was thrown wholly on herself for consolation.

In youth our most bitter disappointments, our brightest hopes and ambitions are known only to ourselves; even our friendship and love we never fully share with another; there is something of every passion, in every situation we conceal. Even so in our triumphs and our defeats.

The successful candidate for the Presidency and his opponent each have a solitude peculiarly his own, and good form forbids either to speak of his pleasure or regret. The solitude of the king on his throne and the prisoner in his cell differs in character and degree, but it is solitude nevertheless.

We ask no sympathy from others in the anxiety and agony of a broken friendship or shattered love. When death sunders our nearest ties, alone we sit in the shadow of our affliction. Alike mid the greatest triumphs and darkest tragedies of life we walk alone. On the divine heights of human attainments, eulogized and worshiped as a hero or saint, we stand alone. In ignorance, poverty, and vice, as a pauper or criminal alone we starve or steal; alone we suffer the sneers and rebuffs of our fellows; alone we are hunted and hounded through dark courts and alleys, in by-ways and highways; alone we stand before the judgment seat; alone in the prison cell we lament our crimes and misfortunes; alone we expiate them on the gallows. In hours like these we realize the awful solitude of individual life—its pains, its penalties, its responsibilities—hours in which the youngest and most helpless are thrown on their own resources for guidance and consolation. Seeing then that life must ever be a march and a battle, that each soldier must be equipped for his own protection, it is the height of cruelty to rob the individual of a single natural right.

To throw obstacles in the way of a complete education is like putting out the eyes; to deny the rights of property, like cutting off the hands. To deny political equality is to rob the ostracised of all self-respect; of credit in the market place; of recompense in the world of work; of a voice among those who make and administer the law; a choice in the jury before whom they are tried, and in the judge who decides their punishment. Shakespeare's play of Titus and Andronicus contains a terrible satire on woman's position in the nineteenth century—"Rude men" (the play tells us) "seized the king's daughter, cut out her tongue, cut off her hands, and then bade her go call for water and wash her hands." What a picture of woman's position. Robbed of her natural rights, handicapped by law and custom at every turn, yet compelled to fight her own battles, and in the emergencies of life to fall back on herself for protections.

The girl of sixteen, thrown on the world to support herself, to make her own place in society, to resist the temptations that surround her and maintain a spotless integrity, must do all this by native force or superior education. She does not acquire this power by being trained to trust others and distrust herself. If she wearies of the struggle, finding it hard work to swim upstream, and allows herself to drift with the current, she will find plenty of company, but not one to share her misery in the hour of her deepest humiliation. If she tries to retrieve her position, to conceal the past, her life is hedged about with fears lest willing hands should tear the veil from what she fain would hide. Young and friendless, *she* knows the bitter solitude of self.

How the little courtesies of life on the surface of society, deemed so important from man towards woman, fade into utter insignificance in view of the deeper tragedies in which she must play her part alone, where no human aid is possible.

The young wife and mother, at the head of some establishment with a kind husband to shield her from the adverse winds of life, with wealth, fortune and position, has a certain harbor of safety, secure against the ordinary ills of life. But to manage a household, have a desirable influence in society, keep her friends and the affections of her husband, train her children and servants well, she must have rare common sense, wisdom, diplomacy, and a knowledge of human nature. To do all this she needs the cardinal virtues and the strong points of character that the most successful statesman possesses.

An uneducated woman, trained to dependence, with no resources in herself must make a failure of any position in life. But society says women do not need a knowledge of the world, the liberal training that experience in public life must give, all the advantages of collegiate education; but when for the lack of all these, the woman's happiness is wrecked, alone she bears her humiliation. The solitude of the weak and the ignorant is indeed pitiable; in the wild chase for the prizes of life they are ground to powder.

In age, when the pleasures of youth are passed, children grown up, married and gone, the hurry and bustle of life in a measure over, when the hands are weary of active service, when the old arm chair and the fireside are the chosen resorts, then men and women alike must fall back on their own resources. If they cannot find companionship in books, if they have no interest in the vital questions of the hour, no interest in watching the consummation of reforms, with which they might have been identified, they soon pass into their dotage. The more fully the faculties of the mind are developed and kept in use, the longer the period of vigor and active interest in all around us continues. If from a lifelong participation in public affairs a woman feels responsible for the laws regulating our system of education, the discipline of our jails and prisons, the sanitary condition of our private homes, public buildings, and thoroughfares, an interest in commerce, finance, our foreign relations, in any or all of these questions, her solitude will at least be respectable, and she will not be driven to gossip or scandal for entertainment.

The chief reason for opening to every soul the doors to the whole round of human duties and pleasures, is the individual development thus attained, the resources thus provided under all circumstances to mitigate the solitude that at times must come to everyone. I once asked Prince Krapotkin, the Russian nihilist, how he endured his long years in prison, deprived of books, pen, ink, and paper. "Ah," he said, "I thought out many questions in which I had a deep interest. In the pursuit of an idea I took no note of time. When tired of solving knotty problems, I recited all the beautiful passages in prose or verse I had ever learned. I became acquainted with myself and my own resources. I had a world of my own, a vast empire, that no Russian jailor or Czar could invade." Such is the value of liberal thought and broad culture when shut off from all human companionship, bringing comfort and sunshine within even the four walls of a prison cell.

As women of times share a similar fate, should they not have all the consolation that the most liberal education can give? Their suffering in the prisons of St. Petersburg, in the long, weary marches to Siberia, and in the mines, working side by side with men, surely call for all the self-support that the most exalted sentiments of heroism can give. When suddenly roused at midnight, with the startling cry of "fire! fire!" to find the house over their heads in flames, do women wait for men to point the way to safety? And are the men, equally bewildered and half suffocated with smoke, in a position to more than try to save themselves?

At such times the most timid women have shown a courage and heroism in saving their husbands and children that has surprised everybody. Inasmuch, then, as woman shares equally the joys and sorrows of time and eternity, is it not the height of presumption in man to propose to represent her at the ballot box and the throne of grace, to do her voting in the state, her praying in the church, and to assume the position of high priest at the family altar?

Nothing strengthens the judgment and quickens the conscience like individual responsibility. Nothing adds such dignity to character as the recognition of one's self-sovereignty; the right to an equal place, everywhere conceded; a place earned by personal merit, not an artificial attainment by inheritance, wealth, family, and position. Seeing, then, that the responsibilities of life rest equally on man and woman, that their destiny is the same, they need the same preparation for time and eternity. The talk of sheltering woman from the fierce storms of life is the sheerest mockery, for they beat on her from every point of the compass, just as they do on man, and with more fatal results, for he has been trained to protect himself, to resist, to conquer. Such are the facts in human experience, the responsibilities of individual sovereignty. Rich and poor, intelligent and ignorant, wise and foolish, virtuous and vicious, man and woman, it is ever the same, each soul must depend wholly on itself.

Whatever the theories may be of woman's dependence on man, in the supreme moments of her life he cannot bear her burdens. Alone she goes to the gates of death to give life to every man that is born to the world. No one can share her fears, no one can mitigate her pangs; and if her sorrow is greater than she can bear, alone she passes beyond the gates into the vast known.

From the mountain tops of Judea, long ago, a heavenly voice bade his disciples, "Bear ye one another's burdens," but humanity has not yet risen to that point of self-sacrifice, and if ever so willing, how few the burdens are that one soul can bear for another. In the highways of Palestine; in prayer and fasting on the solitary mountain top; in the Garden of Gethsemane; before the judgment seat of Pilate; betrayed by one of his trusted disciples at his last supper; in his agonies on the cross, even Jesus of Nazareth, in these last sad days on earth, felt the awful solitude of self. Deserted by man, in agony he cries, "My God! My God! why hast Thou forsaken me?" And so it ever must be in the conflicting scenes of life, in the long, weary march, each one walks alone. We may have many friends, love, kindness, sympathy and charity to smooth our pathway in everyday life, but in the tragedies and triumphs of human experience each mortal stands alone.

But when all artificial trammels are removed, and women are recognized as individuals, responsible for their own environments, thoroughly educated for all positions in life they may be called to fill; with all the resources in themselves that liberal thought and broad culture can give; guided by their own conscience and judgment trained to self-protection by a healthy development of the muscular system and skill in the use of weapons of defense, and stimulated to self-support by a knowledge of the business world and the pleasure that pecuniary independence must ever give; when women are trained in this way they will, in a measure, be fitted for those hours of solitude that come alike to all, whether prepared or otherwise. As in our extremity we must depend on ourselves, the dictates of wisdom point to complete individual development.

In talking of education how shallow the argument that each class must be educated for the special work it proposes to do and all those faculties not needed in this special walk must lie dormant and utterly wither for want of use, when, perhaps, these will be the very faculties needed in life's greatest emergencies. Some say "Where is the use of drilling girls in the languages, the sciences, in law, medicine, theology? As wives, mothers, housekeepers, cooks, they need a different curriculum from boys who are to fill all positions." The chief cooks in our great hotels and ocean steamers are men. In our large cities men run the bakeries, they make our bread, cake and pies, they manage the laundries, they are now considered our best milliners and dressmakers. Because some men fill these departments of usefulness, shall we regulate the curriculum in Harvard and Yale to their present necessities? If not, why this talk in our best colleges of a curriculum for girls who are crowding into the trades and professions, teachers in all our public schools, rapidly filling many lucrative and honorable positions in life? They are showing, too, their calmness and courage in the most trying hours of human experience.

You have probably all read in the daily papers of the terrible storm in the Bay of Biscay when a tidal wave made such havoc on the shore, wrecking vessels, unroofing houses, and carrying destruction everywhere. Among other buildings the woman's prison was demolished. Those who escaped saw men struggling to reach the shore. They promptly by clasping hands made a chain of themselves and pushed out into the sea, again and again, at the risk of their lives until they had brought six men to shore, carried them to a shelter, and did all in their power for their comfort and protection.

What especial school of training could have prepared these women for this sublime moment in their lives? In times like this humanity rises above all college curriculums and recognizes Nature as the greatest of all teachers in the hour of danger and death. Women are already the equals of men in the whole realm of thought, in art, science, literature, and government. With telescopic vision they explore the starry firmament and bring back the history of the planetary world. With chart and compass they pilot ships across the mighty deep, and with skillful finger send electric messages around the globe. In galleries of art the beauties of nature and the virtues of humanity are immortalized by them on canvas, and by their inspired touch dull blocks of marble are transformed into angels of light.

In music they speak again the language of Mendelssohn, Beethoven, Chopin, Schumann, and are worthy interpreters of their great thoughts. The poetry and novels of the century are theirs, and they have touched the keynote of reform in religion, politics, and social life. They fill the editor's and professor's chair, and plead at the bar of justice, walk the wards of the hospital, and speak from the pulpit and the platform; such is the type of womanhood that an enlightened public sentiment welcomes to-day, and such the triumph of the facts of life over the false theories of the past.

Is it, then, consistent to hold the developed woman of this day within the same narrow political limits as the dame with the spinning wheel and knitting needle occupied in the past? No! no! Machinery has taken the labors of woman as well as man on its tireless shoulders; the loom and the spinning wheel are but dreams of the past; the pen, the brush, the easel, the chisel, have taken their places, while the hopes and ambitions of women are essentially changed.

We see reason sufficient in the outer conditions of human beings for individual liberty and development, but when we consider the self-dependence of every human soul we see the need of courage, judgment, and the exercise of every faculty of mind and body, strengthened and developed by use, in woman as well as man.

Whatever may be said of man's protecting power in ordinary conditions, mid all the terrible disasters by land and sea, in the supreme moments of danger, alone, woman must ever meet the horrors of the situation, the Angel of Death even makes no royal pathway for her. Man's love and sympathy enter only into the sunshine of our lives. In that solemn solitude of self that links us with the immeasurable and the eternal, each soul lives alone forever. A recent writer says:

> I remember once, in crossing the Atlantic to have gone upon the deck of the ship at midnight, when a dense black cloud enveloped the sky, and the great deep was roaring madly under the lashes of demoniac winds. My feeling was not of danger or fear (which is a base surrender of the immortal soul), but of utter desolation and loneliness; a little speck of life shut in by a tremendous darkness. Again I remember to have climbed the slopes of the Swiss Alps up beyond the point where vegetation ceases, and the stunted conifers no longer struggle against the unfeeling blasts. Around me lay a huge confusion of rocks, out of which the gigantic ice peaks shot into the measureless blue of the heavens, and again my only feeling was the awful solitude.
>
> And yet, there is a solitude, which each and every one of us has always carried with him, more inaccessible than the ice-cold mountains, more profound than the midnight sea; the solitude of self. Our inner being, which we call ourself, no eye nor touch of man or angel has ever pierced. It is more hidden than the caves of the gnome; the sacred adytum of the oracle; the hidden chamber of eleusinian mystery, for to it only omniscience is permitted to enter.
>
> Such is individual life. Who, I ask you, can take, dare take, on himself the rights, the duties, the responsibilities of another human soul?

ALASDAIR MACINTYRE

(1929-)

AFTER VIRTUE

(1981)

Born 1929 in Glasgow, Scotland, the son of two physicians, Alasdair MacIntyre received an M.A. from Victoria University in Manchester, England (1951) and from Oxford University (1961). He immigrated to the United States in 1970 and has taught at numerous universities in Britain and the U.S., including Oxford, Boston, Brandeis, Princeton, Vanderbilt, and, most recently, Notre Dame. He has been professor of moral philosophy, sociology, and political science.

In his early career he was attracted to Marxist thought, but he later came to critique its morality as part of an overall critique of all modern morality, but especially of liberal individualism. He bitingly criticized modern moral thought as hopelessly fragmented, torn apart by competing and incommensurable systems, yet still clinging to remnants of the early Greek and Christian morality of virtue, the unity of which the modern world had rejected. He sought to rehabilitate the moral thought of Aristotle and Saint Augustine for our modern age; *After Virtue* was the first of a trilogy of books which carried out this effort. MacIntyre hoped to lay the basis for a universal morality based on virtue which would maintain the integrity of the individual and also of the community. His emphasis on community has caused him to be seen as one of the founders of the "communitarian" movement that has grown during the past three decades, although MacIntyre himself eschewed this label.

MacIntyre wants to revive a morality based on virtues, rather than on rules or utility. He believes that the loss of such a moral system has led to an inability in the modern world to come to any agreements concerning morality, because the different moral systems that have replaced the older virtue-based morality are fundamentally incommensurable with one another, and we are left with only fragments of the older views that are detached from any comprehensive context. The virtue-based morality which MacIntyre seeks to rehabilitate would be one like that of Aristotle, based on human nature, not as it is, but on what humans should become through the acquisition of the virtues as habits. It is through acquisition of these virtues that we achieve the goal of becoming what we should be as humans, not just as isolated individuals, but as part of communities. MacIntyre recognizes that Aristotle's ethical system could not be revived, for numerous reasons. Aristotle's theories of human nature have been challenged (especially his views about slavery and about women; MacIntyre says far too little about the latter, though); and the community which Aristotle believed to be the only one in which human beings could reach their ethical goals—the Greek city-state—no longer exists. But MacIntyre believes that it is possible to retain the most fundamental aspects of Aristotle's morality—the acquisition of virtues which enable us to attain our essential goals as humans— and in the selection below he suggests the outlines of such a virtue-based morality for our own time.

In the first excerpt below MacIntyre first acknowledges that different societies have very different moral codes. However, he believes that human beings in these different societies can possess common virtues—such as courage, justice, and truthfulness—that enable them to participate in a variety of different practices in such a way that they can achieve goods that are internal to those practices. Such a practice might be a sport; one cannot truly excel in a sport unless one exercises virtues like courage and fairness.

This identification of virtues that enable us to achieve the internal goods associated with practices is only the first of three stages in his argument. In the second stage, he argues that we need to ask how virtues enable us to achieve the highest good in the unified life of a person. The account of virtues associated with the practices is insufficient because it does not enable us to distinguish between virtues that are more and less important (for example, when the virtues required for one practice conflict with the virtues required for another practice) and it does not offer an over-riding goal for an entire life that would enable us to put each other virtue in its place. Finally, one highly significant virtue—integrity—is not associated with the practices at all.

In asking what constitutes the highest good of a human life MacIntyre first asks what constitutes the identity of a single human life, and he concludes that it is the unity of the narrative of that life. This narrative consists not of isolated actions, but of intentional and intelligible acts that occur in the context of the narratives of the other lives of those with whom the individual interacts. The second excerpt below explains this fundamental role of narrative. Each person is both the actor and the author of his or her own narrative, or rather he or she is the co-actor and co-author. We are accountable for our actions, and we can hold others accountable for theirs.

MacIntyre then goes on to show that when we ask what is the highest good for each person, we are asking how that person might live out the unity of the narrative of their life and bring it to completion. He sees the answer in terms of the medieval idea of the quest, a quest for the highest good, but one which is not precisely defined in advance. We learn what that good is by pursuing it and encountering all the obstacles, hardships, and detours involved in the quest. Thus "the good life for man is the life spent in seeking for the good life for man, and the virtues necessary for the seeking are those which will enable us to understand what more and what else the good life for man is."

In the third part of his argument, MacIntyre goes on to demonstrate that this good life cannot be thought of in terms of the individual alone because in the narrative of his or her life the individual is defined by his or her actions with a community.

SOURCE

MacIntyre, Alasdair. 1981. *After Virtue: A Study in Moral Theory.* Notre Dame, Indiana: University of Notre Dame Press.

Selections from:
> Chapter 14: The Nature of the Virtues (excerpted 169-180)
> Chapter 15: The Virtues, the Unity of a Human Life and the Concept of a Tradition (excerpted 192-197)

CHAPTER 14

THE NATURE OF THE VIRTUES

One response to the history which I have narrated so far might well be to suggest that even within the relatively coherent tradition of thought which I have sketched there are just too many different and incompatible conceptions of a virtue for there to be any real unity to the concept or indeed to the history. Homer, Sophocles, Aristotle, the New Testament and medieval thinkers differ from each other in too many ways. They offer us different and incompatible lists of the virtues; they give a different rank order of importance to different virtues; and they have different and incompatible theories of the virtues. If we were to consider later Western writers on the virtues, the list of differences and incompatibilities would be enlarged still further; and if we extended our enquiry to Japanese, say, or American Indian cultures, the differences would become greater still. It would be all too easy to conclude that there are a number of rival and alternative conceptions of the virtues, but, even within the tradition which I have been delineating, no single core conception.

The case for such a conclusion could not be better constructed than by beginning from a consideration of the very different lists of items which different authors in different times and places have included in their catalogues of virtues. Some of these catalogues—Homer's, Aristotle's and the New Testament's—I have already noticed at greater or lesser length. Let me at the risk of some repetition recall some of their key features and then introduce for further comparison the catalogues of two later Western writers, Benjamin Franklin and Jane Austen.

The first example is that of Homer. At least some of the items in a Homeric list of *aretai* would clearly not be counted by most of us nowadays as virtues at all, physical strength being the most obvious example. To this it might be replied that perhaps we ought not to translate the word *aretê* in Homer by our word 'virtue', but instead by our word 'excellence'; and perhaps, if we were so to translate it, the apparently surprising difference between Homer and ourselves would at first sight have been removed. For we could allow without any kind of oddity that the possession of physical strength is the possession of an excellence. But in fact we would not have removed, but instead would merely have relocated, the difference between Homer and ourselves. For we would now seem to be saying that Homer's concept of an *aretê*, an excellence, is one thing and that our concept of a virtue is quite another since a particular quality can be an excellence in Homer's eyes, but not a virtue in ours and *vice versa*.

But of course it is not that Homer's list of virtues differs only from our own; it also notably differs from Aristotle's. And Aristotle's of course also differs from our own. For one thing, as I noted earlier, some Greek virtue-words are not easily translatable into English or rather out of Greek. Moreover consider the importance of friendship as a virtue in Aristotle's list—how different from us! Or the place of *phronêsis*—how different from Homer and from us! The mind receives from Aristotle the kind of tribute which the body receives from Homer. But it is not just the case that the difference between Aristotle and Homer lies in the inclusion of some items and the omission of others in their respective catalogues. It turns out also in the way in which those catalogues are ordered, in which items are ranked as relatively central to human excellence and which marginal. Moreover the relationship of virtues to the social order has changed. For Homer the paradigm of human excellence is the warrior; for Aristotle it is the Athenian gentleman. Indeed according to Aristotle certain virtues are only available to those of great riches and of high social status; there are virtues which are unavailable to the poor man, even if he is a free man. And those virtues are on Aristotle's view ones central to human life; magnanimity—and once again, any translation of *megalopsuchia* is unsatisfactory—and munificence are not just virtues, but important virtues within the Aristotelian scheme.

At once it is impossible to delay the remark that the most striking contrast with Aristotle's catalogue is to be found neither in Homer's nor in our own, but in the New Testament's. For the New Testament not only praises virtues of which Aristotle knows nothing—faith, hope and love— and says nothing about virtues such as *phronêsis* which are crucial for Aristotle, but it praises at least one quality as a virtue which Aristotle seems to count as one of the vices relative to magnanimity, namely humility. Moreover since the New Testament quite clearly sees the rich as destined for the pains of Hell, it is clear that the key virtues cannot be available to them; yet they *are* available to slaves. And the New Testament of course differs from both Homer and Aristotle not only in the items included in its catalogue, but once again in its rank ordering of the virtues.

Turn now to compare all three lists of virtues considered so far—the Homeric, the Aristotelian, and the New Testament's—with two much later lists, one which can be compiled from Jane Austen's novels and the other which Benjamin Franklin constructed for himself. Two features stand out in Jane Austen's list. The first is the importance that she allots to the virtue which she calls 'constancy', a virtue about which I shall say more in a later chapter. In some ways constancy plays a role in Jane Austen analogous to that of *phronêsis* in Aristotle; it is a virtue the possession of which is a prerequisite for the possession of other virtues. The second is the fact that what Aristotle treats as the virtue of agreeableness (a virtue for which he says there is no name) she treats as only the simulacrum of a genuine virtue—the genuine virtue in question is the one she calls amiability. For the man who practices agreeableness does so from considerations of honour and expediency, according to Aristotle; whereas Jane Austen thought it possible and necessary for the possessor of that virtue to have a certain real affection for the people as such. (It matters here that Jane Austen is a Christian.) Remember that Aristotle himself had treated military courage as a simulacrum of true courage. Thus we find here yet another type of disagreement over the virtues; namely, one as to which human qualities are genuine virtues and which mere simulacra.

In Benjamin Franklin's list we find almost all the types of difference from at least one of the other catalogues we have considered and one more. Franklin includes virtues which are new to our consideration such as cleanliness, silence and industry; he clearly considers the drive to acquire itself a part of virtue, whereas for most ancient Greeks this is the vice of *pleonexia*; he treats some virtues which earlier ages had considered minor as major; but he also redefines some familiar virtues. In the list of thirteen virtues which Franklin compiled as part of his system of private moral accounting, he elucidates each virtue by citing a maxim obedience to which *is* the virtue in question. In the case of chastity the maxim is 'Rarely use venery but for health or offspring—never to dullness, weakness or the injury of your own or another's peace or reputation'. This is clearly not what earlier writers had meant by 'chastity'.

We have therefore accumulated a startling number of differences and incompatibilities in the five stated and implied accounts of the virtues. So the question which I raised at the outset becomes more urgent. If different writers in different times and places, but all within the history of Western culture, include such different sets and types of items in their lists, what grounds have we for supposing that they do indeed aspire to list items of one and the same kind, that there is any shared concept at all? A second kind of consideration reinforces the presumption of a negative answer to this question. It is not just that each of these five writers lists different and differing kinds of items; it is also that each of these lists embodies, is the expression of a different theory about what a virtue is.

In the Homeric poems a virtue is a quality the manifestation of which enables someone to do exactly what their well-defined social role requires. The primary role is that of the warrior king and that Homer lists those virtues which he does becomes intelligible at once when we recognise that the key virtues therefore must be those which enable a man to excel in combat and in the games. It follows that we cannot identify the Homeric virtues until we have first identified the key social roles in Homeric society and the requirements of each of them. The concept of *what anyone filling such-and-such a role ought to do* is prior to the concept of a virtue; the latter concept has application only via the former.

On Aristotle's account matters are very different. Even though some virtues are available only to certain types of people, none the less virtues attach not to men as inhabiting social roles, but to man as such. It is the *telos* of man as a species which determines what human qualities are virtues. We need to remember however that although Aristotle treats the acquisition and exercise of the virtues as means to an end, the relationship of means to end is internal and not external. I call a means internal to a given end when the end cannot be adequately characterised independently of a characterisation of the means. So it is with the virtues and the *telos* which is the good life for man on Aristotle's account. The exercise of the virtues is itself a crucial component of the good life for man. This distinction between internal and external means to an end is not drawn by Aristotle himself in the *Nicomachean Ethics*, as I noticed earlier, but it is an essential distinction to be drawn if we are to understand what Aristotle intended. The distinction *is* drawn explicitly by Aquinas in the course of his defence of St Augustine's definition of a virtue, and it is clear that Aquinas understood that in drawing it he was maintaining an Aristotelian point of view.

The New Testament's account of the virtues, even if it differs as much as it does in content from Aristotle's— Aristotle would certainly not have admired Jesus Christ and he would have been horrified by St Paul—does have the same logical and conceptual structure as Aristotle's account. A virtue is, as with Aristotle, a quality the exercise of which leads to the achievement of the human *telos*. *The* good for man is of course a supernatural and not only a natural good, but supernature redeems and completes nature. Moreover the relationship of virtues as means to the end which is human incorporation in the divine kingdom of the age to come is internal and not external, just as it is in Aristotle. It is of course this parallelism which allows Aquinas to synthesise Aristotle and the New Testament. A key feature of this parallelism is the way in which the concept of the *good life for man* is prior to the concept of a virtue in just the way in which on the Homeric account the concept of a social role was prior. Once again it is the way in which the former concept is applied which determines how the latter is to be applied. In both cases the concept of a virtue is a secondary concept.

The intent of Jane Austen's theory of the virtues is of another kind. C.S. Lewis has rightly emphasised how profoundly Christian her moral vision is and Gilbert Ryle has equally rightly emphasised her inheritance from Shaftesbury and from Aristotle. In fact her views combine elements from Homer as well, since she is concerned with social roles in a way that neither the New Testament nor Aristotle are. She is therefore important for the way in which she finds it possible to combine what are at first sight disparate theoretical accounts of the virtues. But for the moment any attempt to assess the significance of Jane Austen's systhesis must be delayed. Instead we must notice the quite different style of theory articulated in Benjamin Franklin's account of the virtues.

Franklin's account, like Aristotle's, is teleological; but unlike Aristotle's, it is utilitarian. According to Franklin in his *Autobiography* the virtues are means to an end, but he envisages the means-ends relationship as external rather than internal. The end to which the cultivation of the virtues ministers is happiness, but happiness understood as success, prosperity in Philadelphia and ultimately in heaven. The virtues are to be useful and Franklin's account continuously stresses utility as a criterion in individual cases: 'Make no expence but to do good to others or yourself; i.e. waste nothing', 'Speak not but what may benefit others or yourself. Avoid trifling conversation' and, as we have already seen, 'Rarely use venery but for health or offspring. . . .' When Franklin was in Paris he was horrified by Parisian architecture: 'Marble, porcelain and gilt are squandered without utility.'

We thus have at least three very different conceptions of a virtue to confront: a virtue is a quality which enables an individual to discharge his or her social role (Homer); a virtue is a quality which enables an individual to move towards the achievement of the specifically human *telos*, whether natural or supernatural (Aristotle, the New Testament and Aquinas); a virtue is a quality which has utility in achieving earthly and heavenly success (Franklin). Are we to take these as three rival accounts of the same thing? Or are they instead accounts of three different things? Perhaps the moral structures in archaic Greece, in fourth-century Greece, and in eighteenth-century Pennsylvania were so different from each other that we should treat them as embodying quite different concepts, whose difference is initially disguised from us by the historical accident of an inherited vocabulary which misleads us by linguistic resemblance long after conceptual identity and similarity have failed. Our initial question has come back to us with redoubled force.

Yet although I have dwelt upon the *prima facie* case for holding that the differences and incompatibilities between different accounts at least suggest that there is no single, central, core conception of the virtues which might make a claim for universal allegiance, I ought also to point out that each of the five moral accounts which I have sketched so summarily does embody just such a claim. It is indeed just this feature of those accounts that makes them of more than sociological or antiquarian interest. Every one of these accounts claims not only theoretical, but also an institutional hegemony. For Odysseus the Cyclopes stand condemned because they lack agriculture, on *agora* and *themis*. For Aristotle the barbarians stand condemned because they lack the *polis* and are therefore incapable of politics. For New Testament Christians there is no salvation outside the apostolic church. And we know that Benjamin Franklin found the virtues more at home in Philadelphia than in Paris and that for Jane Austen the touchstone of the virtues is a certain kind of marriage and indeed a certain kind of naval officer (that is, a certain kind of *English* naval officer).

The question can therefore now be posed directly: are we or are we not able to disentangle from these rival and various claims a unitary core concept of the virtues of which we can give a more compelling account than any of the other accounts so far? I am going to argue that we can in fact discover such a core concept and that it turns out to provide the tradition of which I have written the history with its conceptual unity. It will indeed enable us to distinguish in a clear way those beliefs about the virtues which genuinely belong to the tradition from those which do not. Unsurprisingly perhaps it is a complex concept, different parts of which derive from different stages in the development of the tradition. Thus the concept itself in some sense embodies the history of which it is the outcome.

One of the features of the concept of a virtue which has emerged with some clarity from the argument so far is that it always requires for its application the acceptance of some prior account of certain features of social and moral life in terms of which it has to be defined and explained. So in the Homeric account the concept of a virtue is secondary to that of *a social role*, in Aristotle's account it is secondary to that of *the good life for man* conceived as the *telos* of human action and in Franklin's much later account it is secondary to that of utility. What is it in the account which I am about to give which provides in a similar way the necessary background against which the concept of a virtue has to be made intelligible? It is in answering this question that the complex, historical, multilayered character of the core concept of virtue becomes clear. For there are no less than three stages in the logical development of the concept which have to be identified in order, if the core conception of a virtue is to be understood, and each of these stages has its own conceptual background. The first stage requires a background account of what I shall call a practice, the second an account of what I have already characterised as the narrative order of a single human life and the third an account a good deal fuller than I have given up to now of what constitutes a moral tradition. Each later stage presupposes the earlier, but not *vice versa*. Each earlier stage is both modified by and reinterpreted in the light of, but also provides an essential constituent of each later stage. The progress in the development of the concept is closely related to, although it does not recapitulate in any straightforward way, the history of the tradition of which it forms the core.

In the Homeric account of the virtues—and in heroic societies more generally—the exercise of a virtue exhibits qualities which are required for sustaining a social role and for exhibiting excellence in some well-marked area of social practice: to excel is to excel at war or in the games, as Achilles does, in sustaining a household, as Penelope does, in giving counsel in the assembly, as Nestor does, in the telling of a tale, as Homer himself does. When Aristotle speaks of excellence in human activity, he sometimes though not always, refers to some well-defined type of human practice: flute-playing, or war, or geometry. I am going to suggest that this notion of a particular type of practice as providing the arena in which the virtues are exhibited and in terms of which they are to receive their primary, if incomplete, definition is crucial to the whole enterprise of identifying a core concept of the virtues. I hasten to add two *caveats* however.

The first is to point out that my argument will not in any way imply that virtues are *only* exercised in the course of what I am calling practices. The second is to warn that I shall be using the word 'practice' in a specially defined way which does not completely agree with current ordinary usage, including my own previous use of that word. What am I going to mean by it?

By a 'practice' I am going to mean any coherent and complex form of socially established cooperative human activity through which goods internal to that form of activity are realised in the course of trying to achieve those standards of excellence which are appropriate to, and partially definitive of, that form of activity, with the result that human powers to achieve excellence, and human conceptions of the ends and goods involved, are systematically extended. Tic-tac-toe is not an example of a practice in this sense, nor is throwing a football with skill; but the game of football is, and so is chess. Bricklaying is not a practice; architecture is. Planting turnips is not a practice; farming is. So are the enquiries of physics, chemistry and biology, and so is the work of the historian, and so are painting and music. In the ancient and medieval worlds the creation and sustaining of human communities—of households, cities, nations—is generally taken to be a practice in the sense in which I have defined it. Thus the range of practices is wide: arts, sciences, games, politics in the Aristotelian sense, the making and sustaining of family life, all fall under the concept. But the question of the precise range of practices is not at this stage of the first importance. Instead let me explain some of the key terms involved in my definition, beginning with the notion of goods internal to a practice.

Consider the example of a highly intelligent seven-year-old child whom I wish to teach to play chess, although the child has no particular desire to learn the game. The child does however have a very strong desire for candy and little chance of obtaining it. I therefore tell the child that if the child will play chess with me once a week I will give the child 50¢ worth of candy; moreover I tell the child that I will always play in such a way that it will be difficult, but not impossible, for the child to win and that, if the child wins, the child will receive an extra 50¢ worth of candy. Thus motivated the child plays and plays to win. Notice however that, so long as it is the candy alone which provides the child with a good reason for playing chess, the child has no reason not to cheat and every reason to cheat, provided he or she can do so successfully. But, so we may hope, there will come a time when the child will find in those goods specific to chess, in the achievement of a certain highly particular kind of analytical skill, strategic imagination and competitive intensity, a new set of reasons, reasons now not just for winning on a particular occasion, but for trying to excel in whatever way the game of chess demands. Now if the child cheats, he or she will be defeating not me, but himself or herself.

There are thus two kinds of good possibly to be gained by playing chess. On the one hand there are those goods externally and contingently attached to chess-playing and to other practices by the accidents of social circumstance— in the case of the imaginary child candy, in the case of real adults such goods as prestige, status and money. There are always alternative ways for achieving such goods, and their achievement is never to be had *only* by engaging in some particular kind of practice. On the other hand there are the goods internal to the practice of chess which cannot be had in any way but by playing chess or some other game of that specific kind. We call them internal for two reasons: first, as I have already suggested, because we can only specify them in terms of chess or some other game of that specific kind and by means of examples from such games (otherwise the meagerness of our vocabulary for speaking of such goods forces us into such devices as my own resort to writing of 'a certain highly particular kind of'); and secondly because they can only be identified and recognised by the experience of participating in the practice in question. Those who lack the relevant experience are incompetent thereby as judges of internal goods.

This is clearly the case with all the major examples of practices: consider for example—even if briefly and inadequately—the practice of portrait painting as it developed in Western Europe from the late middle ages to the eighteenth century. The successful portrait painter is able to achieve many goods which are in the sense just defined external to the practice of portrait painting—fame, wealth, social status, even a measure of power and influence at courts upon occasion. But those external goods are not to be confused with the goods which are internal to the practice. The internal goods are those which result from an extended attempt to show how Wittgenstein's dictum 'The human body is the best picture of the human soul' (*Investigations*, p.178e) might be made to become true by teaching us 'to regard . . . the picture on our all as the object itself (the men, landscape and so on) depicted there' (p.205e) in a quite new way. What is misleading about Wittgenstein's dictum as it stands is its neglect of the truth in George Orwell's thesis 'At 50 everyone has the face he deserves'. What painters from Giotto to Rembrandt learnt to show was how the face at any age may be revealed as the face that the subject of a portrait deserves.

Originally in medieval paintings of the saints the face was an icon; the question of a resemblance between the depicted face of Christ or St Peter and the face that Jesus or Peter actually possessed at some particular age did not even arise. The antithesis to this iconography was the relative naturalism of certain fifteenth-century Flemish and German painting. The heavy eyelids, the coifed hair, the lines around the mouth undeniably represent some particular woman, either actual or envisaged. Resemblance has usurped the iconic relationship. But with Rembrandt there is, so to speak, synthesis: the naturalistic portrait is now rendered as an icon, but an icon of a new and hitherto inconceivable kind. Similarly in a very different kind of sequence mythological faces in a certain kind of seventeenth-century French painting become aristocratic faces in the eighteenth century. Within each of these sequences at least two different kinds of good internal to the painting of human faces and bodies are achieved.

There is first of all the excellence of the products, both the excellence in performance by the painters and that of each portrait itself. This excellence—the very verb 'excel' suggests it—has to be understood historically. The sequences of development find their point and purpose in a progress towards and beyond a variety of types and modes of excellence. There are of course sequences of decline as well as of progress, and progress is rarely to be understood as straightforwardly linear. But it is in participation in the attempts to sustain progress and to respond creatively to moments that the second kind of good internal to the practices of portrait painting is to be found. For what the artist discovers within the pursuit of excellence in portrait painting—and what is true of portrait painting is true of the practice of the fine arts in general—is the good of a certain kind of life. That life may not constitute the whole of life for someone who is a painter by a very long way or it may at least for a period, Gauguin-like, absorb him or her at the expense of almost everything else. But it is the painter's living out of a greater or lesser part of his or her life *as a painter* that is the second kind of good internal to painting. And judgment upon these goods requires at the very least the kind of competence that is only to be acquired either as a painter or as someone willing to learn systematically what the portrait painter has to teach.

A practice involves standards of excellence and obedience to rules as well as the achievement of goods. To enter into a practice is to accept the authority of those standards and the inadequacy of my own performance as judged by them. It is to subject my own attitudes, choices, preferences and tastes to the standards which currently and partially define the practice. Practices of course, as I have just noticed, have a history: games, sciences and arts all have histories. Thus the standards are not themselves immune from criticism, but none the less we cannot be initiated into a practice without accepting the authority of the best standards realised so far. If, on starting to listen to music, I do not accept my own incapacity to judge correctly, I will never learn to hear, let alone to appreciate, Bartok's last quartets. If, on starting to play baseball, I do not accept that others know better than I when to throw a fast ball and when not, I will never learn to appreciate good pitching let alone to pitch. In the realm of practices the authority of both goods and standards operates in such a way as to rule out all subjectivist and emotivist analyses of judgment. De gustibus *est* disputandum.

We are now in a position to notice an important difference between what I have called internal and what I have called external goods. It is characteristic of what I have called external goods that when achieved they are always some individual's property and possession. Moreover characteristically they are such that the more someone has of them, the less there is for other people. This is sometimes necessarily the case, as with power and fame, and sometimes the case by reason of contingent circumstance as with money. External goods are therefore characteristically objects of competition in which there must be losers as well as winners. Internal goods are indeed the outcome of competition to excel, but it is characteristic of them that their achievement is a good for the whole community who participate in the practice. So when Turner transformed the seascape in painting or W.G. Grace advanced the art of batting in cricket in a quite new way their achievement enriched the whole relevant community.

But what does all or any of this have to do with the concept of the virtues? It turns out that we are now in a position to formulate a first, even if partial and tentative definition of a virtue: *A virtue is an acquired human quality the possession and exercise of which tends to enable us to achieve those goods which are internal to practices and the lack of which effectively prevents us from achieving any such goods.* Later this definition will need amplification and amendment. But as a first approximation to an adequate definition it already illuminates the place of the virtues in human life. For it is not difficult to show for a whole range of key virtues that without them the goods internal to practices are barred to us, but not just barred to us generally, barred in a very particular way.

It belongs to the concept of a practice as I have outlined it—and as we are all familiar with it already in our actual lives, whether we are painters or physicists or quarterbacks or indeed just lovers of good painting or first-rate experiments or a well-thrown pass—that its goods can only be achieved by subordinating ourselves to the best standard so far achieved, and that entails subordinating ourselves within the practice in our relationship to other practitioners. We have to learn to recognise what is due to whom; we have to be prepared to take whatever self-endangering risks are demanded along the way; and we have to listen carefully to what we are told about our own inadequacies and to reply with the same carefulness for the facts. In other words we have to accept as necessary components of any practice with internal goods and standards of excellence the virtues of justice, courage and honesty. For not to accept these, to be willing to cheat as our imagined child was willing to cheat in his or her early days at chess, so far bars us from achieving the standards of excellence or the goods internal to the practice that it renders the practice pointless except as a device for achieving external goods.

We can put the same point in another way. Every practice requires a certain kind of relationship between those who participate in it. Now the virtues are those goods by reference to which, whether we like it or not, we define our relationships to those other people with whom we share the kind of purposes and standards which inform practices. Consider an example of how reference to the virtues has to be made in certain kinds of human relationship.

A, B, C, and D are friends in that sense of friendship which Aristotle takes to be primary: they share in the pursuit of certain goods. In my terms they share in a practice. D dies in obscure circumstances, A discovers how D died and tells the truth about it to B while lying to C. C discovers the lie. What A cannot then intelligibly claim is that he stands in the same relationship of friendship to both B and C. By telling the truth to one and lying to the other he has partially defined a difference in the relationship. Of course it is open to A to explain this difference in a number of ways; perhaps he was trying to spare C pain or perhaps he is simply cheating C. But some difference in the relationship now exists as a result of the lie. For their allegiance to each other in the pursuit of common goods has been put in question.

Just as, so long as we share the standards and purposes characteristic of practices, we define our relationships to each other, whether we acknowledge it or not, by reference to standards of truthfulness and trust, so we define them too by reference to standards of justice and of courage. If A, a professor, gives B and C the grades that their papers deserve, but grades D because he is attracted by D's blue eyes or is repelled by D's dandruff, he has defined his relationship to D differently from his relationship to the other members of the class, whether he wishes it or not. Justice requires that we treat others in respect of merit or desert according to uniform and impersonal standards; to depart from the standards of justice in some particular instance defines our relationship with the relevant person as in some way special or distinctive.

The case with courage is a little different. We hold courage to be a virtue because the care and concern for individuals, communities and causes which is so crucial to so much in practices requires the existence of such a virtue. If someone says that he cares for some individual, community or cause, but is unwilling to risk harm or danger on his, her or its own behalf, he puts in question the genuineness of his care and concern. Courage, the capacity to risk harm or danger to oneself, has its role in human life because of this connection with care and concern. This is not to say that a man cannot genuinely care and also be a coward. It is in part to say that a man who genuinely cares and has not the capacity for risking harm or danger has to define himself, both to himself and to others, as a coward.

I take it then that from the standpoint of those types of relationship without which practices cannot be sustained truthfulness, justice and courage—and perhaps some others—are genuine excellences, are virtues in the light of which we have to characterise ourselves and others, whatever our private moral standpoint or our society's particular codes may be. For this recognition that we cannot escape the definition of our relationships in terms of such goods is perfectly compatible with the acknowledgment that different societies have and have had different codes of truthfulness, justice and courage. Lutheran pietists brought up their children to believe that one ought to tell the truth to everybody at all times, whatever the circumstances or consequences, and Kant was one of their children. Traditional Bantu parents brought up their children not to tell the truth to unknown strangers, since they believed that this could render the family vulnerable to witchcraft. In our culture many of us have been brought up not to tell the truth to elderly great-aunts who invite us to admire their new hats. But each of these codes embodies an acknowledgment of the virtue of truthfulness. So it is also with varying codes of justice and of courage.

Practices then might flourish in societies with very different codes; what they could not do is flourish in societies in which the virtues were not valued, although institutions and technical skills serving unified purposes might well continue to flourish. . . .

CHAPTER 15

THE VIRTUES, THE UNITY OF A HUMAN LIFE AND THE CONCEPT OF A TRADITION

... It is a conceptual commonplace, both for philosophers and for ordinary agents, that one and the same segment of human behaviour may be correctly characterised in a number of different ways. To the question 'What is he doing?' the answers may with equal truth and appropriateness be 'Digging', 'Gardening', 'Taking exercise', 'Preparing for winter' or 'Pleasing his wife'. Some of these answers will characterise the agent's intentions, others unintended consequences of his actions, and of these unintended consequences some may be such that the agent is aware of them and others not. What is important to notice immediately is that any answer to the questions of how we are to understand or to explain a given segment of behaviour will presuppose some prior answer to the question of how these different correct answers to the question 'What is he doing?' are related to each other. For if someone's primary intention is to put the garden in order before the winter and it is only incidentally the case that in so doing he is taking exercise and pleasing his wife, we have one type of behaviour to be explained; but if the agent's primary intention is to please his wife by taking exercise, we have quite another type of behaviour to be explained and we will have to look in a different direction for understanding and explanation.

In the first place the episode has been situated in an annual cycle of domestic activity, and the behaviour embodies an intention which presupposes a particular type of household-cum-garden setting with the peculiar narrative history of that setting in which this segment of behaviour now becomes an episode. In the second instance the episode has been situated in the narrative history of a marriage, a very different, even if related, social setting. We cannot, that is to say, characterise behaviour independently of intentions, and we cannot characterise intentions independently of the settings which make those intentions intelligible both to agents themselves and to others.

I use the word 'setting' here as a relatively inclusive term. A social setting may be an institution, it may be what I have called a practice, or it may be a milieu of some other human kind. But it is central to the notion of a setting as I am going to understand it that a setting has a history, a history within which the histories of individual agents not only are, but have to be, situated, just because without the setting and its changes through time the history of the individual agent and his changes through time will be unintelligible. Of course one and the same piece of behaviour may belong to more than one setting. There are at least two different ways in which this may be so.

In my earlier example the agent's activity may be part of the history both of the cycle of household activity and of his marriage, two histories which have happened to intersect. The household may have its own history stretching back through hundreds of years, as do the histories of some European farms, where the farm has had a life of its own, even though different families have in different periods inhabited it; and the marriage will certainly have its own history, a history which itself presupposes that a particular point has been reached in the history of the institution of marriage. If we are to relate some particular segment of behaviour in any precise way to an agent's intentions and thus to the settings which that agent inhabits, we shall have to understand in a precise way how the variety of correct characterisations of the agent's behaviour relate to each other first by identifying which characteristics refer us to an intention and which do not and then by classifying further the items in both categories.

Where intentions are concerned, we need to know which intention or intentions were primary, that is to say, of which it is the case that, had the agent intended otherwise, he would not have performed that action. Thus if we know that a man is gardening with the self-avowed purposes of healthful exercise and of pleasing his wife, we do not yet know how to understand what he is doing until we know the answer to such questions as whether he would continue gardening if he continued to believe that gardening was healthful exercise, but discovered that his gardening no longer pleased his wife, *and* whether he would continue gardening, if he ceased to believe that gardening was healthful exercise, but continued to believe that it pleased his wife, *and* whether he would continue gardening if he changed his beliefs on both points. That is to say, we need to know both what certain of his beliefs are and which of them are causally effective; and, that is to say, we need to know whether certain contrary-to-fact hypothetical statements are true or false. And until we know this, we shall not know how to characterise correctly what the agent is doing.

Consider another equally trivial example of a set of compatibly correct answers to the question 'What is he doing?' 'Writing a sentence'; 'Finishing his book'; 'Contributing to the debate on the theory of action'; 'Trying to get tenure'. Here the intentions can be ordered in terms of the stretch of time to which reference is made. Each of the shorter-term intentions is, and can only be made, intelligible by reference to some longer-term intentions; and the characterisation of the behaviour in terms of the longer-term intentions can only be correct if some of the characterisations in terms of shorter-term intentions are also correct. Hence the behaviour is only characterised adequately when we know what the longer and longest-term intentions invoked are and how the shorter-term intentions are related to the longer. Once again we are involved in writing a narrative history.

Intentions thus need to be ordered both causally and temporally and both orderings will make references to settings, references already made obliquely by such elementary terms as 'gardening', 'wife', 'book' and 'tenure'. Moreover the correct identification of the agent's beliefs will be an essential constituent of this task; failure at this point would mean failure in the whole enterprise. (The conclusion may seem obvious; but it already entails one important consequence. There is no such thing as 'behaviour', to be identified prior to and independently of intentions, beliefs and settings. Hence the project of a science of behaviour takes on a mysterious and somewhat outré character. It is not that such a science is impossible; but there is nothing for it to be but a science of uninterpreted physical movement such as B.F. Skinner aspires to. It is no part of my task here to examine Skinner's problems; but it is worth noticing that it is not at all clear what a scientific experiment could be, if one were a Skinnerian; since the conception of an experiment is certainly one of intention—and belief-informed behaviour. And what would be utterly doomed to failure would be the project of a science of, say, *political* behaviour, detached from a study of intentions, beliefs and settings. It is perhaps worth noting that when the expression 'the behavioural sciences' was given its first influential use in a Ford Foundation Report of 1953, the term 'behaviour' was defined so as to include what were called 'such subjective behaviour as attitudes, beliefs, expectations, motivations and aspirations' as well as 'overt acts'. But what the Report's wording seems to imply is that it is cataloguing two distinct sets of items, available for independent study. If the argument so far is correct, then there is only one set of items.)

Consider what the argument so far implies about the interrelationships of the intentional, the social and the historical. We identify a particular action only by invoking two kinds of context, implicitly if not explicitly. We place the agent's intentions, I have suggested, in causal and temporal order with reference to their role in his or her history; and we also place them with reference to their role in the history of the setting or settings to which they belong. In doing this, in determining what causal efficacy the agent's intentions had in one or more directions, and how his short-term intentions succeeded or failed to be constitutive of long-term intentions, we ourselves write a further part of these histories. Narrative history of a certain kind turns out to be the basic and essential genre for the characterisation of human actions.

It is important to be clear how different the standpoint presupposed by the argument so far is from that of those analytical philosophers who have constructed accounts of human actions which make central the notion of 'a' human action. A course of human events is then seen as a complex sequence of individual actions, and a natural question is: How do we individuate human actions? Now there are contexts in which such notions are at home. In the recipes of a cookery book for instance actions are individuated in just the way that some analytical philosophers have supposed to be possible of all actions. 'Take six eggs. Then break them into a bowl. Add flour, salt, sugar, etc.' But the point about such sequences is that each element in them is intelligible as an action only as a-possible-element-in-a-sequence. Moreover even such a sequence requires a context to be intelligible. If in the middle of my lecture on Kant's ethics I suddenly broke six eggs into a bowl and added flour and sugar, proceeding all the while with my Kantian exegesis, I have *not*, simply in virtue of the fact that I was following a sequence prescribed by Fanny Farmer, performed an intelligible action.

To this it might be related that I certainly performed an action or a set of actions, if not an intelligible action. But to this I want to reply that the concept of an intelligible action is a more fundamental concept than that of an action as such. Unintelligible actions are failed candidates for the status of intelligible action; and to lump unintelligible actions and intelligible actions together in a single class of actions and then to characterise action in terms of what items of both sets have in common is to make the mistake of ignoring this. It is also to neglect the central importance of the concept of intelligibility.

The importance of the concept of intelligibility is closely related to the fact that the most basic distinction of all embedded in our discourse and our practice in this area is that between human beings and other beings. Human beings can be held to account for that of which they are the authors; other beings cannot. To identify an occurrence as an action is in the paradigmatic instances to identify it under a type of description which enables us to see that occurrence as flowing intelligibly from a human agent's intentions, motives, passions and purposes. It is therefore to understand an action as something for which someone is accountable, about which it is always appropriate to ask the agent for an intelligible account. When an occurrence is apparently the intended action of a human agent, but none the less we cannot so identify it, we are both intellectually and practically baffled. We do not know how to respond; we do not know how to explain; we do not even know how to characterise minimally as an intelligible action; our distinction between the humanly accountable and the merely natural seems to have broken down. And this kind of bafflement does indeed occur in a number of different kinds of situation; when we enter alien cultures or even alien social structures within our own culture, in our encounters with certain types of neurotic or psychotic patient (it is indeed the unintelligibility of such patient's actions that leads to their being treated as patients; actions unintelligible to the agent as well as to everyone else are understood—rightly—as a kind of suffering), but also in everyday situations. Consider an example.

I am standing waiting for a bus and the young man standing next to me suddenly says: 'The name of the common wild duck is *Histrionicus histrionicus histrionicus.*' There is no problem as to the meaning of the sentence he uttered: the problem is, how to answer the question, what was he doing in uttering it? Suppose he just uttered such sentences at random intervals; this would be one possible form of madness. We would render his act of utterance intelligible if one of the following turned out to be true. He has mistaken me for someone who yesterday had approached him in the library and asked: 'Do you by any chance know the Latin name of the common wild duck?' *Or* he has just come from a session with his psychotherapist who has urged him to break down his shyness by talking to strangers. 'But what shall I say?' 'Oh, anything at all.' *Or* he is a Soviet spy waiting at a prearranged rendez-vous and uttering the ill-chosen code sentence which will identify him to his contact. In each case the act of utterance becomes intelligible by finding its place in a narrative.

To this it may be replied that the supplying of a narrative is not necessary to make such an act intelligible. All that is required is that we can identify the relevant type of speech act (e.g. 'He was answering a question') or some purpose served by his utterance (e.g. 'He was trying to attract your attention'). But speech acts and purposes too can be intelligible or unintelligible. Suppose that the man at the bus stop explains his act of utterance by saying 'I was answering a question.' I reply: 'But I never asked you any question to which that could have been the answer.' He says, 'Oh, I know *that.*' Once again his action becomes unintelligible. And a parallel example could easily be constructed to show that the mere fact that an action serves some purpose of a recognised type is not sufficient to render an action intelligible. Both purposes and speech-acts require contexts.

The most familiar type of context in and by reference to which speech-acts and purposes are rendered intelligible is the conversation. Conversation is so all-pervasive a feature of the human world that it tends to escape philosophical attention. Yet remove conversation from human life and what would be left? Consider then what is involved in following a conversation and finding it intelligible or unintelligible. (To find a conversation intelligible is not the same as to understand it; for a conversation which I overhear may be intelligible, but I may fail to understand it.) If I listen to a conversation between two other people my ability to grasp the thread of the conversation will involve an ability to bring it under some one out of a set of descriptions in which the degree and kind of coherence in the conversation is brought out: 'a drunken, rambling quarrel', 'a serious intellectual disagreement', 'a tragic misunderstanding of each other', 'a comic, even farcical misconstrual of each other's motives', 'a penetrating interchange of views', 'a struggle to dominate each other', 'a trivial exchange of gossip.'

The use of words such as 'tragic', 'comic', and 'farcical' is not marginal to such evaluations. We allocate conversations to genres, just as we do literary narratives. Indeed a conversation is a dramatic work, even if a very short one, in which the participants are not only the actors, but also the joint authors, working out in agreement or disagreement the mode of their production. For it is not just that conversations belong to genres in just the way that plays and novels do; but they have beginnings, middles and endings just as do literary works. They embody reversals and recognitions; they move towards and away from climaxes. There may within a longer conversation be digressions and subplots, indeed digressions within digressions and subplots within subplots.

But if this is true of conversations, it is true also *mutatis mutandis* of battles, chess games, courtships, philosophy seminars, families at the dinner table, businessmen negotiating contracts—that is, of human transactions in general. For conversation, understood widely enough, is the form of human transactions in general. Conversational behaviour is not a special sort or aspect of human behaviour, even though the forms of language-using and of human life are such that the deeds of others speak for them as much as do their words. For that is possible only because they are the deeds of those who have words.

I am presenting both conversations in particular then and human actions in general as enacted narratives. Narrative is not the work of poets, dramatists and novelists reflecting upon events which had no narrative order before one was imposed by the singer or the writer; narrative form is neither disguise nor decoration. Barbara Hardy has written that 'we dream in narrative, daydream in narrative, remember, anticipate, hope, despair, believe, doubt, plan, revise, criticise, construct, gossip, learn, hate and love by narrative' in arguing the same point (Hardy 1968, p.5).

At the beginning of this chapter I argued that in successfully identifying and understanding what someone else is doing we always move towards placing a particular episode in the context of a set of narrative histories, histories both of the individuals concerned and of the settings in which they act and suffer. It is now becoming clear that we render the actions of others intelligible in this way because action itself has a basically historical character. It is because we all live out narratives in our lives and because we understand our own lives in terms of the narratives that we live out that the form of narrative is appropriate for understanding the actions of others. Stories are lived before they are told— except in the case of fiction. . . .

MARIE DE FRANCE

TWELFTH CENTURY

THE LAIS OF MARIE DE FRANCE

Very little certain biographical information exists on Marie de France. Though she was from France (probably the region around Paris known as the Ile-de-France), she wrote in England. Some authors have tentatively identified her with an illegitimate daughter of Geoffrey of Anjou, the father of King Henry II of England. Most recent scholars believe that she wrote during the last third of the twelfth century and some argue that she was an abbess. But all this is uncertain, so much so that R. Howard Bloch, the author of the most recent comprehensive study of Marie de France and her works, says that she "comes as close as one can imagine to being anonymous." (R. Howard Bloch, *The Anonymous Marie de France*. Chicago and London: University of Chicago Press, 2003, p. 7.)

Yet, in the prologues to her works she clearly identifies herself as "Marie de France," and her contemporaries were so well aware of her that she was envied by other poets. Bloch believes that analysis of the internal evidence of all three of her major works reveals a single flesh-and-blood woman who was intensely conscious of herself as an author and of the profound effect her writings would have. Her other two works were a collection of *Fables* based on Aesop and a longer work known as the *Purgatory of St. Patrick*. But Marie de France was and is most famous for her *Lais*, which are short narrative poems. She seems to have produced the first written narrative lays in Europe, though they may well be based on earlier oral narrative ballads. In her prologues Marie writes that she took the lays from the Bretons (people of Celtic origin who inhabited the peninsula of Brittany on the West coast of France), but scholars have searched in vain for Breton lays with the same stories Marie tells. Breton place names, traditions, and customs do appear in Marie's lays, and Welsh ones as well. Only three of the lays are clearly based on Breton materials, but all have Celtic trappings in one way or another. It seems most likely that Marie's lays, while incorporating earlier Celtic oral traditions, are the unique and brilliant creation of her own genius.

SOURCE

de France, Marie. *The Lais of Marie de France.* Trans. Robert Hanning and Joan Ferrante. New York: E.P. Dutton, 1978.

Selections from:

Guigemar (30-55)
Le Fresne (73-87)
Chevrefoil (190-193)

Guigemar

ᛜ Whoever deals with good material
feels pain if it's treated improperly.
Listen, my lords, to the words of Marie,
who does not forget her responsibilities when her
turn comes.[1]

---

[1] The French *en sun tens* could also be rendered, "in her day"; Rychner opts for this sense, seeing in it an implied contrast between Marie as a modern writer and the ancient writers and sages referred to in the Prologue to the whole collection.

5 People should praise anyone
 who wins admiring comments for herself.
 But anywhere there is
 a man or a woman of great worth,
 people who envy their good fortune
10 often say evil things about them;
 they want to ruin their reputations.
 Thus they act like
 vicious, cowardly dogs
 who bite people treacherously.
15 I don't propose to give up because of that;
 if spiteful critics or slanderers
 wish to turn my accomplishments against me,
 they have a right to their evil talk.
 ℞ The tales—and I know they're true—
20 from which the Bretons made their *lais*
 I'll now recount for you briefly;
 and at the very beginning of this enterprise,
 just the way it was written down,
 I'll relate an adventure
25 that took place in Brittany,
 in the old days.
 ℞ At that time, Hoel ruled Brittany,
 sometimes peacefully, sometimes at war.
 The king had a vassal
30 who was lord of Leonnais;
 his name was Oridial
 and he was on very intimate terms with his lord.
 A worthy and valiant knight,
 he had, by his wife, two children,
35 a son and a beautiful daughter.
 The girl's name was Noguent;
 they called the boy Guigemar.
 There wasn't a more handsome youngster in the
 kingdom.
 His mother had a wonderful love for him,

40   and his father a great devotion;
        when he could bring himself to part with the boy,
        his father sent him to serve the king.
        The boy was intelligent and brave,
        and made himself loved by all.
45   When his time of probation was at an end,
        and he was mature in body and mind,
        the king dubbed him knight,
        giving him luxurious armor, which was exactly what
        he desired.
        Guigemar left the court,
50   but not before dispensing many rich gifts.
        ℞ He journeyed to Flanders to seek his fame;
        there was always a war, or a battle raging there.
        Neither in Lorraine nor in Burgundy,
        in Anjou nor in Gascony,
55   could one find, in those days,
        Guigemar's equal as a fine knight.
        But in forming him nature had so badly erred
        that he never gave any thought to love.
        There wasn't a lady or a maid on earth,
60   no matter how noble, or how beautiful,
        who wouldn't have willingly granted him her love,
        had he asked her for it.
        Many maids asked him,
        but he wasn't interested in such things;
65   no one could discover in him
        the slightest desire to love.
        Therefore both friends and strangers
        gave him up for lost.
        ℞ At the height of his fame,
70   this baron, Guigemar, returned to his own land
        to visit his father and his lord,
        his good mother and his sister,
        all of whom were most eager to see him.
        Guigemar stayed with them,

75   I believe, an entire month.
Then he was seized by a desire to hunt;
that night he summoned his companions in arms,
his huntsmen, and his beaters;
next morning he set out for the woods
80   to indulge in the sport that gave him much pleasure.
They gathered in pursuit of a great stag;
the dogs were unleashed.
The hunters ran ahead
while the young man lingered behind;
85   a squire carried his bow,
his hunting knife, and his quiver.[2]
He wanted to fire some arrows, if he had the opportunity,
before he left that spot.
In the thickest part of a great bush
90   Guigemar saw a hind with a fawn;
a completely white beast,
with deer's antlers on her head.
Spurred by the barking of the dogs, she sprang into the open.
Guigemar took his bow and shot at her,
95   striking her in the breastbone.[3]
She fell at once,
but the arrow rebounded,
gave Guigemar such a wound—
it went through his thigh right into the horse's flank—
100   that he had to dismount.
He collapsed on the thick grass

---

[2]   As practiced by the medieval aristocracy, the hunt proceeded according to precise, complicated rules that governed the actions of each participant.

[3]   "Breastbone": so Rychner glosses *esclot*; Ewert reads, "front hoof."

beside the hind he'd struck.
The hind, wounded as she was,
suffered pain and groaned.
105   Then she spoke, in this fashion:
"Alas! I'm dying!
And you, vassal, who wounded me,
this be your destiny:
may you never get medicine for your wound!
110   Neither herb nor root,
neither physician nor potion,
will cure you
of that wound in your thigh,
until a woman heals you,
115   one who will suffer, out of love for you,
pain and grief
such as no woman ever suffered before.
And out of love for her, you'll suffer as much;
the affair will be a marvel
120   to lovers, past and present,
and to all those yet to come.
Now go away, leave me in peace!"
    ﻉ Guigemar was badly wounded;
what he had heard dismayed him.
125   He began to consider carefully
what land he might set out for
to have his wound healed.
He didn't want to remain there and die.
He knew, he reminded himself,
130   that he'd never seen a woman
to whom he wanted to offer his love,
nor one who could cure his pain.
He called his squire to him;
"Friend," he said, "go quickly!
135   Bring my companions back here;
I want to talk to them."

The squire rode off and Guigemar remained;
he complained bitterly to himself.
Making his shirt into a bandage,
140   he bound his wound tightly;
Then he mounted his horse and left that spot.
He was anxious to get far away;
he didn't want any of his men to come along,
who might interfere, or try to detain him.
145   Through the woods he followed
a grassy path, which led him
out into open country; there, at the edge of the plain,
he saw a cliff and a steep bank
overlooking a body of water below:
150   a bay that formed a harbor.
There was a solitary ship in the harbor;
Guigemar saw its sail.
It was fit and ready to go,
calked outside and in—
155   no one could discover a seam in its hull.
Every deck rail and peg
was solid ebony;
no gold under the sun could be worth more.
The sail was pure silk;
160   it would look beautiful when unfurled.
 C3 The knight was troubled;
he had never heard it said
anywhere in that region
that ships could land there.
165   He went down to the harbor
and, in great pain, boarded the ship.
He expected to discover men inside,
guarding the vessel,
but he saw no one, no one at all.
170   Amidships he found a bed
whose posts and frame

were wrought in the fashion of Solomon,[4]
of cypress and ivory, with designs in inlaid gold.
175 The quilt on the bed was made
of silken cloth, woven with gold.
I don't know how to estimate the value of the other
bedclothes,
but I'll tell you this much about the pillow:
whoever rested his head on it
180 would never have white hair.
The sable bedspread
was lined with Alexandrian silk.
Two candelabra of fine gold—
the lesser of the two worth a fortune—
185 were placed at the head of the cabin,
lighted tapers placed in them.
ꝯ Guigemar, astonished by all this,
reclined on the bed
and rested; his wound hurt.
190 Then he rose and tried to leave the ship,
but he couldn't return to land.
The vessel was already on the high seas,
carrying him swiftly with it.
A good, gentle wind was blowing,
195 so turning back now was out of the question.
Guigemar was very upset; he didn't know what to do.
It's no wonder he was frightened,
especially as his wound was paining him a great deal.
Still, he had to see the adventure through.

---

[4] Rychner notes that this term referred during the Middle Ages to
a certain type of inlaid work. There is, however, also a widely diffused
medieval legend about a marvelous ship made by Solomon that
intrudes into some versions of the story of the Grail, and moreover
the description of the bed contains reminiscences of the biblical
Song of Solomon (see Ewert's note).

200   He prayed to God to watch over him,
to use his power to bring him back to land,
and to protect him from death.
He lay down on the bed, and fell asleep.
That day he'd survived the worst;
205   before sundown he would arrive
at the place where he'd be cured—
near an ancient city,
the capital of its realm.
ᘓ The lord who ruled over that city
210   was a very aged man who had a wife,
a woman of high lineage,
noble, courteous, beautiful, intelligent;
he was extremely jealous,
which accorded with his nature.
215   (All old folk are jealous;
every one of them hates the thought of being cuckolded,
such is the perversity of age.)
The watch he kept over her was no joke.
The grove beneath the tower
220   was enclosed all around
with walls of green marble,
very high and thick.
There was only one entrance,
and it was guarded day and night.
225   On the other side, the sea enclosed it;
no one could enter, no one leave,
except by means of a boat,
as the castle might require it.
Inside the castle walls,
230   the lord had built a chamber—
none more beautiful anywhere—to keep his wife
under guard—
At its entrance was a chapel.
The room was painted with images all around;
Venus the goddess of love

235 was skillfully depicted in the painting,
   her nature and her traits were illustrated,
   whereby men might learn how to behave in love,
   and to serve love loyally.
   Ovid's book, the one in which he instructs
240 lovers how to control their love,
   was being thrown by Venus into a fire,
   and she was excommunicating all those
   who ever perused this book
   or followed its teachings.[5]
245 That's where the wife was locked up.
   Her husband had given her
   a girl to serve her,
   one who was noble and well educated—
   she was his niece, the daughter of his sister.[6]
250 There was great affection between the two women.
   She stayed with her mistress when he went off,
   remaining with her until he returned.
   No one else came there, man or woman,
   nor could the wife leave the walls of the enclosure.
255 An old priest, hoary with age,
   kept the gate key;
   he'd lost his nether member
   or he wouldn't have been trusted.
   He said mass for her

---

[5] The book in question is Ovid's *Remedia amoris* (Remedies for Love),
a companion volume to the Roman poet's equally tongue-in-cheek
Ars amatoria. E. J. Mickel notes the irony of this mural, presumably
commissioned by the husband to encourage his wife to love him,
but, as Marie describes it, predictive of the coming relationship
between Guigemar and the young wife.

[6] The French text is ambiguous as to whether the girl is the niece of
the husband or the wife.

260 and served her her food.

ℭ That same day, as soon as she rose from a nap,
the wife went into the grove;
she had slept after dinner,
and now she set out to amuse herself,

265 taking her maid with her.
Looking out to sea,
they saw the ship on the rising tide
come sailing into the harbor.
They could see nothing guiding it.

270 The lady started to flee—
it's not surprising if she was afraid;
her face grew red from fear.
But the girl, who was wise
and more courageous,

275 comforted and reassured her,
and they went toward the water, fast as they could.
The damsel removed her cloak, and boarded the
beautiful ship.
She found no living thing

280 except the sleeping knight.
She saw how pale he was and thought him dead;
she stopped and looked at him.
Then she went back
quickly, and called her mistress,

285 told her what she'd found,
and lamented the dead man she'd seen.
The lady answered, "Let's go see him!
If he's dead, we'll bury him;
the priest will help us.

290 If I find that he's alive, he'll tell us all about this."
ℭ Without tarrying any longer, they returned together,
the lady first, then the girl.
When the lady entered the ship,
she stopped in front of the bed.

295   She examined the knight,
    lamenting his beauty and fine body;
    she was full of sorrow on his account,
    and said it was a shame he'd died so young.
    She put her hand on his breast,
300   and felt that it was warm, and his heart healthy,
    beating beneath his ribs.
    The knight, who was only asleep,
    now woke up and saw her;
    he was delighted, and greeted her—
305   he realized he'd come to land.
    The lady, upset and weeping,
    answered him politely
    and asked him how
    he got there, what country he came from,
310   if he'd been exiled because of war.
    "My lady," he said, "not at all.
    But if you'd like me to tell you
    the truth, I'll do so;
    I'll hide nothing from you.
315   ଔ I come from Brittany.
    Today I went out hunting in the woods,
    and shot a white hind;
    the arrow rebounded,
    giving me such a wound in the thigh
320   that I've given up hope of being cured.
    The hind complained and spoke to me,
    cursed me, swore
    that I'd never be healed
    except by a girl;
325   I don't know where she might be found.
    ଔ When I heard my destiny,
    I quickly left the woods:
    I found this boat in a harbor,
    and made a big mistake: I went on board.

330   The boat raced off to sea with me on it;
       I don't know where I've arrived,
       or what this city's called.
       Beautiful one, I beg you, for God's sake,
       please advise me!
335   I don't know where to go,
       and I can't even steer this ship!"
       ൦ She answered him, "My dear lord,
       I'll be happy to advise you;
       this is my husband's city,
340   and so is the region around it.
       He is a rich man of high lineage,
       but extremely old;
       he's also terribly jealous.
       On my word of honor,
345   he has locked me up in this stronghold.
       There's only one entrance,
       and an old priest guards the gate:
       may God let him burn in hell!
       I'm shut in here night and day.
350   I'd never dare
       to leave except at his command,
       when my lord asks for me.
       Here I have my room and my chapel,
       and this girl lives with me.
355   If it pleases you to stay here
       until you're better able to travel,
       we'll be happy to put you up,
       we'll serve you willingly."
       When he hears this,
360   Guigemar thanks the lady warmly,
       and says he'll stay with her.
       He rose from the bed;
       with some difficulty they supported him,
       and the lady brought him to her chamber.

365   The young man lay down
     on the girl's bed,
     behind a drape that was hung
     across her room like a curtain.
     They brought him water in a golden basin,
370   washed his thigh,
     and with a fine, white silk cloth
     they wiped the blood from his wound.
     Then they bound it tightly.
     They treated him very kindly.
375   When their evening meal came,
     the girl left enough of hers
     for the knight to have some;
     he ate and drank quite well.
     ∞ But now love struck him to the quick;
380   great strife was in his heart
     because the lady had wounded him so badly
     that he forgot his homeland.
     His other wound no longer bothered him,
     but he sighed with new anguish.
385   He begged the girl, who was assigned to take care
     of him, to let him sleep.
     She left him and went away,
     since he had requested it,
     returning to her mistress,
390   who was also feeling somewhat scorched
     by the same fire Guigemar felt
     igniting and consuming his heart.
     ∞ The knight was alone now,
     preoccupied and in distress.
395   He didn't yet know what was wrong,
     but this much he could tell:
     if the lady didn't cure him,
     he was sure to die.
     "Alas!" he said, "what shall I do?

400 I'll go to her and tell her
that she should have mercy and pity
on a poor, disconsolate wretch like me.
If she refuses my plea,
shows herself so proud and scornful,
405 then I'll have to die of grief,
languishing forever in this pain."
He sighed; but a little later
formed a new resolution,
and said to himself he'd have to keep suffering;
410 you have to endure what you can't change.
He lay awake all night, sighing and in distress.
He turned over in his mind
her words and appearance,
415 the bright eyes, the fair mouth
whose sweetness had touched his heart.[7]
Under his breath he cried for mercy;
he almost called her his beloved.
If he only knew what she was feeling—
420 how love was torturing her—
I think he would have been very happy;
that little bit of consolation
would have diminished the pain
that drained him of his color.
425 If he was suffering from love of her,
she had nothing to gloat about, either.
Next morning, before dawn,
the lady arose.
She'd been awake all night, that was her complaint.
430 It was the fault of love, pressing her hard.
The damsel, who was with her,
noticed from the appearance of her lady
that she was in love
with the knight who was staying

---

[7] Reading *doucors* with MS (P), instead of Ewert's *dolur* from (H).

435   in her chamber until he was healed;
           but her mistress didn't know whether or not he
           loved her.
           The lady went off to church
           and the girl went off to the knight.
           ℭ She sat down by the bed;
440   he spoke to her, saying,
           "My dear friend, where has my lady gone?
           Why did she rise so early?"
           He paused, and sighed.
           The girl spoke frankly:
445   "My lord," she said, "you're in love;
           take care not to hide it too well!
           The love you offer
           may in fact be well received.
           Anyone whom my lady chooses to love
450   certainly ought to think well of her.
           This love would be suitable
           if both of you were constant:
           you're handsome and she's beautiful."
           He answered the girl,
455   "I'm so in love with her
           that if I don't get relief soon
           I'll be in a very bad way.
           Advise me, dear friend!
           What should I do about my passion?"
460   The girl very sweetly
           comforted the knight,
           promised to help him
           in every way she could;
           she was very good-hearted and well bred.
465   ℭ When the lady had heard mass
           she returned; she was anything but neglectful:
           she wanted to know whether the man
           whom she couldn't help loving
           was awake or asleep.

470   The girl called her
        and brought her to the knight;
        now she'll have all the time she needs
        to tell him what she's feeling,
        for better or for worse.
475   He greeted her and she him;
        they were both very scared now.
        He didn't dare ask anything from her,
        for he was a foreigner
        and was afraid, if he told her what he felt,
480   she'd hate him for it, send him away.
        But he who hides his sickness
        can hardly be brought back to health;
        love is a wound in the body,
        and yet nothing appears on the outside.
485   It's a sickness that lasts a long time,
        because it comes from nature.
        Many people treat it lightly,
        like these false courtiers
        who have affairs everywhere they go,
490   then boast about their conquests;
        that's not love but folly,
        evil and lechery.
        If you can find a loyal love,
        you should love and serve it faithfully,
495   be at its command.
        Guigemar was deeply in love;
        he must either get help quickly
        or live in misery.
        So love inspires bravery in him:
500   he reveals his desires to the lady.
        ଔ "Lady," he said, "I'm dying because of you;
        my heart is full of anguish.
        If you won't cure me,
        I'll have to perish sooner or later.

505   I beg you to love me—
        fair one, don't deny me!"
        When she had heard him out,
        she gave a fitting answer.
        She laughed, and said, "My love,
510   I'd be ill advised to act too quickly
        in granting your prayer.
        I'm not accustomed to such a request."
        "My lady," he replied, "for God's sake, have mercy!
        Don't be annoyed if I speak like this to you.
515   It's appropriate for an inconstant woman
        to make some one plead with her a long time
        to enhance her worth; that way he won't think
        she's used to such sport.
        But a woman of good character,
520   sensible as well as virtuous,
        if she finds a man to her liking,
        oughtn't to treat him too disdainfully.
        Rather she should love and enjoy him;
        this way, before anyone knows or hears of it,
525   they'll have done a lot that's to their advantage.
        Now, dear lady, let's end this discussion."
        The lady realized he was telling the truth,
        and immediately granted him
        her love; then he kissed her.
530   From now on, Guigemar is at ease.
        They lie down together and converse,
        kissing and embracing often.
        I hope they also enjoy whatever else
        others do on such occasions.
535   It appears to me that Guigemar
        stayed with her a year and a half.
        Their life was full of pleasure.
        But Fortune, who never forgets her duty,
        turns her wheel suddenly,

540   raising one person up while casting another down;
      and so it happened with the lovers,
      because suddenly they were discovered.
      ℭ One summer morning,
      the lady was lying beside her young lover;
545   she kissed his mouth and eyes,
      and said to him, "Dear, sweet love,
      my heart tells me I'm going to lose you.
      We're going to be found out.
      If you die, I want to die, too,
550   but if you can escape,
      you'll go find another love
      while I stay here in misery."
      "Lady," he said, "don't say such a thing!
      I would never have any joy or peace
555   if I turned to another woman.
      You needn't be afraid of that!"
      "Beloved, I need your promise.
      Give me your shirt;
      I'll make a knot in the tail.
560   You have my leave to love the woman,
      whoever she may be,
      who will be able to undo it."
      He gave her the shirt, and his promise;
      she made the knot in such a way
565   that no woman could untie it
      except with scissors or knife.
      She gave him back the shirt,
      and he took it on condition
      that she should make a similar pledge to him,
570   by means of a belt
      that she would wear next to her bare flesh,
      tightened about her flanks.
      Whoever could open the buckle
      without breaking it or severing it from the belt,

575   would be the one he would urge her to love.
         He kissed her, and left it at that.
         ଔ That day they were discovered—
         spied upon and found out
         by an evil, cunning chamberlain,
580   sent by the husband.
         He wanted to speak with the lady,
         and couldn't get into her chamber;
         he looked in a window and saw the lovers,
         he went and told his lord.
585   When he heard about it,
         the lord was sorrier than he'd ever been before.
         He called for three of his henchmen
         and straightaway went to the wife's chamber;
         he had the door broken down.
590   Inside he found the knight.
         He was so furious
         that he gave orders to kill the stranger.
         Guigemar got up,
         not at all afraid.
595   He grabbed a wooden rod
         on which clothes were usually hung,
         and waited for his assailants.
         Guigemar will make some of them suffer for this;
         before they get close to him,
600   he'll have maimed them all.
         ଔ The lord stared at him for a long time,
         and finally asked him
         who he was, where he came from,
         how he'd gotten in there.
605   Guigemar told him how he'd come there
         and how the lady had received him;
         he told him all about the adventure
         of the wounded hind,
         about his wound and the ship;

610   now he is entirely in the other's power.
         The lord replied that he didn't believe him,
         but if it really was the way he had told it
         and if he could find the ship,
         he'd send Guigemar back out to sea.
615   If he survived, that would be a shame;
         he'd be happier if Guigemar drowned.
         ℞ When he had made this pledge,
         they went together to the harbor,
         and found the ship; they put Guigemar on it—
620   it will take him back to his own land.
         The ship got under way without waiting.
         The knight sighed and cried,
         often lamenting his lady
         and praying to almighty God
625   to grant him a quick death,
         and never let him come to port
         if he couldn't regain his mistress,
         whom he desired more than his own life.
         He persisted in his grief
630   until the ship came to the port
         where he'd first found it;
         he was now very near his native land.
         He left the ship as quickly as he could.
         ℞ A boy whom Guigemar had raised
635   came by, following a knight,
         and leading a war-horse.
         Guigemar recognized him and called to him;
         the squire looked at him,
         recognized his lord, dismounted,
640   and presented the charger to him.
         Guigemar went off with him; all his friends
         rejoiced that they had found him again.
         He was highly honored in his land,
         but through it all he was sad and distracted.

645   His friends wanted him to take a wife,
      but he refused them altogether;
      he'll never have to do with a woman,
      for love or money,
      if she can't untie
650   his knotted shirt without tearing it.
      The news traveled throughout Brittany;
      all the women and girls
      came to try their luck,
      but none could untie the knot.
655   ℭ Now I want to tell you about the lady
      whom Guigemar loved so dearly.
      On the advice of one of his barons,
      her husband had her imprisoned
      in a dark marble tower.
660   There she passed bad days, worse nights.
      No one in the world could describe
      the pain, the suffering,
      the anguish and the grief,
      that she endured in that tower.
665   She remained there two years and more, I believe,
      without ever having a moment of pleasure.
      Often, she mourned for her lover:
      "Guigemar, my lord, why did I ever lay eyes on you?
      I'd rather die quickly
670   than suffer this lingering torture.
      My love, if I could escape,
      I'd go to where you put out to sea
      and drown myself." Then she got up;
      in astonishment she went to the door
675   and found it unlocked;
      by good fortune, she got outside—
      no one bothered her.
      She came to the harbor, and found the boat.
      It was tied to the rock

680   where she had intended to drown herself.
When she saw it there, she went aboard;
she could think of only one thing—
that this was where her lover had perished.
Suddenly, she couldn't stand up.
685   If she could have gotten back up on deck,
she would have thrown herself overboard,
so great was her suffering.
The boat set out, taking her with it.
It came to port in Brittany,
690   beneath a strong, well-built castle.
ᘓ The lord of the castle
was named Meriaduc.
He was fighting a war with a neighbor,
and had risen early that morning
695   because he wanted to dispatch his troops
to attack his enemy.
Standing at a window,
he saw the ship arrive.
He went downstairs
700   and called his chamberlain;
quickly they went to the ship,
climbed up its ladder;
inside they found the woman
who had a fairylike beauty.
705   He took her by the cloak
and brought her with him to his castle.
He was delighted with his discovery,
for she was incredibly beautiful;
whoever had put her on the boat,
710   he could tell she came from high lineage.
He felt for her a love
as great as he'd ever had for a woman.
ᘓ He had a young sister,
a beautiful maiden, in his care;

715 he commended the lady to her attention.
So she was waited on and made much of
the damsel dressed her richly.
But she remained constantly sad and preoccupied.
The lord often came to speak with her,
720 since he wanted to love her with all his heart.
He pleaded for her love; she didn't want it,
instead she showed him her belt:
she would never love any man
except the one who could open the belt
725 without breaking it. When he heard that,
Meriaduc replied angrily,
"There's another one like you in this land,
a very worthy knight,
who avoids, in a similar manner, taking a wife
730 by means of a shirt
the right tail of which is knotted;
it can't be untied except by using scissors or a knife.
I think you must have made that knot!"
735 ℭℛ When the lady heard this, she sighed,
and almost fainted.
He took her in his arms,
cut the laces of her tunic,
and tried to open the belt.
740 But he didn't succeed.
There wasn't a knight in the region
whom he didn't summon to try his luck.
ℭℛ Things went on like this for quite a while,
up to the time of a tournament
745 that Meriaduc had proclaimed
against the lord he was fighting.
He sent for knights and enlisted them in his service,
knowing very well that Guigemar would come.
He asked him as a special favor,

750   as his friend and companion,
    not to let him down in this hour of need,
    but to come help him.
    So Guigemar set out, richly supplied,
    leading more than one hundred knights.
755   Meriaduc entertained him
    as an honored guest in his stronghold.
    He then sent two knights to his sister,
    and commanded her
    to prepare herself and come to him,
760   bringing with her the woman he so much loved.
    The girl obeyed his order.
    Lavishly outfitted,
    they came hand in hand into the great hall.
    The lady was pale and upset;
765   she heard Guigemar's name
    and couldn't stand up.
    If the damsel hadn't supported her,
    she'd have fallen to the ground.
    Guigemar arose when the women entered;
770   he looked at the lady and noticed
    her appearance and behavior;
    involuntarily, he shrank back a bit.
    "Is this," he said, "my dear love,
    my hope, my heart, and my life—
775   my beautiful lady who loved me?
    Where did she come from? Who brought her here?
    Now, that was a foolish thought!
    I know it can't be she;
    women often look alike—
780   I got all excited for no reason.
    But because she looks like the one
    for whom my heart aches and sighs,
    I'll gladly speak to her."
    Then the knight came forward,

785   he kissed her and sat her down beside him;
he didn't say another word,
except that he asked her to sit down.
Meriaduc looked at them closely,
upset by the sight of them together.

790   He called Guigemar cheerfully:
"My lord," he said, "please
let this girl try
to untie your shirt,
to see if she can manage to do it."

795   Guigemar answered, "Certainly."
ᚩ He summoned a chamberlain
who was in charge of the shirt
and commanded him to bring it.
It was given to the girl,

800   but she couldn't untie it at all.
The lady knew the knot very well;
her heart is greatly agitated,
for she would love to try to untie it,
if she dared and could.

805   Meriaduc saw this clearly;
he was as sorry as he could be.
"My lady," he said, "now try
to untie it, if you can."
When she heard his order,

810   she took the shirttail
and easily untied the knot.
Guigemar was thunderstruck;
he knew her very well, and yet
he couldn't bring himself to believe firmly it was she.

815   So he spoke to her in this way:
"Beloved, sweet creature,
is that you? Tell me truly!
Let me see your body,
and the belt I put on you."

820 He put his hands on her hips,
 and found the belt.
 "My beautiful one," he said, "what a lucky adventure
 that I've found you like this!
 Who brought you here?"
825 She told him about the grief,
 the great pains, the monotony
 of the prison where she was held captive,
 and everything that had happened to her—
 how she escaped,
830 how she wished to drown, but found the ship instead,
 and how she entered it and was brought to this port;
 and how the lord of the castle kept her in custody,
 guarding her in luxury
 but constantly asking for her love.
835 Now her joy has returned:
 "My love, take back your beloved!"
 ଔ Guigemar got up.
 "My lords," he said, "listen to me!
 Here I have the mistress
840 I thought I had lost forever.
 Now I ask and implore Meriaduc
 to give her back to me out of kindness.
 I will become his vassal,
 serve him two or three years,
845 with one hundred knights, or more!"
 Meriaduc answered,
 "Guigemar," he said, "my handsome friend,
 I'm not so harried
 or so afflicted by any war
850 that you can bargain with me about this.
 I found this woman and I propose to take care of her
 and defend her against you."
 ଔ When Guigemar heard that, he quickly
 commanded his men to mount.

855 He galloped away, defying Meriaduc.[8]
It upset him to leave his beloved behind.
Guigemar took with him
every knight who had come
to the town for the tournament.
860 Each declared his loyalty to Guigemar;
they'll accompany him wherever he goes.
Whoever fails him now will truly be dishonored!
That night they came to the castle
Of Meriaduc's opponent.
865 The lord of the castle put them up;
he was joyful and delighted
that Guigemar came over to his side, bringing help
with him.
Now he's sure the war's as good as over.
❧ The next morning they arose,
870 and equipped themselves at their lodgings.
They departed from the village, noisily;
Guigemar came first, leading them.
Arriving at Meriaduc's castle, they assaulted it;
but it was very strong and they failed to take it.
875 Guigemar besieged the town;
he won't leave until it has fallen.
His friends and other troops increased so greatly
that he was able to starve everyone inside.
He captured and destroyed the castle,
880 killed its lord.
Guigemar led away his mistress with great rejoicing;
all his pain was now at an end.
❧ From this story that you have heard
the *lai* of Guigemar was composed,

---

[8] The *defi* was a formal gesture, renouncing feudal bonds of alliance or
dependency and making it possible for one knight to attack another
(or a vassal his former lord) without incurring charges of treason.

885   which is now recited to the harp and rote;
      the music is a pleasure to hear.

Le Fresne (The Ash Tree)

      I shall tell you the *lai* of Le Fresne
      according to the story as I know it.
      In olden days there lived in Brittany
      two knights who were neighbors;
5   both were rich men,
      brave and worthy knights.
      They lived close by, within the same region;
      each was married.
      Now one of the wives became pregnant;
10   so when her time came
      she gave birth to twins.
      Her husband was absolutely delighted;
      in his joy at the event
      he sent word to his good neighbor
15   that his wife had had two sons—
      he had that many more children now.
      He would send one to him to raise,
      and name the child after him.
      The rich neighbor was sitting down to eat
20   when the messenger arrived;
      he knelt before the high table
      to announce his news.
      The lord thanked God for it
      and rewarded him with a fine horse.
25   The knight's wife laughed
      (she was seated next to him at dinner)
      because she was deceitful and proud,
      evil-tongued and envious.
      She spoke very foolishly,

30   saying, for all her household to hear,
         "So help me God, I can't imagine
         where this worthy man got such advice
         to announce to my lord,
         to his own shame and dishonor,
35   that his wife has had twin sons.
         Both he and she are disgraced by this;
         we know the truth of the matter all too well:
         it never was and never will be
         possible for such a thing to happen[9]
40   that a woman could have
         two sons in one birth—
         unless two men had lain with her."
         Her lord stared fiercely at her,
         reproached her bitterly for what she said.
45   "Wife," he said, "stop that!
         You mustn't talk that way!
         The fact is that she's a woman
         who's always had a good reputation."
         But the people in the household
50   repeated the wife's words;
         the matter was widely spoken of
         and became known throughout Brittany.
         The slanderous wife was hated for it,
         and later made to suffer for it.
55   Every woman who heard about it,
         rich or poor, hated her.
         The messenger who had brought the news
         went home and told his lord everything.
         When he heard the messenger's report,

---

[9]   Marie uses the word *aventure* here and throughout the *lai* to refer to
    unexpected circumstances of the kind that test the endurance and moral
    worth of human beings, and bring them to happiness if they deserve it.

60 he became so sad he didn't know what to do.
He hated his worthy wife because of it,
strongly suspected her,
and kept her under strict guard,
even though she didn't deserve it.

65 ᛉ The wife who had spoken so evilly
became pregnant herself that same year,
and was carrying twins—
now her neighbor has her vengeance.
She carried them until her time came;

70 then she gave birth to two daughters; she was extremely upset,
and terribly sad about the situation.
She lamented bitterly to herself:
"Alas!" she said, "what shall I do?
I'll never get any honor out of this!

75 I'm in disgrace, that's certain.
My lord and all his kin
will never believe me
when they hear about this bad luck;[10]
indeed, I condemned myself

80 when I slandered all womankind.
Didn't I say it never happened—
at least, we've never seen it happen—
that a woman could have twins
unless she had lain with two men?

85 Now that I have twins, it seems to me
my words have come back to haunt me.
Whoever slanders another
never knows when it will rebound on him;
he may speak badly about someone

90 who's more deserving of praise than he.
Now, to keep from being disgraced,

---

[10] The French text has *aventure*.

I'll have to kill one of my children!
I'd rather make that up to God
than live in shame and dishonor."

95 Those of her household who were in the
bedchamber with her
comforted her and said
they wouldn't allow her to do it;
killing somebody was no joke.
ঙ The lady had an attendant
100 who was of noble birth;
the lady had raised and taken care of her
and was very attached to her.
This girl heard her mistress crying,
bemoaning her situation;
105 it bothered her terribly.
She came and comforted her:
"My lady," she said, "it's not worth carrying on so.
Stop grieving—that's the thing to do.
Give me one of the babies;
100 I'll take care of her for you,
so that you won't be disgraced;
you'll never see the child again.
I'll abandon her at a convent,
to which I'll carry her safe and sound.
115 Some good person will find her,
and, God willing, he'll raise her."
The lady heard what she said;
she was delighted with the idea, and promised her
that if she did her this service
120 she'd be well rewarded for it.
ঙ They wrapped the noble child
in a linen garment,
and then in an embroidered silk robe,
which the lady's husband had brought back to
her

125   from Constantinople,
    where he had been.
    They had never seen anything so fine.
    With a piece of ribbon
    she tied a large ring onto the child's arm;
    it contained a full ounce of pure gold,
130   and had a ruby set in it,
    with lettering around the rim of the setting.
    Wherever the little girl might be found,
    everyone would know beyond doubt
    that she came from a noble family.
135   ❧ The damsel took the baby
    and left the chamber with her.
    That night, after dark,
    she left the town
    and took the highroad
140   that led into the forest.
    She went right through the woods
    with the baby, and out the other side,
    without ever leaving the road.
    Then, far off to the right, she heard
145   dogs barking and cocks crowing;
    she knew she would be able to find a town over there.
    Quickly, she went in the direction
    of the barking.
    Soon she came
150   to a fine, prosperous town.
    There was an abbey there,
    a thriving, well-endowed one;
    I believe it held a community of nuns
    supervised by an abbess.
155   The damsel saw
    the towers, walls, and steeple of the abbey,
    and she hastened toward it,
    stopping at the front gate.
    She put down the child she was carrying

160   and knelt humbly
          to say a prayer.
          "O God," she prayed, "by your holy name,
          if it is your will,
          protect this infant from death."
165   When she'd finished praying,
          she looked behind her,
          saw a broad-limbed ash tree,
          its branches thick with leaves;
          its trunk divided into four boughs.
170   It had been planted as a shade tree.
          The girl took the baby in her arms
          and ran over to the ash tree,
          placed the child up in its branches and left her
          there,
          commending her to the true God.
175   Then the girl returned to her mistress
          and told her what she'd done.
          ଡ଼ There was a porter in the abbey,
          whose job it was to open the abbey gate,
          to let in the people who had come
180   to hear the early service.
          That morning he rose as early as usual,
          lit the candles and the lamps,
          rang the bells and opened the gate.
          He noticed the clothes up in the ash tree,
185   and thought that someone must have stolen them,
          and then left them there.
          He didn't notice anything else.
          As quickly as he could, he went over to the tree,
          touched the clothes, and found the child there.
190   He gave thanks to God;
          he did not leave the child, but took her with him
          to his own dwelling.
          He had a daughter who was a widow;
          her husband was dead and she had a child,

195 still in the cradle, whom she was nursing.
 The good man called her:
 "Daughter," he said, "get up!
 Light the candle, start the fire!
 I've brought home a baby
200 that I found out there in the ash tree.
 Nurse her for me,
 then get her warm and bathe her."
 The daughter obeyed him;
 she lit the fire and took the baby,
205 made her warm and gave her a good bath,
 then nursed her.
 On the child's arm they discovered the ring,
 and they saw her costly, beautiful clothes.
 From these they were certain
210 that she was born of noble lineage.
 CR The next day, after the service,
 when the abbess came out of the chapel,
 the porter went to speak to her;
 he wanted to tell her how, by chance,
215 he had found the child.
 The abbess ordered him
 to bring the child to her
 just as she was found.
 The porter went home,
220 willingly brought the child back,
 and showed her to the abbess.
 She examined the baby closely
 and said she would raise her,
 would treat her as her niece.
225 She strictly forbade the porter
 to tell the truth about the child's discovery.
 She raised the child herself,
 and because she had been found in the ash tree
 the abbess decided to name her "Fresne" [Ash].

230 And so people called her.
    The abbess did indeed treat her as a niece,
    and for a long time she grew up in privacy;
    she was raised
    entirely within the walls of the abbey.
235 When she reached the age
    where nature creates beauty,
    in all of Brittany there wasn't such a beautiful
    or so refined a girl;
    she was noble and cultivated
240 in appearance and speech.
    Everyone who saw her loved her,
    praised her to the skies.
    Now at Dole there lived a good lord—
    there's never been a better, before or since—
245 whose name I'll tell you here:
    they called him Gurun in that region.
    He heard about the young girl
    and he fell in love with her.
    He went to a tournament,
250 and on his way back passed the abbey,
    where he stopped to ask after the damsel.
    The abbess introduced her to him.
    He saw that she was beautiful and cultivated,
    wise, refined, and well educated.
255 If he couldn't win her love
    he'd consider himself very badly off indeed.
    But he was at a loss about how to proceed;
    if he came there often,
    the abbess would notice what was going on,
260 and he'd never lay eyes on the damsel again.
    He hit upon a scheme:
    he would become a benefactor of the abbey,
    give it so much of his land
    that it would be enriched forever;

265 he'd thus establish a patron's right to live there,
 so that he could come and stay whenever he chose.
 To be a member of that community
 he gave generously of his goods—
 but he had a motive
270 other than receiving pardon for his sins.
 ℛ He came there often
 and spoke to the girl;
 he pleaded so well, promised so much
 that she granted him what he desired.
275 When he was sure of her love,
 he spoke seriously with her one day.
 "Beautiful one," he said, "now that
 you've made me your lover,
 come away from here and live with me.
280 I'm sure you know
 that if your aunt found out about us
 she'd be upset,
 especially if you became pregnant right under her
 roof.
 In fact, she'd be furious.
285 If you'll take my advice,
 you'll come away with me.
 I'll never let you down—
 and I'll take good care of you."
 Since she loved him deeply,
290 she willingly granted what he desired.
 She went away with him;
 he took her to his castle.
 She brought her silk swaddling cloth and her ring
 with her;
 that could turn out to be very fortunate for her.
295 The abbess had given them to her
 and told her the circumstances
 in which she had been sent to her:

she was nestled up in the ash tree,
and whoever had abandoned her there
300   had bestowed on her the garments and the ring.
The abbess had received no other possessions with
her;
she had raised her as her niece.
The girl kept the tokens,[11]
locked them in a chest.
305   She took the chest away with her;
she'd no intention of leaving it behind.
  ❧ The knight who took her away
loved and cherished her greatly,
and so did all his men and servants.
310   There wasn't one, big or little,
who didn't love her for her noble character,
and honor her as well.
  ❧ She lived with him for a long time,
until the knight's vassals
315   reproached him for it.
They often urged him
to marry a noble woman,
and to get rid of this mistress of his.
They'd be pleased if he had an heir
320   who could succeed to
his land and inheritance;
it would be much to their disadvantage
if he was deterred by his concubine
from having a child born in wedlock.
325   They would no longer consider him their lord
or willingly serve him
if he didn't do what they wanted.
The knight agreed
to take a wife according to their wishes,

---

[11]   The translation follows Rychner's emendation of *l'esgardat* to *les gardat*.

330   so they began to look about for one.
"My lord," they said, "quite near by
lives a worthy man of your rank;
he has a daughter who is his heiress.
You'll get much land if you take her.

335   The girl's name is Codre [Hazel];
there isn't one so pretty in this region.
In exchange for the ash, when you get rid of her,
you'll have the hazel.
The hazel tree bears nuts and thus gives pleasure;

340   the ash bears no fruit.
Let us make the arrangements for the daughter;
God willing, we will get her for you."
℞ They arranged the marriage,
obtained everyone's promise.

345   Alas! what a misfortune
that these good men didn't know
the real story about these girls[12]—
they were twin sisters!
Fresne was hidden away,

350   and her lover was to marry the other.
When she found out that he had done this,
she didn't sulk about it;
she continued to serve her lord well
and honored all his vassals.

355   The knights of the household,
the squires and serving boys
were all very sad on her account;
sad because they were going to lose her.
℞ On the day of the betrothal,

360   her lord sent for his friends.
The archbishop of Dole,
another of his vassals, was there as well.

---

[12] Again, the text has *aventure.*

They all brought his fiancée to him.
Her mother came with her;
365 she worried about this other girl
whom the lord loved so much,
because she might try to cause trouble, if she could,
between Codre and her husband.
The mother wants her expelled from the house;
370 she'll tell her son-in-law
that he should marry her off to some good man;
that way he'll be rid of her, she thinks.
ᛒ They held the betrothals in grand style;
there was much celebrating.
375 Fresne was in the private chambers.
No matter what she saw,
it didn't seem to bother her;
she didn't even seem a bit angry.
She waited on the bride-to-be
380 courteously and efficiently.
Everybody who saw this
thought it a great marvel.
Her mother inspected her carefully,
and began to love and admire her.
385 She said to herself that if she'd known
what kind of a person Fresne was,
she wouldn't have let her suffer on account of her
daughter Codre,
wouldn't have taken Fresne's lord away from her.
ᛒ That night, Fresne went
390 to make up the bed
in which the new bride was to sleep;
she took off her cloak,
and called the chamberlains to her.
She instructed them concerning the manner
395 in which the lord liked things done,
for she had seen it many times.

When they had prepared the bed,
they threw a coverlet over it.
The cloth was some old dress material;
400   the girl looked at it,
it seemed to her poor stuff;
that bothered her.
She opened a chest, took out her birth garment,
and put it on her lord's bed.
405   She did it to honor him;
the archbishop would be coming there
to bless the newlyweds in bed.
That was part of his duty.
When the chamber was empty,
410   the mother led her daughter in.
She wished to prepare her for bed,
and told her to get undressed.
She looked at the cloth on the bed;
she'd never seen such a fine one
415   except the one she'd given
to her infant daughter when she abandoned her.
Then she suddenly remembered the castaway;
her heart skipped a beat.
She called the chamberlain:
420   "Tell me," she said, "on your honor,
where was this fine silk cloth found?"
"My lady," he replied, "I'll tell you:
the girl brought it,
and threw it over the coverlet
425   because the coverlet didn't seem good enough to her.
I think the silk cloth is hers."
The mother now called Fresne,
and Fresne came to her;
she removed her cloak,
430   and the lady began questioning her:
"My dear, don't hide anything from me!

Where did you find this beautiful cloth?
How did you come by it? Who gave it to you?
Tell me at once where it came from!"
435 The girl answered her,
"My lady, my aunt, who raised me—
she is an abbess—gave it to me
and ordered me to take good care of it;
whoever sent me to be raised by her
440 had given me this, and also a ring."
"Fair one, may I see the ring?"
"Yes, my lady, I'll be happy to show you."
Then Fresne brought her the ring;
she examined it carefully.
445 She recognized it very well,
and the silk cloth too.
No doubt about it, now she knew—
this was her own daughter.
She didn't hide it, but cried out for all to hear,
450 "My dear, you are my daughter!"
Out of pity for Fresne
she fell over in a faint.
When she regained consciousness,
she quickly sent for her husband,
455 and he came, all in a fright.
When he entered the bedroom,
his wife threw herself at his feet,
hugged and kissed him,
asked his forgiveness for her crime.
460 He didn't know what this was all about;[13]
"Wife," he said, "what are you talking about?
There's been nothing but good between us.
I'll pardon you as much as you please!
Tell me what's bothering you."

---

[13] The reading follows MS (S).

465   "My lord, since you've forgiven me,
        I'll tell you—listen!
        Once, in my great wickedness,
        I spoke foolishly about my neighbor,
        slandering her because she had twins.

470   I was really wronging myself.
        The truth is, I then became pregnant
        and had twin daughters; so I hid one,
        had her abandoned in front of an abbey,
        wrapped in our brocaded silk cloth,

475   wearing the ring that you gave me
        when you first courted me.
        I can't hide this from you:
        I've found the ring and the cloth,
        and also discovered our daughter,

480   whom I lost through my folly;
        and this is she, right here,
        the brave, wise, and beautiful girl
        loved by the knight
        who has married her sister."

485   Her husband said, "I'm delighted by this news;
        I was never so pleased.
        Since we've found our daughter,
        God has given us great joy,
        instead of doubling the sin.

490   My daughter," he said, "come here!"
        The girl was overjoyed
        by the story she'd heard.[14]
        Her father won't wait any longer;
        he goes to get his son-in-law,

495   and brings in the archbishop too—
        he tells him the adventure.
        When the knight heard the story

---

[14] "Story" renders *aventure*.

he was happier than he'd ever been.
The archbishop advised
500 that things should be left as they were that night;
in the morning he would separate
the knight from the woman he had married.
They agreed to this plan.
Next morning, the marriage was annulled
505 and the knight married his beloved;
she was given to him by her father,
who was well disposed toward her;
he divided his inheritance with her.
The father and his wife remained at the festivities,
510 for as long as they lasted, with their daughter.
When they returned to their land,
they took their daughter Codre with them;
later, in their country,
she made a rich marriage too.
515 ◇ When this adventure became known
just as it happened,
the *lai* of Fresne was made from it.
It was named after its heroine.

Chevrefoil (The Honeysuckle)

I should like very much
to tell you the truth
about the *lai* men call *Chevrefoil*—
why it was composed and where it came from.
5 Many have told and recited it to me
and I have found it in writing,
about Tristan and the queen
and their love that was so true,
that brought them much suffering
10 and caused them to die the same day.
King Mark was annoyed,

angry at his nephew Tristan;
he exiled Tristan from his land
because of the queen whom he loved.
15   Tristan returned to his own country,
South Wales, where he was born,
he stayed a whole year;
he couldn't come back.
Afterward he began to expose himself
20   to death and destruction.
Don't be surprised at this:
for one who loves very faithfully
is sad and troubled
when he cannot satisfy his desires.
25   Tristan was sad and worried,
so he set out from his land.
He traveled straight to Cornwall,
where the queen lived,
and entered the forest all alone—
30   he didn't want anyone to see him;
he came out only in the evening
when it was time to find shelter.
He took lodging that night,
with peasants, poor people.
35   He asked them for news
of the king—what he was doing.
They told him they had heard
that the barons had been summoned by ban.
They were to come to Tintagel
40   where the king wanted to hold his court;
at Pentecost they would all be there,
there'd be much joy and pleasure,
and the queen would be there too.
Tristan heard and was very happy;
45   she would not be able to go there
without his seeing her pass.
The day the king set out,

Tristan also came to the woods
by the road he knew
50   their assembly must take.
He cut a hazel tree in half,
then he squared it.
When he had prepared the wood,
he wrote his name on it with his knife.
55   If the queen noticed it—
and she should be on the watch for it,
for it had happened before
and she had noticed it then—
she'd know when she saw it,
60   that the piece of wood had come from her love.
This was the message of the writing[15]
that he had sent to her:
he had been there a long time,
had waited and remained
65   to find out and to discover
how he could see her,
for he could not live without her.
With the two of them it was just
as it is with the honeysuckle
70   that attaches itself to the hazel tree:
when it has wound and attached
and worked itself around the trunk,
the two can survive together;
but if someone tries to separate them,

---

[15]   There are several possible explanations of this line: that Tristan
had sent a message to her before she arrived in the forest, which
seems least likely since it is not otherwise mentioned; that his
name on the wood told her every thing because of the
understanding that existed between them; that the message was
written on the wood in runic inscriptions which only the specially
trained could read (see M. Cagnon, "*Chievrefoil* and the Ogamic
Tradition," *Romania* 91 [1970] 238-55).

75 the hazel dies quickly
 and the honeysuckle with it.
 "Sweet love, so it is with us:
 You cannot live without me, nor I without you."
 The queen rode along;
80 she looked at the hillside
 and saw the piece of wood; she knew what it was,
 she recognized all the letters.
 The knights who were accompanying her,
 who were riding with her,
85 she ordered to stop:
 she wanted to dismount and rest.
 They obeyed her command.
 She went far away from her people
 and called her girl
90 Brenguein, who was loyal to her.
 She went a short distance from the road;
 and in the woods she found him
 whom she loved more than any living thing.
 They took great joy in each other.
95 He spoke to her as much as he desired,
 she told him whatever she liked.
 Then she assured him
 that he would be reconciled with the king—
 for it weighed on him
100 that he had sent Tristan away;
 he'd done it because of the accusation.
 Then she departed, she left her love,
 but when it came to the separation,
 they began to weep.
105 Tristan went to Wales,
 to wait until his uncle sent for him.
 For the joy that he'd felt
 from his love when he saw her,
 by means of the stick he inscribed

110   as the queen had instructed,
and in order to remember the words,
Tristan, who played the harp well,
composed a new *lai* about it.
I shall name it briefly:
115   in English they call it *Goat's Leaf*
the French call it *Chevrefoil.*
I have given you the truth
about the *lai* that I have told here.

MARGUERITE DE NAVARRE

1492-1549

HEPTAMÉRON

1546-1549

Marguerite de Navarre was the daughter of the duke and duchess of Angoulême. Her brother, Francis, became King Francis I, the great Renaissance king of France, when his cousin and father-in-law, Louis XII, died without direct male heir. Francis loved his sister and favored her with large grants of lands, making her a peer of the royal blood. In Francis's early years, Marguerite often presided over his court. She personally worked to free her brother when he was captured at the Battle of Pavia in 1525, even traveling to Madrid to negotiate his release.

Her first husband, the duke of Alençon, died of wounds inflicted at this battle. Through his death she inherited two great duchies, and she became a queen when she married her new husband, Henri d'Albret, king of Navarre; together they ruled a swath of territories along France's southern border. Henri was about ten years younger than she; she loved him deeply, but he did not reciprocate. They had one surviving child, Jeanne d'Albret, whose son Henry would become King Henry IV in 1590.

Marguerite was strongly attracted to the circle of French humanists centered on Guillaume Briçonnet, bishop of Meaux, who also were interested in church reform. This group, called "evangelicals" in France, espoused some of Luther's new ideas. Marguerite's deep spirituality was expressed in her poetry and in her book *Mirror of the Sinful Soul*. Francis supported her when this book was attacked by the theologians at the University of Paris. But when a fierce anti-Protestant reaction began in Paris in 1534 she withdrew to her estates, where she protected many humanists and reformers.

In her outward life Marguerite was a product of and participant in the worldly life of Renaissance courts. Most of the stories in the *Heptaméron* reflect this sophisticated world with its morality which was so at odds with Marguerite's religious inclinations.

The Heptaméron

Marguerite seems to have written the first draft of the *Heptaméron* in 1546, one year before the death of her brother, Francis I. She continued to work on it until her own death in 1549. The original plan called for one hundred stories (ten stories each day for ten days), according to the plan of Boccaccio's *Decameron*, which Marguerite took for a model. Only seventy-two stories were completed, hence only seven complete days (and hence the name *Heptaméron* attached to it by its first editor). The structure of the book is carefully planned. In the Prologue, we learn that the ten story-tellers were stranded by flooded rivers when returning from a spa in the Pyrenees Mountains in southern France. They took refuge in a monastery while waiting for a bridge to be built to replace the ones washed out by the river, and they decided to entertain themselves by telling stories to each other. Among the storytellers are three married couples: Parlamente and Hircan, Ennasuite and Simontaut, and Nomerfide and Saffredent. A seventh storyteller,

Longarine, is a widow whose husband was murdered en route from the spa; she is admired by Saffredent. Simontaut secretly loves Parlamente, but is spurned by her. Geburon is a wise older man, Dagoucin apparently a cleric, and Oisille a sage widow, in part modeled on Marguerite's own mother, Louise de Savoie; she assumes a natural role as leader of the group.

The plan was for each person to tell one story each day for ten days. After a person tells his or her story and the others discuss it, she or he designates another member of the group to tell the next story. The storytellers agree at the outset that all the stories they tell must be true. Most scholars agree, however, that this requirement of historicity was only a literary convention. At least a dozen of the tales can probably be securely traced to real historical incidents, but others were invented by Marguerite or adapted from tales told elsewhere. Scholars have also attempted to identify the storytellers with real historical individuals. There is general agreement, for example, that Parlamente is modeled to some degree on Marguerite herself, and Hircan on her husband, Henri d'Albret, King of Navarre. The storytellers also often represent stereotypical points of view toward love and sexual relationships; nevertheless it is possible to observe certain changes in their characters throughout the eight days.

SOURCE

de Navarre, Marquerite. 1549. *The Heptaméron*. Translated by P.A. Chilton. England: Penguin Books, 1984.

Selections from:

>Story 3 (83-89)
>Story 4 (90-97)
>Story 5 (98-101)
>Story 8 (108-114)
>Story 67 (503-506)
>Story 69 (510-512)

STORY THREE

[Told by Saffredent]

I've often wished, Ladies, that I'd been able to share the good fortune of the man in the story I'm about to tell you. So here it is. In the town of Naples in the time of King Alfonso (whose well-known lasciviousness was, one might say, the very sceptre by which he ruled) there lived a nobleman—a handsome, upright and likeable man, a man indeed whose qualities were so excellent that a certain old gentleman granted him the hand of his daughter. In beauty and charm she was in every way her husband's equal, and they lived in deep mutual affection until a carnival, in the course of which the King disguised himself and went round all the houses in the town, where the people vied with one another to give him a good reception. When he came to the house of the gentleman I have referred to, he was entertained more lavishly than in any of the other houses. Preserves, minstrels, music— all were laid before him, but above all there was the presence of the most beautiful lady that the King had ever seen. At the end of the banquet, the lady sang for the King with her husband, and so sweetly did she sing that her beauty was more than ever enhanced. Seeing such physical perfection, the King took less delight in contemplating the gentle harmony that existed between the lady and her husband, than he did in speculating as to how he might go about spoiling it. The great obstacle to his desires was the evident deep mutual love between them, and so, for the time being, he kept his passion hidden and as secret as he could. But in order to obtain at least some relief for his feelings, he held a series of banquets for the lords and ladies of Naples, to which he did not, of course, omit to invite the gentleman and his fair wife.

As everyone knows, men see and believe just what they want to, and the King thought he caught something in the lady's eyes which augured well—if only the husband were not in the way. To find out if his surmise was correct, therefore, he sent the husband off for two or three weeks to attend to some business in Rome. Up till then the wife had never had him out of her sight, and she was heartbroken the moment he walked out of the door. The King took the opportunity to console her as often as possible, showering blandishments and gifts of all kinds upon her, with the result that in the end she felt not only consoled, but even content in her husband's absence. Before the three weeks were up she had fallen so much in love with the King that she was every bit as upset about her husband's imminent return as she had been about his departure. So, in order that she should not be deprived of the King after her husband's return, it was agreed that she would let her royal lover know whenever her husband was going to his estates in the country. He could then come to see her without running any risks, and in complete secrecy, so that her honour and reputation—which gave her more concern than her conscience—could not possibly be damaged in any way.

Dwelling on the prospect of the King's visits with considerable pleasure, the lady gave her husband such an affectionate reception that, although he had heard during his absence that the King had been paying her a lot of attention, he had not the slightest suspicion of how far things had gone. However, the fire of passion cannot be concealed for long, and as time went by its flames began to be somewhat obvious. He naturally began to guess at the truth, and kept a close watch on his wife until there was no longer any room for doubt. But he decided to keep quiet about it, because he was afraid that if he let on that he knew, he might suffer even worse things at the hands of the King than he had already. He considered, in short, that it was better to put up with the affront, than to risk his life for the sake of a woman who apparently no longer loved him. He was, all the same, angry and bitter, and determined to get his own back if at all possible.

Now he was well aware of the fact that bitterness and jealousy can drive women to do things that love alone will never make them do, and that this is particularly true of women with strong feelings and high principles of honour. So one day, while he was conversing with the Queen, he made so bold as to say that he felt very sorry for her when he saw how little the King really loved her. The Queen had heard all about the affair between the King and the gentleman's wife, and merely replied:

'I do not expect to be able to combine both honour and pleasure in my position. I am perfectly well aware that while I receive honour and respect, it is *she* who has all the pleasure. But then, I know too that while she may have the pleasure, she does not receive the honour and respect.'

He knew, of course, to whom she was referring, and this was his reply: 'Madame, you were born to honour and respect. You are after all of such high birth that, being queen or being empress could scarcely add to your nobility. But you are also beautiful, charming and refined, and you deserve to have your pleasures as well. The woman who is depriving you of those pleasures which are yours by right, is in fact doing herself more harm—because her moment of glory will eventually turn to shame and she will forfeit as much pleasure as she, you or any woman in the Kingdom of Naples could ever have. And if I may say so, Madame, if the King didn't have a crown on his head, he wouldn't have the slightest advantage over me as far as giving pleasure to ladies is concerned. What is more, I'm quite sure that in order to satisfy a refined person such as yourself he really ought to be wishing he could exchange his constitution for one more like my own!'

The Queen laughed, and said: 'The King may have a more delicate constitution than your own. Even so, the love which he bears me gives me so much satisfaction that I prefer it to all else.'

'Madame, if that were the case, then I would not feel so sorry for you, because I know that you would derive great happiness from the pure love you feel within you, if it were matched by an equally pure love on the part of the King. But God has denied you this, in order that you should not find in this man the answer to all your wants and so make him your god on earth.'

'I admit,' said the Queen, 'that my love for him is so deep that you will never find its like, wherever you may look.'

'Forgive me,' said the gentleman, 'but there are hearts whose love you've never sounded. May I be so bold as to tell you that there is a certain person who loves you, and loves you so deeply and so desperately, that in comparison your love for the King is as nothing? And his love grows and goes on growing in proportion as he sees the King's love for you diminishing. So, if it were, Madame, to please you, and you were to receive his love, you would be more than compensated for all that you have lost.'

The Queen began to realize, both from what he was saying, and from the expression on his face, that he was speaking from the depths of his heart. She remembered that he had some time ago sought to do her service, and that he had felt so deeply about it that he had become quite melancholy. At the time she had assumed the cause of his mood lay with his wife, but she was now quite convinced that the real reason was his love for her. Love is a powerful force, and will make itself felt whenever it is more than mere pretence, and it was this powerful force that now made her certain of what remained hidden from the rest of the world. She looked at him again. He was certainly more attractive than her husband. He had been left by his wife, too, just as she had been left by the King. Tormented by jealousy and bitterness, allured by the gentleman's passion, she sighed, tears came to her eyes, and she began: 'Oh God! Must it take the desire for revenge to drive me to do what love alone would never have driven me to?'

Her words were not lost on the gentleman who replied: 'Madame, vengeance is sweet indeed, when instead of taking one's enemy's life, one gives life to a lover who is true. It is time, I think, that the truth freed you from this foolish love for a man who certainly has no love for you. It is time that a just and reasonable love banished from you these fears that so ill become one whose spirit is so strong and so virtuous. Why hesitate, Madame? Let us set aside rank and station. Let us look upon ourselves as a man and a woman, as the two most wronged people in the world, as two people who have been betrayed and mocked by those whom we loved with all our hearts. Let us, Madame, take our revenge, not in order to punish them as they deserve, but in order to do justice to our love. My love for you is unbearable. If it is not requited I shall die. Unless your heart is as hard as diamond or as stone, it is impossible that you should not feel some spark from this fire that burns the more fiercely within me the more I try to stifle it. I am dying for love of you! And if that cannot move you to take pity on me and grant me your love, then at least your own love for yourself must surely force you to do so. For you, who are so perfect that you merit the devotion of all the honourable and worthy men in all the world, have been despised and deserted by the very man for whose sake you have disdained all others!'

At this speech the Queen was quite beside herself. Lest her face betray the turmoil of her mind, she took his arm and led him into the garden adjoining her room. For a long time she walked up and down with him saying nothing. But he knew that the conquest was almost complete, and when they reached the end of the path, where no one could see them, he expressed in the clearest possible way the love that for so long he had kept concealed. At last they were of one mind. And so it was, one might say, that together they enacted a Vengeance, having found the Passion too much to bear.*

---

* An allusion to medieval mystery plays: after the Passion and Resurrection, the mystery of the Vengeance depicted the punishment of Christ's slayers.

Before they parted they arranged that whenever the husband made his trips to his village, he would, if the King had gone off to the town, go straight to the castle to see the Queen. Thus they would fool the very people who were trying to fool them. Moreover, there would now be four people joining in the fun, instead of just two thinking they had it all to themselves. Once this was settled, the Queen retired to her room and the gentleman went home, both of them now sufficiently cheered up to forget all their previous troubles. No longer did the King's visits to the gentleman's lady distress either of them. Dread had now turned to desire, and the gentleman started to make trips to his village rather more often than he had in the past. It was, after all, only half a league [out of the town]. Whenever the King heard that the gentleman had gone to the country, he would make his way straight to his lady. Similarly, whenever the gentleman heard that the King had left his castle, he would wait till nightfall and then go straight to the Queen—to act, so to speak, as the King's viceroy. He managed to do this in such secrecy that no one had the slightest inkling of what was going on. They proceeded in this fashion for quite a while, but the King, being a public person, had much greater difficulty concealing his love-affair sufficiently to prevent anyone at all getting wind of it. In fact, there were a few unpleasant wags who started to make fun of the gentleman, saying he was a cuckold, and putting up their fingers like cuckold's horns whenever his back was turned. Anyone with any decency felt very sorry for the man. He knew what they were saying, of course, but derived a good deal of amusement from it, and reckoned his horns were surely as good as the King's crown.

One day when the King was visiting the gentleman and his wife at their home, he noticed a set of antlers mounted on the wall. He burst out laughing, and could not resist the temptation to remark that the horns went very well with the house. The gentleman was a match for the King, however. He had an inscription placed on the antlers which read as follows:

Io porto le corna, ciascun lo vede,
Ma tal le porta, che no lo crede.

Next time the king was in the house, he saw the inscription, and asked what it meant.

The gentleman simply said: 'If the King doesn't tell his secrets to his subjects, then there's no reason why his subjects should tell their secrets to the King. And so far as horns are concerned, you should bear in mind that they don't always stick up and push their wearers' hats off. Sometimes they're so soft that you can wear a hat on top of them, without being troubled by them, and even without knowing they're there at all!'

From these words the King realized that the gentleman knew about his affair with his wife. But he never suspected that the gentleman was having an affair with *his* wife. For her part, the Queen was careful to feign displeasure at her husband's behaviour, though secretly she was pleased, and the more she was pleased, the more displeasure she affected. This amicable arrangement permitted the continuation of their amours for many years to come, until at length old age brought them to order.

*

'Well, Ladies,' concluded Saffredent, 'let that story be a lesson to you. When your husbands give you little roe-deer horns, make sure that you give them great big stag's antlers!'

'Saffredent,' said Ennasuite, laughing, 'I'm quite sure that if you were still such an ardent lover as you used to be, you wouldn't mind putting up with horns as big as oaks, as long as you could give a pair back when the fancy took you.

But you're starting to go grey, you know, and it really is time you began to give your appetites a rest!'

'Mademoiselle,' he replied, 'even if the lady I love gives me no hope, and even if age has dampened my ardour somewhat, my desires are as strong as ever. But seeing that you object to my harbouring such noble desires, let me invite you to tell the fourth story, and let's see if you can produce an example to refute what I say.'

During this exchange one of the ladies had started to laugh. She knew that the lady who had just taken Saffredent's words to be aimed at her was not in fact so much the object of his affections that he would put up with cuckoldry, disgrace or injury of any kind for her sake. When Saffredent saw that she was laughing and that she had understood him, he was [highly] pleased, and let Ennasuite go on. This is what she said:

'I have a story to tell, Ladies, which will show Saffredent and everyone else here that not *all* women are like the Queen he has told us about, and that not all men who are rash enough to try their tricks get what they want. It's a story that ought not to be kept back, and it tells of a lady in whose eyes failure in love was worse than death itself. I shan't mention the real names of the people involved, because it's not long since it all happened, and I should be afraid of giving offence to their close relatives.'

STORY FOUR

In Flanders there once lived a lady of high birth, of birth so high, indeed, that there was no one higher in the land. She had no children and had been twice widowed. After her second husband's death she had gone to live with her brother, who was very fond of her. He was himself a noble lord of high estate, married to the daughter of a King. This young Prince was much given to his pleasures, being fond of the ladies, of hunting and generally enjoying himself, just as one would expect of a young man. His wife, however, was rather difficult, and did not enjoy the same things as he did, so he always used to take his sister along as well, because she, while being a sensible and virtuous woman, was also the most cheerful and lively company one could imagine.

Now there was a certain gentleman attached to the household, an extremely tall man, whose charm and good looks made him stand out among his companions. Taking careful note of the fact that his master's sister was a very lively lady who liked to enjoy herself, it occurred to him that it might be worth seeing if an amorous overture from a well-bred gentleman might not be to her taste. So he approached her, only to find that her reply was not what he would have expected. Nevertheless, in spite of the fact that she had given him the sort of answer that becomes an honest woman and a princess, she had had no difficulty in forgiving this good-looking and well-bred man for having been so presumptuous. Indeed, she made it plain that she did not at all mind his talking to her, though she also frequently reminded him that he must be careful what he said. In order to continue to enjoy the honour and pleasure of her company, he was only too glad to promise not to return to his earlier overtures. But as time went by his passion grew stronger, until he forgot his promises altogether. Not that he dared risk opening the subject again verbally—he had already to his cost had a taste of her ability to answer him back with her words of wisdom. No, what he had in mind was this. If he could find the right time and place, then might she not relent and indulge him a little, and indulge herself at the same time? After all, she was a widow and young, healthy and vivacious. To this end he mentioned to his master that he had lands adjoining his home that offered excellent hunting, and assured him that if he came and hunted a stag or two in May he would have the time of his life. Partly because he liked the gentleman and partly because he was addicted to hunting, the Prince accepted this invitation, and went to stay at his house, which was, as one would expect of the richest man in the land, a very fine place and very well maintained. In one wing of the house the gentleman accommodated the Prince and his wife. In the other wing opposite he accommodated the lady whom by now he loved more than he loved life itself. Her room had been luxuriously decorated from top to bottom with tapestries, and the floor was thickly covered with matting—so that it was impossible to see the trap-door by the side of the bed which led down to the room beneath. The gentleman's mother, who normally slept in this room, was old, and her catarrh made her cough in the night, so, in order to avoid disturbing the Princess, she had exchanged rooms with her son. Every evening this old lady took preserves up to the Princess, accompanied by her son, who, being very close to the brother of the Princess, was naturally permitted to attend both her *coucher* and her *lever*. Needless to say, these occasions constantly served to inflame his passion.

So it was that one evening he kept her up very late, and only left her room when he saw she was falling asleep. Back in his own room, he put on the most magnificent and most highly perfumed nightshirt he possessed, and on his head he placed the most beautifully decorated nightcap you ever saw. As he admired himself in his mirror, he was absolutely convinced that there was not a woman in the world who could possibly resist such a handsome and elegant sight. He looked forward with satisfaction to the success of his little plan, and went off to his bed. Not that he expected to stay there long, burning with desire as he was, and quite confident that he was soon to win his place in a bed that was both more pleasurable and more honourable than his own. Once he had dismissed his attendants, he got up to lock the door, and listened carefully for noises in the Princess's room above. When he was sure all was quiet, he turned to the task. Bit by bit he gently lowered the trap-door. It had been well constructed and was so densely covered with cloth, that not a sound was made. He hoisted himself through the aperture and into the room above. The Princess was just falling asleep. Without more ado, without a thought for her rank and station, or for the duty and respect he owed her, without, indeed, so much as a by-your-leave, he jumped into bed with her. Before she knew where she was he was lying there between her arms. But she was a strong woman. Struggling out of his clutches, she demanded to know who he was, and proceeded to lash out, scratching and biting for all she was worth. He was terrified she would call for help, and felt obliged to stuff the bedclothes into her mouth in a vain attempt to prevent her doing so. She realized that he would use all his strength to dishonour her, and fought back with all *her* strength in order to stop him. She shouted at the top of her lungs for her lady-in-waiting, a respectable elderly lady, who was sleeping in the next room, and who, as soon as she heard the shout, rushed to her mistress's rescue, still wearing her night attire.

When the gentleman realized that he had been caught, terrified of being recognized by the Princess, he beat a hasty retreat down through his trap-door. He arrived back in his room in a very sorry state indeed. It was a shattering experience for a man who had set out burning with desire, fully confident that his lady was going to receive him with open arms. He picked up his mirror from the table and examined himself in the candlelight. His face was streaming with blood from the bites and scratches she had inflicted. His beautiful embroidered nightshirt had more streaks of blood in it than it had gold thread.

'So much for good looks!' he groaned. 'I suppose you've got what you deserve. I shouldn't have expected so much from my appearance. Now it's made me attempt something that I should have realized was impossible from the start. It might even make my situation worse, instead of making it better! If she realizes that it was I who did this senseless thing, breaking all the promises I had made, I know I shall lose even my privilege of visiting her chastely and openly. That's what my vanity's done for me! To make the most of my charm and good looks, and win her heart and her love, I ought not to have kept it so dark. I ought not to have tried to take her chaste body by force! I ought to have devoted myself to her service, in humility and with patience, accepting that I must wait till love should triumph. For without love, what good to a man are prowess and physical strength?'

And so he sat the whole night through, weeping, gnashing his teeth and wishing the incident had never happened. In the morning he looked at himself again in the mirror, and seeing that his face was lacerated all over, he took to his bed, pretending he was desperately ill and could not bear to go out into the light. There he remained until his visitors had gone home.

Meanwhile, the Princess was triumphant. She knew that the only person at her brother's court who would dare to do such an extraordinary thing was the man who had already once made so bold as to declare his love. In other words, she knew perfectly well that the culprit was her host. With the help of her lady-in-waiting she looked round all the possible hiding-places in the room, without, of course, finding anybody. She was beside herself with rage. 'I know very well who it is!' she fumed. 'It's the master of the house himself! That's the only person it can be. And mark my words, I shall speak to my brother in the morning, and I'll have the man's head as proof of my chastity!'

Seeing how angry she was, her lady-in-waiting just said: 'I am pleased to see that your honour means so much to you, Madame, and that in order to enhance it you have no intention of sparing this man's life—he has already taken too many risks with it because of his violent love for you. But it very often happens that when people try to enhance their honour, they only end up doing the opposite. I would therefore urge you, Madame, to tell me the plain truth about the whole affair.'

When she had heard the whole story, she asked: 'Do you assure me that all he got from you was blows and scratches?'

'I do assure you,' came the reply, 'that that was all he got, and unless he manages to find a very good doctor indeed, we'll see the marks on his face tomorrow.'

'Well, that being so,' the old lady went on, 'it seems to me that you should be thinking about giving thanks to the Lord, rather than talking about revenge. It must have taken some courage, you know, to make such a daring attempt, and at this moment he must be feeling so mortified by his failure, that death would be a good deal easier for him to bear! If what you want is revenge, then you should just leave him to his passion and his humiliation—he'll torture himself much more than you could. And if you're concerned about your honour, then be careful not to fall into the same trap as he did. He promised himself all kinds of pleasures and delights, and what he actually got was the worst disappointment that any gentleman could ever suffer. So take care, Madame—if you try to make your honour even more impressive, you may only end up doing the opposite. If you make an official complaint against him, you will have to bring the whole thing into the open, whereas at the moment nobody knows anything, and he certainly won't go and tell anybody. What is more, just suppose you did go ahead, and Monseigneur, your brother, did bring the case to justice, and the poor man was put to death—people will say that he *must* have had his way with you. Most people will argue that it's not very easy to accept that a man can carry out such an act,—unless he has been given a certain amount of encouragement by the lady concerned. You're young and attractive, you're very lively and sociable in all kinds of company. There isn't a single person at this court who hasn't seen the encouraging way you treat the man you are now suspecting. That could only make people conclude that if he did indeed do what you say, then it couldn't have been without some blame being due to you as well. Your honour, which up till now has been such that you've been able to hold your head high wherever you went, would be put in doubt wherever this story was heard.'

As she listened to the wise reasonings of her lady-in-waiting, the Princess knew that what she was saying was true. She would indeed be criticized and blamed, in view of the encouraging and intimate way she had always treated the gentleman, so she asked her lady-in-waiting what she thought she ought to do.

'It is most gracious of you, Madame,' the old lady replied, 'to heed my advice. You know that I have great affection for you. Well, it seems to me that you should rejoice in your heart that this man—and he is the most handsome and best-bred gentleman I saw in my life—has been completely unable to turn you from the path of virtue, in spite of his love for you, and in spite of using physical violence against you. For this you should humble yourself before God, and acknowledge that it was not your virtue that saved you. For there have been many women, women who have led a far more austere life than you have, who have been humiliated by men far less worthy of affection than the man we are talking of. From now on you should be even more cautious when men make overtures to you, and bear in mind that there are plenty of women who have escaped from danger the first time, only to succumb the second. Never forget that Love is blind, Madame, and descends upon his victims at the very moment when they are treading a path which they think is safe, but which in reality is slippery and treacherous. I think also that you should never allude in any way to what has happened, either to him or anyone else, and even if *he* were to bring it up, I think you should pretend not to understand what he is talking about. In this way there are two dangers that you will be able to avoid. First of all, there's the danger of glorying in your triumph. And then there's the danger that you might enjoy being reminded of the pleasures of the flesh. Even the most chaste of women have a hard time preventing some spark of pleasure being aroused by such things, however much they strive to avoid them. Finally, Madame, so that he should not get it into his head that you in some way enjoyed what he tried to do, I would advise you to gradually stop seeing so much of him. In that way you will bring home to him what a low opinion you have of his foolish and wicked behaviour. At the same time he will be brought to see what a good person you are to have been satisfied with the triumph that God has already granted you, without seeking any further revenge. May God grant you the grace, Madame, to continue in the path of virtue wherein he has placed you, to continue to love and to serve Him even better than hitherto, in the knowledge that it is from Him alone that all goodness flows.'

The Princess made up her mind to follow the wise counsel of her lady-in-waiting, and slept peacefully for the rest of the night, while the wretched gentleman below spent a night of sleepless torment.

The next day the Princess's brother was ready to depart, and asked if he could take his leave of the master of the house. He was astonished to hear that he was ill, could not tolerate the light of day and refused to be seen by anyone. He would have gone to see him, but was told that he was sleeping, and decided not to disturb him. So together with his wife and his sister he left the house without being able to say goodbye. When his sister, the Princess, heard about their host's excuses for not seeing them before they left, she knew for certain that he was the one who had caused her so much distress. Obviously he did not dare to show his face because of the scratches he had received. Indeed, he refused all subsequent invitations to attend court until all his wounds—except, that is, for those he had suffered to his heart and to his pride— had healed. When eventually he did go back to court to face his triumphant enemy, he could not do so with out blushing. He, who was the boldest man at court, would completely lose his self-assurance in her presence, and would frequently go quite to pieces. This only made the Princess the more sure that her suspicions had been well-founded. Gently, and little by little, she withdrew her attentions—but not so gently that he failed to appreciate what she was doing. Scared lest anything worse befell him, he dared not breathe a word. He simply had to nurse his passion in the depths of his heart, and put up with a rebuff that had been justly deserved.

*

'And that, Ladies, is a story that should strike fear into the hearts of any man who thinks he can help himself to what doesn't belong to him. The Princess's virtue and the good sense of her lady-in-waiting should inspire courage in the hearts of all women. So if anything like this should ever happen to any of you, you now know what the remedy is!'

'In my opinion,' said Hircan, 'the tall lord of your story lacked nerve, and didn't deserve to have his memory preserved. What an opportunity he had! He should never have been content to eat or sleep till he'd succeeded. And one really can't say that his love was very great, if there was still room in his heart for the fear of death and dishonour.'

'And what,' asked Nomerfide, 'could the poor man have done with two women against him?'

'He should have killed the old one, and when the young one realized there was no one to help her, he'd have been half-way there!'

'Kill her!' Nomerfide cried. 'You wouldn't mind him being murderer as well, then? If that's what you think, we'd better watch out we don't fall into *your* clutches!'

'If I'd gone that far,' he replied, 'I'd consider my honour ruined if I didn't go through with it!'

Then Geburon spoke up: 'So you find it strange that a princess of high birth who's been brought up in the strict school of honour should be too much for one man? In that case you'd find it even stranger that a woman of poor birth should manage to get away from *two* men!'

'I invite you to tell the fifth story, Geburon,' said Ennasuite, 'because it sounds as if you have one about some poor woman that will be far from dull.'

'Since you've chosen me [to speak],' he began, 'I shall tell a story that I know to be true because I conducted an inquiry into it at the very place where it happened. As you'll see, it isn't only princesses who've got good sense in their heads and virtue in their heart. And love and resourcefulness aren't always to be found where you'd expect them, either.'

STORY FIVE

At the port of Coulon near Niort, there was once a woman whose job it was to ferry people night and day across the river. One day she found herself alone in her boat with two Franciscan friars from Niort. Now this is one of the longest crossings on any river in France, and the two friars took it into their heads that she would find it less boring if they made amorous proposals to her. But, as only right and proper, she refused to listen. However, the two were not to be deterred. They had not exactly had their strength sapped by rowing, nor their ardours chilled by the chilly water nor, indeed, their consciences pricked by the woman's refusals. So they decided to rape her, both of them, and if she resisted, to throw her into the river. But she was as sensible and shrewd as they were vicious and stupid.

'I'm not as ungracious as you might think,' she said to them, 'and if you'll just grant me two little things, you'll see I'm just as keen to do what you want as you are.'

The Cordeliers swore by the good Saint Francis that they'd let her have anything she asked for, if she'd just let them have what they wanted.

'First of all, you must promise on your oath that neither of you will tell a soul about it,' she said.

To this they readily agreed.

'Secondly, you must do what you want with me one at a time—I'd be too embarrassed to have both of you looking at me. So decide between you who's to have me first.'

They thought this too was a very reasonable request, and the younger of the two offered to let the older man go first. As they sailed past a small island in the river, the ferrywoman said to the younger one: 'Now my good father, jump ashore and say your prayers while I take your friend here to another island. If he's satisfied with me when he gets back, we'll drop him off here, and then you can come with me.'

So he jumped out of the boat to wait on the island till his companion came back. The ferrywoman then took the other one to another island in the river, and while she pretended to be making the boat fast to a tree, told him to go and find a convenient spot.

He jumped out, and went off to look for a good place. No sooner was he on dry land than the ferrywoman shoved off with a kick against the tree, and sailed off down the river, leaving the two good friars stranded.

'You can wait till God sends an angel to console you, Messieurs!' she bawled at them. 'You're not going to get any thing out of me today!'

The poor friars saw they had been hoodwinked. They ran to the water's edge and pleaded on bended knees that she would take them to the port. They promised not to ask her for any more favours. But she went on rowing, and called back: 'I'd be even more stupid to let myself get caught again, now I've escaped!'

As soon as she landed on the other side, she went into the village, fetched her husband and called out the officers of the law to go and round up these two ravenous wolves, from whose jaws she had just by the grace of God been delivered. They had plenty of willing helpers. There was no one in the village, great or small, who was not anxious to join in the hunt and have his share of the fun. When the two good brothers, each on his own island, saw this huge band coming after them, they did their best to hide—even as Adam hid from the presence of the Lord God, when he saw that he was naked. They were half dead for shame at this exposure of their sins, and trembled in terror at the thought of the punishment that surely awaited them. But there was nothing they could do. They were seized and bound, and led through the village to the shouts and jeers of every man and woman in the place. Some people said: 'There they go, those good fathers who preach chastity to us yet want to take it from our wives!* Others said: 'They are whited sepulchres, outwardly beautiful, but within full of dead men's bones and all uncleanness!' And someone else called out, 'Every tree is known by his own fruit!' In fact, they hurled at the two captives every text in the Gospels that condemns hypocrites. In the end their Father Superior came to the rescue. He lost no time in requesting their custody, reassuring the officers of the law that he would punish them more severely than secular law could. By way of reparation, they would, he promised, be made to say as many prayers and masses as might be required! [The Father Superior was a worthy man, so the judge granted his request and sent the two prisoners back to their convent, where they were brought before the full Chapter and severely reprimanded.] Never again did they take a ferry across a river, without making the sign of the cross and commending their souls to God!

*

'Now consider this story carefully, Ladies. We have here a humble ferrywoman who had the sense to frustrate the evil intentions of two vicious men. What then ought we to expect from women who all their lives have seen nothing but good

---

*   The 1559 edition adds: The husband said: 'They dare not touch
    money with their bare hands, but they like to feel our wives' thighs,
    which are even more dangerous.'

examples, read of nothing but good examples and, in short, had examples of feminine virtue constantly paraded before them? If well-fed women are virtuous, is it not just as much a matter of custom as of virtue? But it's quite another matter if you're talking about women who have no education, who probably don't hear two decent sermons in a year, who have time for nothing but thinking how to make a meagre living, and who, in spite of all this, diligently resist all pressures in order to preserve their chastity. It is in the heart of such women as these that one finds pure virtue, for in the hearts of those we regard as inferior in body and mind the spirit of God performs his greatest works. Woe to those women who do not guard their treasure with the utmost care, for it is a treasure that brings them great honour if it is well guarded and great dishonour if it is squandered!'

'If you ask me, Geburon,' observed Longarine, 'there's nothing very virtuous in rejecting the advances of a friar. I don't know how anyone could possibly feel any affection at all for them.'

'Longarine,' he replied, 'women who are not so used as you are to having refined gentlemen to serve them find friars far from unpleasant. They're often just as good-looking as we are, just as well-built and less worn out, because they've not been knocked about in battle. What is more, they talk like angels and are as persistent as devils. That's why I think that any woman who's seen nothing better than the coarse cloth of monks' habits should be considered extremely virtuous if she manages to escape their clutches.'

'Good Heavens!' exclaimed Nomerfide loudly. You may say what you like, but I'd rather be thrown in the river any day, than go to bed with a friar!'

'*So you're a strong swimmer, are you then!*'* said Oisille, laughing.

---

* The original is: vous scavez doncques bien nouer. 'Nouer' meant both 'to swim' and 'to tie' In the second sense it had sexual connotations.

Nomerfide took this in bad part, thinking that Oisille did not give her as much credit as she would have liked, and said heatedly: 'There *are* plenty of people who've refused better men than friars, without blowing their trumpets about it!'

'Yes, and they've been even more careful not to beat their drums about ones they've accepted and given in to!' retorted Oisille, amused to see that she was annoyed.

'I can see that Nomerfide would like to speak,' Geburon intervened, 'so I invite her to take over from me, in order that she may unburden herself by telling us a good story.'

'I couldn't care less about people's remarks,' she snapped, 'they neither please nor annoy me. But since you ask me to speak, will you listen carefully, because I want to tell a story to show you that women can exercise their [cleverness] for bad purposes as well as for good ones. As we've sworn to tell the truth, I have no desire to conceal it. After all, just as the ferrywoman's virtue does not redound to the honour of other women unless they actually follow in her footsteps, so the *vice* of one woman does not bring dishonour on all other women. So, if you will listen . . .'

STORY EIGHT

[Told by Longarine]

In the county of Alès there was once a man by the name of Bornet, who had married a very decent and respectable woman. He held her honour and reputation very dear, as I am sure all husbands here hold the honour and reputation of *their* wives dear. He wanted her to be faithful to him, but was not so keen on having the rule applied to them both equally. He had become enamoured of his chambermaid, though the only benefit he got from transferring his affections in this way was the sort of pleasure one gets from varying one's diet. He had a neighbour called Sendras, who was of similar station and temperament to himself—he was a tailor and a drummer. These two were such close friends that, with the exception of the wife, there was nothing that they did not share between them. Naturally he told him that he had designs on the chambermaid.

Not only did his friend wholeheartedly approve of this, but did his best to help him, in the hope that he too might get a share in the spoils.

The chambermaid herself refused to have anything to do with him, although he was constantly pestering her, and in the end she went to tell her mistress about it. She told her that she could not stand being badgered by him any longer, and asked permission to go home to her parents. Now the good lady of the house, who was really very much in love with her husband, had often had occasion to suspect him, and was therefore rather pleased to be one up on him, and to be able to show him that she had found out what he was up to. So she said to her maid: 'Be nice to him, dear, encourage him a little bit, and then make a date to go to bed with him in my dressing-room. Don't forget to tell me which night he's supposed to be coming, and make sure you don't tell anyone else.'

The maid did exactly as her mistress had instructed. As for her master, he was so pleased with himself that he went off to tell his friend about his stroke of luck, whereupon the friend insisted on taking his share afterwards, since he had been in on the business from the beginning. When the appointed time came, off went the master, as had been agreed, to get into bed, as he thought, with his little chambermaid. But his wife, having abandoned her position of authority in order to serve in a more pleasurable one, had taken her maid's place in the bed. When he got in with her, she did not act like a wife, but like a bashful young girl, and he was not in the slightest suspicious. It would be impossible to say which of them enjoyed themselves more— the wife deceiving her husband, or the husband who thought he was deceiving his wife. He stayed in bed with her for some time, not as long as he might have wished (many years of marriage were beginning to tell on him), but as long as he could manage. Then he went out to rejoin his accomplice, and tell him what a good time he had had. The lustiest piece of goods he had ever come across, he declared. His friend, who was younger and more active than he was, said: 'Remember what you promised?'

'Hurry up, then,' replied the master, 'in case she gets up, or my wife wants her for something.

Off he went and climbed into bed with the supposed chambermaid his friend had just failed to recognize as his wife. *She* thought it was her husband again, and did not refuse anything he asked for (I say 'asked', but 'took' would be nearer the mark, because he did not dare open his mouth). He made a much longer business of it than the husband, to the surprise of the wife, who was not used to these long nights of pleasure. However, she did not complain, and looked forward to what she was planning to say to him in the morning, and the fun she would have teasing him. When dawn came, the man got up, and fondling her as he got out of bed, pulled off a ring she wore on her finger, a ring that her husband had given her at their marriage. Now the women in this part of the world are very superstitious about such things. They have great respect for women who hang on to their wedding rings till the day they die, and if a woman loses her ring, she is dishonoured, and is looked upon as having given her faith to another man. But she did not mind him taking it, because she thought it would be sure evidence against her husband of the way she had hoodwinked him.

The husband was waiting outside for his friend, and asked him how he had got on. The man said he shared the husband's opinion, and added that he would have stayed longer, had he not been afraid of getting caught by the daylight. The pair of them then went off to get as much sleep as they could. When morning came, and they were getting dressed together, the husband noticed that his friend had on his finger a ring that was identical to the one he had given his wife on their wedding day. He asked him where he had got it, and when he was told it had come from the chambermaid the night before, he was aghast. He began banging his head against the wall, and shouted: 'Oh my God! Have I gone and made myself a cuckold without my wife even knowing about it?'

His friend tried to calm him down. 'Perhaps your wife had given the ring to the girl to look after before going to bed?' he suggested. The husband made no reply, but marched straight out and went back to his house.

There he found his wife looking unusually gay and attractive. Had she not saved her chambermaid from staining her conscience, and had she not put her husband to the ultimate test, without any more cost to herself than a night's sleep? Seeing her in such good spirits, the husband thought to himself:

'She wouldn't be greeting me so cheerfully if she knew what I'd been up to.'

As they chatted, he took hold of her hand and saw that the ring, which normally never left her finger, had disappeared. Horrified, he stammered: 'What have you done with your ring?'

She was pleased that he was giving her the opportunity to say what she had to say.

'Oh! You're the most dreadful man I ever met! Who do you think you got it from? You think you got it from the chambermaid, don't you? You think you got it from that girl you're so much in love with, the girl who gets more out of you than I've ever had! The first time you got into bed you were so passionate that I thought you must be about as madly in love with her as it was possible for any man to be! But when you came back the *second* time, after getting up, you were an absolute devil! Completely uncontrolled you were, didn't know when to stop! You miserable man! You must have been blinded by desire to pay such tribute to my body—

after all you've had me long enough without showing much appreciation for my figure. So it wasn't because that young girl is so pretty and so shapely that you were enjoying yourself so much. Oh no! You enjoyed it so much because you were seething with some depraved pent-up lust—in short the sin of concupiscence was raging within you, and your senses were dulled as a result. In fact you'd worked yourself up into such a state that I think any old nanny-goat would have done for you, pretty or otherwise! Well, my dear, it's time you mended your ways. It's high time you were content with me for what I am—your own wife and an honest woman, and it's high time that you found *that* just as satisfying as when you thought I was a poor little erring chambermaid. I did what I did in order to save you from your wicked ways, so that when you get old, we can live happily and peacefully together without anything on our consciences. Because if you go on in the way you have been, I'd rather leave you altogether than see you destroying your soul day by day, and at the same time destroying your physical health and squandering everything you have before my very eyes! But if you will acknowledge that you've been in the wrong, and make up your mind to live according to the ways of God and His commandments, then I'll overlook all your past misbehaviour, even as I hope God will forgive me *my* ingratitude to Him, and failure to love Him as I ought.'

If there was ever a man who was dumbfounded and despairing, it was this poor husband. There was his wife, looking so pretty, and yet so sensible and so chaste, and he had gone and left her for a girl who did not love him. What was worse, he had had the misfortune to have gone and made her do something wicked without her even realizing what was happening. He had gone and let another man share pleasures which, rightly, were his alone to enjoy. He had gone and given himself cuckold's horns and made himself look ridiculous for evermore. But he could see she was already angry enough about the chambermaid, and he did not dare tell her about the other dirty trick he had played. So he promised that he would leave his wicked ways behind him, asked her to forgive him and gave her the ring back. He told his friend not to breathe a word to anybody, but secrets of this sort nearly always end up being proclaimed from the [roof-tops,] and it was not long before the facts became public knowledge. The husband was branded as a cuckold without his wife having done a single thing to disgrace herself.

*

'Ladies, it strikes me that if all the men who offend their wives like that got a punishment like that, then Hircan and Saffredent ought to be feeling a bit nervous.'

Come now, Longarine,' said Saffredent, 'Hircan and I aren't the only married men here, you know.'

'True,' she replied, 'but you're the only two who'd play a trick like that.'

'And just when have you heard of us chasing our wives' maids?' he retorted.

If the ladies in question were to tell us the facts,' Longarine said, 'then you'd soon find plenty of maids who'd been dismissed before their pay-day!'

'Really,' intervened Geburon, 'a fine one you are! You promise to make us all laugh, and you end up making these two gentlemen annoyed.'

It comes to the same thing,' said Longarine. 'As long as they don't get their swords out, their getting angry makes it all the more amusing.'

'But the fact remains,' said Hircan, 'that if our wives were to listen to what this lady here has to say, she'd make trouble for every married couple here!'

'I know what I'm saying, and who I'm saying it to,' Longarine replied. 'Your wives are so good, and they love you so much, that even if you gave them horns like a stag's, they'd still convince themselves, and everybody else, that they were garlands of roses!'

Everyone found this remark highly amusing, even the people it was aimed at, and the subject was brought to a close. Dagoucin, however, who had not yet said a word, could not resist saying: 'When a man already has everything he needs in order to be contented, it is very unreasonable of him to go off and seek satisfaction elsewhere. It has often struck me that when people are not satisfied with what they already have, and think they can find something better, then they only make themselves worse off. And they do not get any sympathy, because inconstancy is one thing that is universally condemned.'

'But what about people who have not yet found their "other half"?' asked Simontaut. 'Would you still say it was inconstancy if they seek her wherever she may be found?'

'No man can know,' replied Dagoucin, 'where his other half is to be found, this other half with whom he may find a union so equal that between [the parts] there is no difference; which being so, a man must hold fast where Love constrains him an whatever may befall him, he must remain steadfast in heart and will. For if she whom you love is your true likeness, if she is of the same will, then it will be your own self that you love, and not her alone.'

'Dagoucin, I think you've adopting a position that is completely wrong,' said Hircan. 'You make it sound as if we ought to love women without being loved in return!'

'What I mean, Hircan, is this. If love is based on a woman's beauty, charm and favours, and if our aim is merely pleasure, ambition or profit, then such love can never last. For if the whole foundation on which our love is based should collapse, then love will fly from us and there will he no love left in us. But I am utterly convinced that if a man loves with no other aim, no other desire, than to love truly, he will abandon his soul in death rather than allow his love to abandon his heart.'

'Quite honestly, Dagoucin, I don't think you've ever really been in love,' said Simontaut, 'because if you had felt the fire of passion, as the rest of us have, you wouldn't have been doing what you've just been doing—describing Plato's republic, which sounds all very fine in writing, but is hardly true to experience.'

'If I have loved,' he replied, 'I love still, and shall love till the day I die. But my love is a perfect love, and I fear lest showing it openly should betray it. So greatly do I fear this, that I shrink to make it known to the lady whose love and friendship I cannot but desire to be equal to my own. I scarcely dare think my own thoughts, lest something should be revealed in my eyes, for the longer I conceal the fire of my love, the stronger grows the pleasure in knowing that it is indeed a perfect love.'

'Ah, but all the same,' said Geburon, 'I don't think you'd be sorry if she did return your love!'

'I do not deny it. But even if I were loved as deeply as I myself love, my love could not possibly increase, just as it could not possibly decrease if I were loved less deeply than I love.'

At this point, Parlamente, who was suspicious of these flights of fancy, said: 'Watch your step, Dagoucin. I've seen plenty of men who've died rather than speak what's in their minds.'

'Such men as those,' he replied, 'I would count happy indeed.'

'Indeed,' said Saffredent, 'and worthy to be placed among the ranks of the Innocents—of whom the Church chants "*Non loquendo, sed moriendo confessi sunt*"! I've heard a lot of talk about these languishing lovers, but I've never seen a single one actually die. I've suffered enough from such torture, but I got over it in the end, and that's why I've always assumed that nobody else ever really dies from it either.*

---

* Saffredent quotes from the *Oratio* for the Feast of the Holy Innocents: 'not by speaking, but by dying have they confessed'.

'Ah! Saffredent, the trouble is that you desire your love to be returned,' Dagoucin replied, 'and men of your opinions never die for love. But I know of many who have died, and died for no other cause than that they have loved, and loved perfectly.'

'As you seem to know some stories on the subject,' said Longarine, 'I would like to ask you to take over from me and tell us one. That will be the ninth story of the day.'

'In order that signs and wonders may prove the truth of my words, and bring you to believe in them,' he began, 'I shall recount to you something that happened not three years ago.' . . .

STORY SIXTY-SEVEN

[Told by Simontaut]

It happened during the aforementioned Captain Robertval's voyage to the island of Canada. He had been appointed leader of the expedition by the King, and, provided the climate was favourable, his orders were to stay in Canada and establish towns and forts. You all probably know how he took the first steps in carrying out these orders. In order to populate the land with Christians he took with him artisans of all types. Amongst these people there was a certain individual who was low enough to betray his master, and almost caused him to be taken prisoner by the natives. But by God's will the plot was uncovered before it could harm Captain Robertval, who had the wicked traitor seized, with the intention of punishing him as he deserved. And he certainly would have punished him, had it not been for the man's wife, who had braved all the perils of the sea with him, and could not now bear to see him die. She wept and pleaded with the Captain and the whole crew, until, partly out of compassion, partly because she at least had served faithfully, they granted her request. The couple were to be left together on a little island inhabited only by wild animals, and with them they would be allowed to take only a few basic necessities.

Finding themselves alone with only the ferocious beasts of the island for company, these unfortunate people had no help but in God, who had always been the sure hope of the poor wife. She was a woman who placed all her trust in Him, and for her preservation, nourishment and consolation she had brought the New Testament, in which she read unceasingly. But she also laboured alongside her husband to build as best they could a little hut in which to live. When the lions and other wild animals came close to devour them, they defended themselves so well, he with his arquebus and she with stones, that not only did they succeed in repelling them, but they were often also able to kill them for food. With the meat of the animals they killed and the herbs they gathered, they were able to live for a while, even [after] the bread they had brought with them had run out. [But] as time went on the husband found it increasingly difficult to take this diet. Eventually, he fell ill from the water they had to drink, and his stomach became distended. He died in a very short space of time, without any rites or any consolation other than those provided by his wife, who served him both as physician and as confessor. And thus he passed joyously from this desolate island into the regions of Heaven. All alone, the poor woman buried the body as deeply in the ground as she was able. But the lions at once caught the scent and came looking for the decaying corpse. From the protection of her little house, determined that her husband's mortal remains should have a decent resting-place, she fought off the wild animals with shots from his arquebus. And so she lived on, her bodily existence no higher than that of the beasts, but her soul in the sphere of the angels. For she spent her time in reading the Scriptures, in contemplation, prayer and other devotions. Her soul, within her emaciated and half-dead body, was joyous and contented. But He who will never abandon his people, He who shows His strength in the midst of man's despair, did not suffer that the virtue He had bestowed upon this woman should remain hidden from men, but willed that to His glory it should be made known. And after a certain time had elapsed He brought it to pass that one of the ships of Robertval's fleet should sail by the island. The crew, catching sight of smoke, were reminded of the couple who had been left there, and decided to go and see how God had dealt with them. The poor woman saw the ship approach, and dragged herself to the water's edge, where the sailors found her as they landed. Giving thanks to God, she led them into her humble abode, and showed them how she had been living. They would have found it beyond belief, without the knowledge that God is almighty to nourish His servants in the barren desert even as in the finest banquets in the world. Unable to remain there any longer, they took the poor creature with them on their [long] voyage to La Rochelle. When they had arrived and told the inhabitants of the town of her fidelity and steadfastness, she was received with great honour by all the ladies, who were glad to send their daughters to her to learn to read and write. In this worthy manner she earned her livelihood for the rest of her days and her sole desire was to exhort all people to love Our Lord and place their trust in Him, holding forth as an example the great mercy He had shown to her.

*

'Now, Ladies, will you not admit that I have fairly praised the virtues that the Lord has endowed you with—virtues which are all the worthier to be praised as their recipients are the weaker?'

'Far be it from us,' replied Oisille, 'to be sorry that you praise the graces of Our Lord in us, for in truth all goodness flows from Him; but it must be avowed that neither man nor woman is favoured in the work of God, for in their endeavours, both do but plant, and God alone gives the increase.'

'If you've read Scripture properly,' said Saffredent, 'you will know that Saint Paul wrote that Apollos planted and that he watered, but he says nothing about *women* lending a hand in God's labour!'

'You're as bad as all the other men who take a passage from Scripture which serves their purposes, and leave out anything that contradicts it. If you had read everything Saint Paul says, you would find that he commends himself to those women who have laboured with him in the Gospel.'

'Be that as it may,' said Longarine, 'the woman in the story certainly deserves praise, both because she loved her husband and risked her life for him, and because she loved God, who, as we've seen, never abandoned her.'

'As to the first point,' came in Ennasuite, 'I think there is not a woman amongst us who would not do the same to save her husband's life.'

'And I think,' said Parlamente, 'that some husbands are such stupid beasts that women who live with them should not find anything odd about living with their wild cousins!'

Ennasuite took this remark to be aimed at her, and could not resist replying: 'Provided they didn't bite, I'd prefer the company of wild beasts to the company of men who are bad-tempered and unbearable! But as I was going to say, if my husband were in danger, like the man in this story, I would not leave him, no, not if it cost me my life.'

'You should be careful not to love him too much,' said Nomerfide. 'Too much love could lead you both astray. There's a happy medium for everything. If there's a failure of understanding, love may engender hatred.'

'I don't think you would have made that point,' said Simontaut, 'if you weren't intending to confirm it with some example. So if you have one, I invite you to take my place and tell it to us.'

Well then,' she answered, 'I shall make it short and sweet, as is my wont.' . . .

STORY SIXTY-NINE

[Told by Hircan]

In the chateau of Odos, in Bigorre, there lived an equerry of the King, one Carlo by name, an Italian, who had married a noble and virtuous lady. Unfortunately she had now aged somewhat, having borne him a number of children. Not being all that young himself, he was content to live with her on peaceable and friendly terms. However, from time to time he would chat to her maids. She never made a fuss about this, but just quietly dismissed them whenever they seemed to be getting too friendly with [him]. One of the maids she took on was a very good, well-behaved young girl, and she decided to tell her what her husband was like, warning her that she was in the habit of turning girls out if she found them misbehaving. The maid wanted to stay in her mistress's good books and not lose her position, so she made up her mind to be an honest woman. The master often accosted her, of course, but she would turn a deaf ear and run straight off to tell her mistress. They used to laugh together about his silly behaviour.

One day the chambermaid was sifting grain in a room at the back of the house. She was wearing her smock over her head as they do in that part of the world—it's a garment like a hood, but it covers the shoulders and falls full length at the back. Well, along comes the master, and seeing her in this attire, he eagerly starts to make overtures. She would not for a moment have given in, but she led him on by asking if she could first of all go to make sure that his wife was busy—so that they should not be caught, she said. He agreed, and she suggested that he put her smock over his own head, and get on with the sifting in the meantime, so that the mistress would not wonder why the noise had stopped. He was only too eager to agree to this plan. At last he was going to have what he wanted. But the girl, who was certainly not devoid of a sense of humour, ran off at once to the lady of the house. 'Come and have a look at that husband of yours,' she said, 'I've shown him how to sift, to get rid of him!' They hurried back to see this newly acquired servant. When the wife saw him, with the hood of the smock over his head and the sieve in his hands, she burst out laughing, and clapped her hands in glee. She eventually managed to say: 'Well, lass, how much a month do you want me to pay you?' The husband recognized the voice and realized he had been tricked. He threw his smock and his sieve to the ground in a rage, and turned on the maid, calling her all the names under the sun. If his wife had not intervened he would have paid her her due and turned her out then and there. However, in the end everyone calmed down, and from then on they lived under the same roof without a cross word.

*

'What do you say about that woman, Ladies? Wasn't it sensible of her to have fun when her husband was trying to have fun too?'

'I don't see that he had much fun,' commented Saffredent, 'if he failed in his intentions.'

'I would think,' said Ennasuite, 'that he had more fun laughing at it with his wife, than he would have had if he *had* managed to have his way. It could have killed him at his age!'

'Even so,' said Simontaut, 'I would have been extremely annoyed to be found with my chambermaid's smock over my head!'

'I've heard,' said Parlamente, 'that it was only thanks to your wife that you were *not* caught out in some such attire, in spite of your cunning, and she's not had a moment's peace ever since.'

'Stick to stories about your own household,' said Simontaut, 'without prying into mine—though I would add that my wife has no cause to complain about me. And even if what you say about me *were* true, she would never notice. There's no reason why she should—she has all her needs satisfied.'

'Honest women need nothing,' said Longarine, 'but their husband's love, which alone can content them. And women who seek nothing but animal satisfaction never find it within the limits prescribed by honour.'

'Do you call it animal satisfaction, when a woman wants from her husband what she is entitled to?' demanded Geburon.

'What I say is this,' she answered, 'that a chaste woman whose heart is filled with true love has more satisfaction from being loved perfectly, than she possibly could from all the pleasures that the body could desire.'

'I am entirely of your opinion,' said Dagoucin. 'although the noble lords here would never accept it or admit it. I believe that if a woman is not contented by mutual love in the first place, there is nothing at all a husband can do on his own to content her. I mean, if she does [not] live in accordance with what is honourable for women in matters of love, then she is bound to be tempted by infernal animal concupiscence.

'What you say reminds me,' said Oisille, 'of a lady who was very beautiful, who was well married and who, because she did not live in accordance with what is honourable in love, did in fact become more carnal in her desires than swine and more cruel than the lions.'

'Madame, will you tell us this story, and bring our storytelling to a close for the day?' asked Simontaut.

'There are two reasons why I ought not to.' she replied. 'One is that it is a long story, and the other is that in is not a story of our time, and although it is by a reliable author, we have after all sworn not to tell stories from a written source.'

'That is true,' said Parlamente, 'but if it's the story I think it is, then it's written in such antiquated language, that apart from you and me, there's no one here who will have heard it. So it can be regarded as a new one.'*

Thereupon they all urged Oisille to tell the tale. She should not worry about the length, they assured her, as there was still a good hour to go before vespers. So, at their bidding, she began.

---

* Story 70 is in fact a transposition of the thirteenth-century poem *La chastelaine de Vergi*.

GABRIEL GARCÍA MÁRQUEZ

1928-

ONE HUNDRED YEARS OF SOLITUDE

1967

Gabriel García Márquez was born in Aracataca, a town near the Caribbean coast of Colombia, a region which is the setting for *One Hundred Years of Solitude*, just as the author's own multi-generational family and the stories told by his grandparents helped shape the portrait of the Buendía family in the novel. The Caribbean region of Colombia differs from the rest of the country. A rich fusion of diverse cultural elements—Indian, European, and African—it is an area of extremes and bizarre happenings and shares its character with the other areas around the Caribbean including the Gulf Coast of the American South. García Márquez traveled in the South and loved the novels of Faulkner. He began studying law during the time known as *la violencia* in Colombia, when political and military strife between Conservatives and Liberals almost paralyzed much of Colombian civic life. Two of the universities he attended closed down because of the unrest. In Baranquilla, where he finally moved, he joined a circle of writers who would have a lasting impact on him. He began his writing career as a journalist, taking strong political stances that often got him into trouble. His early fiction did not win him the recognition he deserved, and for much of his life he struggled financially, especially in a period in which he and his new bride, Mercedes Bacha, a Colombian pharmacist of Egyptian descent, moved to Mexico with their young sons. All this was dramatically reversed by the publication of *One Hundred Years of Solitude* in 1967. The book was an instant success in Latin America and the world, gaining him fame, and, in 1982, the Nobel Prize for literature.

The novel traces through seven generations the history of the Buendía family, who founded the town of Macondo. Macondo started as a quaint, backwater village, but in the novel it becomes transformed by the impact of the modern world. The change would seem to interrupt the solitude of Macondo, but, in the end, only increases it. The family, too, with its endogamous sexual relations—the theme of incest haunts the novel—creates its own solitude, its members cut off not only from the rest of the world, but ultimately from each other as well. The history of the Buendía family is cyclical; for it, progress is not progress. History, in the sense of being a memory of the past, is also very much in jeopardy in the novel. García Márquez's view is calculatedly complex and unsettling. As in the tales told by his grandmother and in the excesses of Colombian history, nothing is too strange to be true. The author recounts the most extraordinary things in a very straightforward, deadpan manner; this "magical realism" is one of the novel's most appealing techniques, to be savored for its humor and irony. But the bizarre events that occur in the novel usually have a basis in fact.

Overview of the novel up to the excerpted passage:

José Arcadio Buendía and his wife Úrsula founded Macondo in the hot and rainy lowland region of Northern Colombia. José Arcadio was at first a man of enormous practical energy, overseeing the layout and organization of the town; but, spurred by new inventions brought to Macondo by gypsies, his interest turned to scientific investigations and alchemy, while the practical leadership of the great household fell to Úrsula. One of their two sons, Colonel Aureliano Buendía, fought and lost 32 battles on behalf of the Liberal Party against the Conservative government. His brother, José Arcadio, had an affair with a prostitute, Pilar Ternera; their son, Arcadio, married Santa Sofía de la Piedad. Arcadio and Santa Sofía had twins named Aureliano Segundo and José Arcadio Segundo (the repetition of names emphasizes the family's ingrown character.)

The twins grew to have very different personalities. Aureliano Segundo was an outgoing, extravagant, fun-loving character. He married a beautiful, but haughty woman, Fernanda del Carpo, from a distinguished family in the highlands, who had been educated in a dismal convent. But his real love was his mistress, Petra Cotes, with whom he spent most of his time. Fernanda and Aureliano Segundo had three children together—Renata (or Meme), José Arcadio, and Amaranta Úrsula. During the time they were growing up, the banana company moved into Macondo and built a luxurious compound surrounded by a fence for the North American executives and their families. Meme became friends with the daughter of the company superintendent, Mr. Brown, and often went to parties at their house. She fell in love with a mechanic in the company motorpool, Mauricio Babilonia, and became pregnant. Fernanda was scandalized and arranged to have Mauricio shot, making it appear that he was trespassing as a chicken thief. His spinal column was shattered and, paralyzed for life, he died in solitude.

The other twin, Jose Arcadio Segundo, was a sad, pensive man who spent most of his time outside the family. In his early years he had served the priest in Macondo, helping him raise and train his fighting cocks. It seemed he was becoming a Conservative. But, when he became a leader of the banana company workers' union, he found himself, like his great-uncle, Colonel Aureliano Buendía, a solitary rebel against the established order.

SOURCE

García Márquez, Gabriel. 1967. *One Hundred Years of Solitude.* Trans. Gregory Rabassa. New York: Harper and Row, 1970. 272-290.

Selections from: Chapter 15 (272-290)

CHAPTER 15

THE EVENTS that would deal Macondo its fatal blow were just showing themselves when they brought Meme Buendía's son home. The public situation was so uncertain then that no one had sufficient spirit to become involved with private scandals, so that Fernanda was able to count on an atmosphere that enabled her to keep the child hidden as if he had never existed. She had to take him in because the circumstances under which they brought him made rejection impossible. She had to tolerate him against her will for the rest of her life because at the moment of truth she lacked the courage to go through with her inner determination to drown him in the bathroom cistern. She locked him up in Colonel Aureliano Buendía's old workshop. She succeeded in convincing Santa Sofía de la Piedad that she had found him floating in a basket. Úrsula would die without ever knowing his origin. Little Amaranta Úrsula, who went into the workshop once when Fernanda was feeding the child, also believed the version of the floating basket. Aureliano Segundo, having broken finally with his wife because of the irrational way in which she handled Meme's tragedy, did not know of the existence of his grandson until three years after they brought him home, when the child escaped from captivity through an oversight on Fernanda's part and appeared on the porch for a fraction of a second, naked, with matted hair, and with an impressive sex organ that was like a turkey's wattles, as if he were not a human child but the encyclopedia definition of a cannibal.

Fernanda had not counted on that nasty trick of her incorrigible fate. The child was like the return of a shame that she had thought exiled by her from the house forever. As soon as they carried off Mauricio Babilonia with his shattered spinal column, Fernanda had worked out the most minute details of a plan destined to wipe out all traces of the burden. Without consulting her husband, she packed her bags, put the three changes of clothing that her daughter would need into a small suitcase, and went to get her in her bedroom a half hour before the train arrived.

"Let's go, Renata," she told her.

She gave no explanation. Meme, for her part, did not expect or want any. She not only did not know where they were going, but it would have been the same to her if they had been taking her to the slaughterhouse. She had not spoken again nor would she do so for the rest of her life from the time that she heard the shot in the backyard and the simultaneous cry of pain from Mauricio Babilonia. When her mother ordered her out of the bedroom she did not comb her hair or wash her face and she got into the train as if she were walking in her sleep, not even noticing the yellow butterflies that were still accompanying her. Fernanda never found out, nor did she take the trouble to, whether that stony silence was a determination of her will or whether she had become mute because of the impact of the tragedy. Meme barely took notice of the journey through the formerly enchanted region. She did not see the shady, endless banana groves on both sides of the tracks. She did not see the white houses of the gringos or their gardens, dried out by dust and heat, or the women in shorts and blue-striped shirts playing cards on the terraces. She did not see the oxcarts on the dusty roads loaded down with bunches of bananas. She did not see the girls diving into the transparent rivers like tarpons, leaving the passengers on the train with the bitterness of their splendid breasts, or the miserable huts of the workers all huddled together where Mauricio Babilonia's yellow butterflies fluttered about, and in the doorways of which there were green and squalid children sitting on their pots, and pregnant women who shouted insults at the train. That fleeting vision, which had been a celebration for her when she came home from school, passed through Meme's heart without a quiver. She did not look out of the window, not even when the burning dampness of the groves ended and the train went through a poppy-laden plain where the carbonized skeleton of the Spanish galleon still sat and then came out into the clear air alongside the frothy, dirty sea where almost a century before José Arcadio Buendía's illusions had met defeat.

At five o'clock in the afternoon, when they had come to the last station in the swamp, she got out of the train because Fernanda made her. They got into a small carriage that looked like an enormous bat, drawn by an asthmatic horse, and they went through the desolate city in the endless streets of which, split by saltiness, there was the sound of a piano lesson just like the one that Fernanda heard during the siestas of her adolescence. They went on board a riverboat, the wooden wheel of which had a sound of conflagration, and whose rusted metal plates reverberated like the mouth of an oven. Meme shut herself up in her cabin. Twice a day Fernanda left a plate of food by her bed and twice a day she took it away intact, not because Meme had resolved to die of hunger, but because even the smell of food was repugnant to her and her stomach rejected even water. Not even she herself knew that her fertility had outwitted the mustard vapors, just as Fernanda did not know until almost a year later, when they brought the child. In the suffocating cabin, maddened by the vibration of the metal plates and the unbearable stench of the mud stirred up by the paddle wheel, Meme lost track of the days. Much time had passed when she saw the last yellow butterfly destroyed in the blades of the fan and she admitted as an irremediable truth that Mauricio Babilonia had died. She did not let herself be defeated by resignation, however. She kept on thinking about him during the arduous muleback crossing of the hallucinating plateau where Aureliano Segundo had become lost when he was looking for the most beautiful woman who had ever appeared on the face of the earth, and when they went over the mountains along Indian trails and entered the gloomy city in whose stone alleys the funereal bronze bells of thirty-two churches tolled. That night they slept in the abandoned colonial mansion on boards that Fernanda laid on the floor of a room invaded by weeds, wrapped in the shreds of curtains that they pulled off the windows and that fell to pieces with every turn of the body. Meme knew where they were because in the fright of her insomnia she saw pass by the gentleman dressed in black whom they delivered to the house inside a lead box on one distant Christmas Eve. On the following day, after mass, Fernanda took her to a somber building that Meme recognized immediately from her mother's stories of the convent where they had raised her to be a queen, and then she understood that they had come to the end of the journey. While Fernanda was speaking to someone in the office next door, Meme remained in a parlor checkered with large oil paintings of colonial archbishops, still wearing an etamine dress with small black flowers and stiff high shoes which were swollen by the cold of the uplands. She was standing in the center of the parlor thinking about Mauricio Babilonia under the yellow stream of light from the stained glass windows when a very beautiful novice came out of the office carrying her suitcase with the three changes of clothing. As she passed Meme she took her hand without stopping.

"Come, Renata," she said to her.

Meme took her hand and let herself be led. The last time that Fernanda saw her, trying to keep up with the novice, the iron grating of the cloister had just closed behind her. She was still thinking about Mauricio Babilonia, his smell of grease, and his halo of butterflies, and she would keep on thinking about him for all the days of her life until the remote autumn morning when she died of old age, with her name changed and her head shaved and without ever having spoken a word, in a gloomy hospital in Cracow.

Fernanda returned to Macondo on a train protected by armed police. During the trip she noticed the tension of the passengers, the military preparations in the towns along the line, and an atmosphere rarefied by the certainty that something serious was going to happen, but she had no information until she reached Macondo and they told her that José Arcadio Segundo was inciting the workers of the banana company to strike. "That's all we need," Fernanda said to herself. "An anarchist in the family." The strike broke out two weeks later and it did not have the dramatic consequences that had been feared. The workers demanded that they not be obliged to cut and load bananas on Sundays, and the position seemed so just that even Father Antonio Isabel interceded in its favor because he found it in accordance with the laws of God. That victory, along with other actions that were initiated during the following months, drew the colorless José Arcadio Segundo out of his anonymity, for people had been accustomed to say that he was only good for filling up the town with French whores. With the same impulsive decision with which he had auctioned off his fighting cocks in order to organize a harebrained boat business, he gave up his position as foreman in the banana company and took the side of the workers. Quite soon he was pointed out as the agent of an international conspiracy against public order. One night, during the course of a week darkened by somber rumors, he miraculously escaped four revolver shots taken at him by an unknown party as he was leaving a secret meeting. The atmosphere of the following months was so tense that even Úrsula perceived it in her dark corner, and she had the impression that once more she was living through the dangerous times when her son Aureliano carried the homeopathic pills of subversion in his pocket. She tried to speak to José Arcadio Segundo, to let him know about that precedent, but Aureliano Segundo told her that since the night of the attempt on his life no one knew his whereabouts.

"Just like Aureliano," Úrsula exclaimed. "It's as if the world were repeating itself."

Fernanda was immune to the uncertainty of those days. She had no contact with the outside world since the violent altercation she had had with her husband over her having decided Meme's fate without his consent. Aureliano Segundo was prepared to rescue his daughter with the help of the police if necessary, but Fernanda showed him some papers that were proof that she had entered the convent of her own free will. Meme had indeed signed once she was already behind the iron grating and she did it with the same indifference with which she had allowed herself to be led away. Underneath it all, Aureliano Segundo did not believe in the legitimacy of the proof, just as he never believed that Mauricio Babilonia had gone into the yard to steal chickens, but both expedients served to ease his conscience, and thus he could go back without remorse under the shadow of Petra Cotes, where he revived his noisy revelry and unlimited gourmandizing. Foreign to the restlessness of the town, deaf to Úrsula's quiet predictions, Fernanda gave the last turn to the screw of her preconceived plan. She wrote a long letter to her son José Arcadio, who was then about to take his first orders, and in it she told him that his sister Renata had expired in the peace of the Lord and as a consequence of the black vomit. Then she put Amaranta Úrsula under the care of Santa Sofía de la Piedad and dedicated herself to organizing her correspondence with the invisible doctors, which had been upset by Meme's trouble. The first thing that she did was to set a definite date for the postponed telepathic operation. But the invisible doctors answered her that it was not wise so long as the state of social agitation continued in Macondo. She was so urgent and so poorly informed that she explained to them in another letter that there was no such state of agitation and that everything was the result of the lunacy of a brother-in-law of hers who was fiddling around at that time in that labor union nonsense just as he had been involved with cockfighting and riverboats before. They were still not in agreement on the hot Wednesday when an aged nun knocked at the door bearing a small basket on her arm. When she opened the door Santa Sofía de la Piedad thought that it was a gift and tried to take the small basket that was covered with a lovely lace wrap. But the nun stopped her because she had instructions to give it personally and with the strictest secrecy to Doña Fernanda del Carpio de Buendía. It was Meme's son. Fernanda's former spiritual director explained to her in a letter that he had been born two months before and that they had taken the privilege of baptizing him Aureliano, for his grandfather, because his mother would not open her lips to tell them her wishes. Fernanda rose up inside against that trick of fate, but she had sufficient strength to hide it in front of the nun.

"We'll tell them that we found him floating in the basket," she said, smiling.

"No one will believe it," the nun said.

"If they believe it in the Bible," Fernanda replied, "I don't see why they shouldn't believe it from me."

The nun lunched at the house while she waited for the train back, and in accordance with the discretion they asked of her, she did not mention the child again, but Fernanda viewed her as an undesirable witness of her shame and lamented the fact that they had abandoned the medieval custom of hanging a messenger who bore bad news. It was then that she decided to drown the child in the cistern as soon as the nun left, but her heart was not strong enough and she preferred to wait patiently until the infinite goodness of God would free her from the annoyance.

The new Aureliano was a year old when the tension of the people broke with no forewarning. José Arcadio Segundo and other union leaders who had remained underground until then suddenly appeared one weekend and organized demonstrations in towns throughout the banana region. The police merely maintained public order. But on Monday night the leaders were taken from their homes and sent to jail in the capital of the province with two-pound irons on their legs. Taken among them were José Arcadio Segundo and Lorenzo Gavilán, a colonel in the Mexican revolution, exiled in Macondo, who said that he had been witness to the heroism of his comrade Artemio Cruz. They were set free, however, within three months because of the fact that the government and the banana company could not reach an agreement as to who should feed them in jail. The protests of the workers this time were based on the lack of sanitary facilities in their living quarters, the nonexistence of medical services, and terrible working conditions. They stated, furthermore, that they were not being paid in real money but in scrip, which was good only to buy Virginia ham in the company commissaries. José Arcadio Segundo was put in jail because he revealed that the scrip system was a way for the company to finance its fruit ships, which without the commissary merchandise would have to return empty from New Orleans to the banana ports. The other complaints were common knowledge. The company physicians did not examine the sick but had them line up behind one another in the dispensaries and a nurse would put a pill the color of copper sulfate on their tongues, whether they had malaria, gonorrhea, or constipation. It was a cure that was so common that children would stand in line several times and instead of swallowing the pills would take them home to use as bingo markers. The company workers were crowded together in miserable barracks. The engineers, instead of putting in toilets, had a portable latrine for every fifty people brought to the camps at Christmas time and they held public demonstrations of how to use them so that they would last longer. The decrepit lawyers dressed in black who during other times had besieged Colonel Aureliano Buendía and who now were controlled by the banana company dismissed those demands with decisions that seemed like acts of magic. When the workers drew up a list of unanimous petitions, a long time passed before they were able to notify the banana company officially. As soon as he found out about the agreement, Mr. Brown hitched his luxurious glassed-in coach to the train and disappeared from Macondo along with the more prominent representatives of his company. Nonetheless, some workers found one of them the following Saturday in a brothel and they made him sign a copy of the sheet with the demands while he was naked with the women who had helped to entrap him. The mournful lawyers showed in court that that man had nothing to do with the company and in order that no one doubt their arguments they had him jailed as an impostor. Later on, Mr. Brown was surprised traveling incognito in a third-class coach and they made him sign another copy of the demands. On the following day he appeared before the judges with his hair dyed black and speaking flawless Spanish. The lawyers showed that the man was not Mr. Jack Brown, the superintendent of the banana company, born in Prattville, Alabama, but a harmless vendor of medicinal plants, born in Macondo and baptized there with the name of Dagoberto Fonseca. A while later, faced with a new attempt by the workers, the lawyers publicly exhibited Mr. Brown's death certificate, attested to by consuls and foreign ministers, which bore witness that on June ninth last he had been run over by a fire engine in Chicago. Tired of that hermeneutical delirium, the workers turned away from the authorities in Macondo and brought their complaints up to the higher courts. It was there that the sleight-of-hand lawyers proved that the demands lacked all validity for the simple reason that the banana company did not have, never had had, and never would have any workers in its service because they were all hired on a temporary and occasional basis. So that the fable of the Virginia ham was nonsense, the same as that of the miraculous pills and the Yuletide toilets, and by a decision of the court it was established and set down in solemn decrees that the workers did not exist.

The great strike broke out. Cultivation stopped halfway, the fruit rotted on the trees and the hundred twenty car trains remained on the sidings. The idle workers overflowed the towns. The Street of the Turks echoed with a Saturday that lasted for several days and in the poolroom at the Hotel Jacob they had to arrange twenty-four-hour shifts. That was where José Arcadio Segundo was on the day it was announced that the army had been assigned to reestablish public order. Although he was not a man given to omens, the news was like an announcement of death that he had been waiting for ever since that distant morning when Colonel Gerineldo Márquez had let him see an execution. The bad omen did not change his solemnity, however. He took the shot he had planned and it was good. A short time later the drumbeats, the shrill of the bugle, the shouting and running of the people told him that not only had the game of pool come to an end, but also the silent and solitary game that he had been playing with himself ever since that dawn execution. Then he went out into the street and saw them. There were three regiments, whose march in time to a galley drum made the earth tremble. Their snorting of a many-headed dragon filled the glow of noon with a pestilential vapor. They were short, stocky, and brutelike. They perspired with the sweat of a horse and had a smell of suntanned hide and the taciturn and impenetrable perseverance of men from the uplands.

Although it took them over an hour to pass by, one might have thought that they were only a few squads marching in a circle, because they were all identical, sons of the same bitch, and with the same stolidity they all bore the weight of their packs and canteens, the shame of their rifles with fixed bayonets, and the chancre of blind obedience and a sense of honor. Úrsula heard them pass from her bed in the shadows and she made a cross with her fingers. Santa Sofía de la Piedad existed for an instant, leaning over the embroidered tablecloth that she had just ironed, and she thought of her son, José Arcadio Segundo, who without changing expression watched the last soldiers pass by the door of the Hotel Jacob.

Martial law enabled the army to assume the functions of arbitrator in the controversy, but no effort at conciliation was made. As soon as they appeared in Macondo, the soldiers put aside their rifles and cut and loaded the bananas and started the trains running. The workers, who had been content to wait until then, went into the woods with no other weapons but their working machetes and they began to sabotage the sabotage. They burned plantations and commissaries, tore up tracks to impede the passage of the trains that began to open their path with machine-gun fire, and they cut telegraph and telephone wires. The irrigation ditches were stained with blood. Mr. Brown, who was alive in the electrified chicken coop, was taken out of Macondo with his family and those of his fellow countrymen and brought to a safe place under the protection of the army. The situation was threatening to lead to a bloody and unequal civil war when the authorities called upon the workers to gather in Macondo. The summons announced that the civil and military leader of the province would arrive on the following Friday ready to intercede in the conflict.

José Arcadio Segundo was in the crowd that had gathered at the station on Friday since early in the morning. He had taken part in a meeting of union leaders and had been commissioned, along with Colonel Gavilán, to mingle in the crowd and orient it according to how things went. He did not feel well and a salty paste was beginning to collect on his palate when he noticed that the army had set up machine-gun emplacements around the small square and that the wired city of the banana company was protected by artillery pieces. Around twelve o'clock, waiting for a train that was not arriving, more than three thousand people, workers, women, and children, had spilled out of the open space in front of the station and were pressing into the neighboring streets, which the army had closed off with rows of machine guns. At that time it all seemed more like a jubilant fair than a waiting crowd. They had brought over the fritter and drink stands from the Street of the Turks and the people were in good spirits as they bore the tedium of waiting and the scorching sun. A short time before three o'clock the rumor spread that the official train would not arrive until the following day. The crowd let out a sigh of disappointment. An army lieutenant then climbed up onto the roof of the station where there were four machine gun emplacements aiming at the crowd and called for silence. Next to José Arcadio Segundo there was a barefooted woman, very fat, with two children between the ages of four and seven. She was carrying the smaller one and she asked José Arcadio Segundo, without knowing him, if he would lift up the other one so that he could hear better. José Arcadio Segundo put the child on his shoulder. Many years later that child would still tell, to the disbelief of all, that he had seen the lieutenant reading Decree No. 4 of the civil and military leader of the province through an old phonograph horn. It had been signed by General Carlos Cortes Vargas and his secretary, Major Enrique García Isaza, and in three articles of eighty words he declared the strikers to be a "bunch of hoodlums" and he authorized the army to shoot to kill.

After the decree was read, in the midst of a deafening hoot of protest, a captain took the place of the lieutenant on the roof of the station and with the horn he signaled that he wanted to speak. The crowd was quiet again.

"Ladies and gentlemen," the captain said in a low voice that was slow and a little tired, "you have five minutes to withdraw."

The redoubled hooting and shouting drowned out the bugle call that announced the start of the count. No one moved.

"Five minutes have passed" the captain said in the same tone. "One more minute and we'll open fire."

José Arcadio Segundo, sweating ice, lowered the child and gave him to the woman. "Those bastards might just shoot," she murmured. José Arcadio Segundo did not have time to speak because at that instant he recognized the hoarse voice of Colonel Gavilán echoing the words of the woman with a shout. Intoxicated by the tension, by the miraculous depth of the silence, and furthermore convinced that nothing could move that crowd held tight in a fascination with death, José Arcadio Segundo raised himself up over the heads in front of him and for the first time in his life he raised his voice.

"You bastards!" he shouted. "Take the extra minute and stick it up your ass!"

After his shout something happened that did not bring on fright but a kind of hallucination. The captain gave the order to fire and fourteen machine guns answered at once. But it all seemed like a farce. It was as if the machine guns had been loaded with caps, because their panting rattle could be heard and their incandescent spitting could be seen, but not the slightest reaction was perceived, not a cry, not even a sigh among the compact crowd that seemed petrified by an instantaneous invulnerability. Suddenly, on one side of the station, a cry of death tore open the enchantment: "Aaaagh, Mother." A seismic voice, a volcanic breath, the roar of a cataclysm broke out in the center of the crowd with a great potential of expansion. José Arcadio Segundo barely had time to pick up the child while the mother with the other one was swallowed up by the crowd that swirled about in panic.

Many years later that child would still tell, in spite of people thinking that he was a crazy old man, how José Arcadio Segundo had lifted him over his head and hauled him, almost in the air, as if floating on the terror of the crowd, toward a nearby street. The child's privileged position allowed him to see at that moment that the wild mass was starting to get to the corner and the row of machine guns opened fire. Several voices shouted at the same time:

"Get down! Get down!"

The people in front had already done so, swept down by the wave of bullets. The survivors, instead of getting down, tried to go back to the small square, and the panic became a dragon's tail as one compact wave ran against another which was moving in the opposite direction, toward the other dragon's tail in the street across the way, where the machine guns were also firing without cease. They were penned in, swirling about in a gigantic whirlwind that little by little was being reduced to its epicenter as the edges were systematically being cut off all around like an onion being peeled by the insatiable and methodical shears of the machine guns. The child saw a woman kneeling with her arms in the shape of a cross in an open space, mysteriously free of the stampede. José Arcadio Segundo put him up there at the moment he fell with his face bathed in blood, before the colossal troop wiped out the empty space, the kneeling woman, the light of the high, drought-stricken sky, and the whorish world where Úrsula Iguarán had sold so many little candy animals.

When José Arcadio Segundo came to he was lying face up in the darkness. He realized that he was riding on an endless and silent train and that his head was caked with dry blood and that all his bones ached. He felt an intolerable desire to sleep. Prepared to sleep for many hours, safe from the terror and the horror, he made himself comfortable on the side that pained him less, and only then did he discover that he was lying against dead people. There was no free space in the car except for an aisle in the middle. Several hours must have passed since the massacre because the corpses had the same temperature as a plaster in autumn and the same consistency of petrified foam that it had, and those who had put them in the car had had time to pile them up in the same way in which they transported bunches of bananas. Trying to flee from the nightmare, José Arcadio Segundo dragged himself from one car to another in the direction in which the train was heading, and in the flashes of light that broke through the wooden slats as they went through sleeping towns he saw the man corpses, woman corpses, child corpses who would be thrown into the sea like rejected bananas. He recognized only a woman who sold drinks in the square and Colonel Gavilán, who still held wrapped in his hand the belt with a buckle of Morelia silver with which he had tried to open his way through the panic. When he got to the first car he jumped into the darkness and lay beside the tracks until the train had passed. It was the longest one he had ever seen, with almost two hundred freight cars and a locomotive at either end and a third one in the middle. It had no lights, not even the red and green running lights, and it slipped off with a nocturnal and stealthy velocity. On top of the cars there could be seen the dark shapes of the soldiers with their emplaced machine guns.

After midnight a torrential cloudburst came up. José Arcadio Segundo did not know where it was that he had jumped off, but he knew that by going in the opposite direction to that of the train he would reach Macondo. After walking for more than three hours, soaked to the skin, with a terrible headache, he was able to make out the first houses in the light of dawn. Attracted by the smell of coffee, he went into a kitchen where a woman with a child in her arms was leaning over the stove.

"Hello," he said, exhausted. "I'm José Arcadio Segundo Buendía."

He pronounced his whole name, letter by letter, in order to convince her that he was alive. He was wise in doing so, because the woman had thought that he was an apparition as she saw the dirty, shadowy figure with his head and clothing dirty with blood and touched with the solemnity of death come through the door. She recognized him. She brought him a blanket so that he could wrap himself up while his clothes dried by the fire, she warmed some water to wash his wound, which was only a flesh wound, and she gave him a clean diaper to bandage his head. Then she gave him a mug of coffee without sugar as she had been told the Buendías drank it, and she spread his clothing out near the fire.

José Arcadio Segundo did not speak until he had finished drinking his coffee.

"There must have been three thousand of them," he murmured.

"What?"

"The dead," he clarified. "It must have been all of the people who were at the station."

The woman measured him with a pitying look. "There haven't been any dead here," she said. "Since the time of your uncle, the colonel, nothing has happened in Macondo." In the three kitchens where José Arcadio Segundo stopped before reaching home they told him the same thing: "There weren't any dead." He went through the small square by the station and he saw the fritter stands piled one on top of the other and he could find no trace of the massacre. The streets were deserted under the persistent rain and the houses locked up with no trace of life inside. The only human note was the first tolling of the bells for mass. He knocked at the door at Colonel Gavilán's house. A pregnant woman whom he had seen several times closed the door in his face. "He left," she said, frightened. "He went back to his own country." The main entrance to the wire chicken coop was guarded as always by two local policemen who looked as if they were made of stone under the rain, with raincoats and rubber boots. On their marginal street the West Indian Negroes were singing their Saturday psalms. José Arcadio Segundo jumped over the courtyard wall and entered the house through the kitchen. Santa Sofía de la Piedad barely raised her voice. "Don't let Fernanda see you," she said. "She's just getting up." As if she were fulfilling an implicit pact, she took her son to the "chamberpot room," arranged Melquíades' broken down cot for him, and at two in the afternoon, while Fernanda was taking her siesta, she passed a plate of food in to him through the window.

Aureliano Segundo had slept at home because the rain had caught him there and at three in the afternoon he was still waiting for it to clear. Informed in secret by Santa Sofía de la Piedad, he visited his brother in Melquíades' room at that time. He did not believe the version of the massacre or the nightmare trip of the train loaded with corpses traveling toward the sea either. The night before he had read an extraordinary proclamation to the nation which said that the workers had left the station and had returned home in peaceful groups. The proclamation also stated that the union leaders, with great patriotic spirit, had reduced their demands to two points: a reform of medical services and the building of latrines in the living quarters. It was stated later that when the military authorities obtained the agreement with the workers, they hastened to tell Mr. Brown and he not only accepted the new conditions but offered to pay for three days of public festivities to celebrate the end of the conflict. Except that when the military asked him on what date they could announce the signing of the agreement, he looked out the window at the sky crossed with lightning flashes and made a profound gesture of doubt.

"When the rain stops," he said. "As long as the rain lasts we're suspending all activities."

It had not rained for three months and there had been a drought. But when Mr. Brown announced his decision a torrential downpour spread over the whole banana region. It was the one that caught José Arcadio Segundo on his way to Macondo. A week later it was still raining. The official version, repeated a thousand times and mangled out all over the country by every means of communication the government found at hand, was finally accepted: there were no dead, the satisfied workers had gone back to their families, and the banana company was suspending all activity until the rains stopped. Martial law continued with an eye to the necessity of taking emergency measures for the public disaster of the endless downpour, but the troops were confined to quarters. During the day the soldiers walked through the torrents in the streets with their pant legs rolled up, playing with boats with the children. At night, after taps, they knocked doors down with their rifle butts, hauled suspects out of their beds, and took them off on trips from which there was no return. The search for and extermination of the hoodlums, murderers, arsonists, and rebels of Decree No. 4 was still going on, but the military denied it even to the relatives of the victims who crowded the commandants' offices in search of news. "You must have been dreaming," the officers insisted. "Nothing has happened in Macondo, nothing has ever happened, and nothing ever will happen. This is a happy town." In that way they were finally able to wipe out the union leaders.

The only survivor was José Arcadio Segundo. One February night the unmistakable blows of rifle butts were heard at the door. Aureliano Segundo, who was still waiting for it to clear, opened the door to six soldiers under the command of an officer. Soaking from the rain, without saying a word, they searched the house room by room, closet by closet, from parlor to pantry. Úrsula woke up when they turned on the light in her room and she did not breathe while the search went on but held her fingers in the shape of a cross, pointing them to where the soldiers were moving about. Santa Sofía de la Piedad managed to warn José Arcadio Segundo, who was sleeping in Melquíades' room, but he could see that it was too late to try to escape. So Santa Sofía de la Piedad locked the door again and he put on his shirt and his shoes and sat down on the cot to wait for them. At that moment they were searching the gold workshop. The officer made them open the padlock and with a quick sweep of his lantern he saw the workbench and the glass cupboard with bottles of acid and instruments that were still where their owner had left them and he seemed to understand that no one lived in that room. He wisely asked Aureliano Segundo if he was a silversmith, however, and the latter explained to him that it had been Colonel Aureliano Buendía's workshop. "Oho," the officer said, turned on the lights, and ordered such a minute search that they did not miss the eighteen little gold fishes that had not been melted down and that were hidden behind the bottles in their tin can. The officer examined them one by one on the workbench and then he turned human. "I'd like to take one, if I may," he said. "At one time they were a mark of subversion, but now they're relics." He was young, almost an adolescent, with no sign of timidity and with a natural pleasant manner that had not shown itself until then. Aureliano Segundo gave him the little fish. The officer put it in his shirt pocket with a childlike glow in his eyes and he put the others back in the can and set it back where it had been.

"It's a wonderful memento," he said. "Colonel Aureliano Buendía was one of our greatest men."

Nevertheless, that surge of humanity did not alter his professional conduct. At Melquíades' room, which was locked up again with the padlock, Santa Sofía de la Piedad tried one last hope. "No one has lived in that room for a century," she said. The officer had it opened and flashed the beam of the lantern over it, and Aureliano Segundo and Santa Sofía de la Piedad saw the Arab eyes of José Arcadio Segundo at the moment when the ray of light passed over his face and they understood that it was the end of one anxiety and the beginning of another which would find relief only in resignation. But the officer continued examining the room with the lantern and showed no sign of interest until he discovered the seventy-two chamberpots piled up in the cupboards. Then he turned on the light. José Arcadio Segundo was sitting on the edge of the cot, ready to go, more solemn and pensive than ever. In the background were the shelves with the shredded books, the rolls of parchment, and the clean and orderly worktable with the ink still fresh in the inkwells. There was the same pureness in the air, the same clarity, the same respite from dust and destruction that Aureliano Segundo had known in childhood and that only Colonel Aureliano Buendía could not perceive. But the officer was only interested in the chamberpots.

"How many people live in this house?" he asked.

"Five."

The officer obviously did not understand. He paused with his glance on the space where Aureliano Segundo and Santa Sofía de la Piedad were still seeing José Arcadio Segundo and the latter also realized that the soldier was looking at him without seeing him. Then he turned out the light and closed the door. When he spoke to the soldiers, Aureliano Segundo understood that the young officer had seen the room with the same eyes as Colonel Aureliano Buendía.

"It's obvious that no one has been in that room for at least a hundred years," the officer said to the soldiers. "There must even be snakes in there."

When the door closed, José Arcadio Segundo was sure that the war was over. Years before Colonel Aureliano Buendía had spoken to him about the fascination of war and had tried to show it to him with countless examples drawn from his own experience. He had believed him. But the night when the soldiers looked at him without seeing him while he thought about the tension of the past few months, the misery of jail, the panic at the station, and the train loaded with dead people, José Arcadio Segundo reached the conclusion that Colonel Aureliano Buendía was nothing but a faker or an imbecile. He could not understand why he had needed so many words to explain what he felt in war because one was enough: fear. In Melquíades' room, on the other hand, protected by the supernatural light, by the sound of the rain, by the feeling of being invisible, he found the repose that he had not had for one single instant during his previous life, and the only fear that remained was that they would bury him alive. He told Santa Sofía de la Piedad about it when she brought him his daily meals and she promised to struggle to stay alive even beyond her natural forces in order to make sure that they would bury him dead. Free from all fear, José Arcadio Segundo dedicated himself then to peruse the manuscripts of Melquíades many times, and with so much more pleasure when he could not understand them. He became accustomed to the sound of the rain, which after two months had become another form of silence, and the only thing that disturbed his solitude was the coming and going of Santa Sofía de la Piedad. He asked her, therefore, to leave the meals on the windowsill and padlock the door. The rest of the family forgot about him, including Fernanda, who did not mind leaving him there when she found that the soldiers had seen him without recognizing him. After six months of enclosure, since the soldiers had left Macondo, Aureliano Segundo removed the padlock, looking for someone he could talk to until the rain stopped. As soon as he opened the door, he felt the pestilential attack of the chamberpots, which were placed on the floor and all of which had been used several times. José Arcadio Segundo, devoured by baldness, indifferent to the air that had been sharpened by the nauseating vapors, was still reading and rereading the unintelligible parchments. He was illuminated by a seraphic glow. He scarcely raised his eyes when he heard the door open, but that look was enough for his brother to see repeated in it the irreparable fate of his great-grandfather.

"There were more than three thousand of them," was all that José Arcadio Segundo said. "I'm sure now that they were everybody who had been at the station."

OCTAVIO PAZ

1914-1998

THE LABYRINTH OF SOLITUDE

1959

The works of Octavio Paz (1914-1998) reflect an intense awareness of his identity as a Mexican, but also an effort to understand the Mexican experience as a microcosm of the universal human dilemma. Paz's father and grandfather were important political figures and Mexican nationalists. His father supported the great Mexican Revolution of 1917 and its peasant leader Zapata, and he helped implement agrarian reforms after the revolution. Paz did not often see his father and was raised mainly by his mother. His maternal grandparents had moved to Mexico from Spain; Paz's mother acquainted him with his European literary heritage.

A far stronger European influence on Paz was his experience in the Spanish Civil War in 1937. He saw there first hand a brief experiment in revolutionary government in which poets played a major role and all people were truly free and equal and shared genuine community. That vision continued to haunt him throughout his life—during his years with a circle of surrealist poets in Paris in the late 1940s; during his return to Mexico where he confronted the disillusionment of a revolution that had become institutionalized; during his activity as a diplomat in Paris and as Mexico's ambassador to India from 1962 to 1968; and during his travels to the United States as a Guggenheim Fellow in 1943-45 and as Fulbright Scholar in 1950-52.

The Labyrinth of Solitude was first written in 1947 and published in 1950. In 1959 a revised second edition was published which included a new epilogue entitled "The Dialectic of Solitude." An attempt to analyze his Mexican identity, this work reflects his experience in Europe in the 1940s and his travels in the United States. In his search for solutions to Mexico's identity crisis he draws on the amazingly rich traditions of Mexican culture—its deep religious traditions, myth, and symbol—as well as on modern psychological insights and his own experiences.

Paz is best known as a poet—one of the great poets of this century, winner of the Nobel Prize for literature in 1990—and he much prefers poetry to prose. The prose of *The Labyrinth of Solitude* is, indeed, a poetic prose. In it he consciously opposes poetic understanding to historical understanding, viewing the latter as mortifying, the former as liberating. Paz has said that there are two types of poems, poetry of solitude and poetry of communion. In the excerpts below he explores both, ending with a poetic vision of how love can create true community.

SOURCE

Paz, Octavio. 1959. *The Labyrinth of Solitude: Life and Thought in Mexico.* Trans. Lysander Kemp. New York and London: Grove Press, Inc. and Evergreen Books, Ltd., 1961. 47-54, 89-104, 202-212.

Selections from:

CHAPTER THREE

THE DAY OF THE DEAD

The solitary Mexican loves fiestas and public gatherings. Any occasion for getting together will serve, any pretext to stop the flow of time and commemorate men and events with festivals and ceremonies. We are a ritual people, and this characteristic enriches both our imaginations and our sensibilities, which are equally sharp and alert. The art of the fiesta has been debased almost everywhere else, but not in Mexico. There are few places in the world where it is possible to take part in a spectacle like our great religious fiestas with their violent primary colors, their bizarre costumes and dances, their fireworks and ceremonies, and their inexhaustible welter of surprises: the fruit, candy, toys and other objects sold on these days in the plazas and open-air markets.

Our calendar is crowded with fiestas. There are certain days when the whole country, from the most remote villages to the largest cities, prays, shouts, feasts, gets drunk and kills, in honor of the Virgin of Guadalupe or Benito Juárez. Each year on the fifteenth of September, at eleven o'clock at night, we celebrate the fiesta of the *Grito*[1] in all the plazas of the Republic, and the excited crowds actually shout for a whole hour . . . the better, perhaps, to remain silent for the rest of the year. During the days before and after the twelfth of

---

[1] Padre Hidalgo's call-to-arms against Spain, 1810.—*Tr.*

December,[2] time comes to a full stop, and instead of pushing us toward a deceptive tomorrow that is always beyond our reach, offers us a complete and perfect today of dancing and revelry, of communion with the most ancient and secret Mexico. Time is no longer succession, and becomes what it originally was and is: the present, in which past and future are reconciled.

But the fiestas which the Church and State provide for the country as a whole are not enough. The life of every city and village is ruled by a patron saint whose blessing is celebrated with devout regularity. Neighborhoods and trades also have their annual fiestas, their ceremonies and fairs. And each one of us—atheist, Catholic, or merely indifferent—has his own saint's day, which he observes every year. It is impossible to calculate how many fiestas we have and how much time and money we spend on them. I remember asking the mayor of a village near Mitla, several years ago, "What is the income of the village government?" "About 3,000 pesos a year. We are very poor. But the Governor and the Federal Government always help us to meet our expenses." "And how are the 3,000 pesos spent?" "Mostly on fiestas, señor. We are a small village, but we have two patron saints."

This reply is not surprising. Our poverty can be measured by the frequency and luxuriousness of our holidays. Wealthy countries have very few: there is neither the time nor the desire for them, and they are not necessary. The people have other things to do, and when they amuse themselves they do so in small groups. The modern masses are agglomerations of solitary individuals. On great occasions in Paris or New York, when the populace gathers in the squares or stadiums, the absence of people, in the sense of *a* people, is remarkable: there are couples and small groups, but they never form a living community in which the individual is at once dissolved and redeemed. But how could a poor

---

[2]   Fiesta of the Virgin of Guadalupe.—*Tr.*

Mexican live without the two or three annual fiestas that make up for his poverty and misery? Fiestas are our only luxury. They replace, and are perhaps better than, the theater and vacations, Anglo-Saxon weekends and cocktail parties, the bourgeois reception, the Mediterranean café.

In all of these ceremonies—national or local, trade or family—the Mexican opens out. They all give him a chance to reveal himself and to converse with God, country, friends or relations. During these days the silent Mexican whistles, shouts, sings, shoots off fireworks, discharges his pistol into the air. He discharges his soul. And his shout, like the rockets we love so much, ascends to the heavens, explodes into green, red, blue, and white lights, and falls dizzily to earth with a trail of golden sparks. This is the night when friends who have not exchanged more than the prescribed courtesies for months get drunk together, trade confidences, weep over the same troubles, discover that they are brothers, and sometimes, to prove it, kill each other. The night is full of songs and loud cries. The lover wakes up his sweetheart with an orchestra. There are jokes and conversations from balcony to balcony, sidewalk to sidewalk. Nobody talks quietly. Hats fly in the air. Laughter and curses ring like silver pesos. Guitars are brought out. Now and then, it is true, the happiness ends badly, in quarrels, insults, pistol shots, stabbings. But these too are part of the fiesta, for the Mexican does not seek amusement: he seeks to escape from himself, to leap over the wall of solitude that confines him during the rest of the year. All are possessed by violence and frenzy. Their souls explode like the colors and voices and emotions. Do they forget themselves and show their true faces? Nobody knows. The important thing is to go out, open a way, get drunk on noise, people, colors. Mexico is celebrating a fiesta. And this fiesta, shot through with lightning and delirium, is the brilliant reverse to our silence and apathy, our reticence and gloom.

According to the interpretation of French sociologists, the fiesta is an excess, an expense. By means of this squandering the community protects itself against the envy of the gods or of men. Sacrifices and offerings placate or buy off the gods and the patron saints. Wasting money and expending energy affirms the community's wealth in both. This luxury is a proof of health, a show of abundance and power. Or a magic trap. For squandering is an effort to attract abundance by contagion. Money calls to money. When life is thrown away it increases; the orgy, which is sexual expenditure, is also a ceremony of regeneration; waste gives strength. New Year celebrations, in every culture, signify something beyond the mere observance of a date on the calendar. The day is a pause: time is stopped, is actually annihilated. The rites that celebrate its death are intended to provoke its rebirth, because they mark not only the end of an old year but also the beginning of a new. Everything attracts its opposite. The fiesta's function, then, is more utilitarian than we think: waste attracts or promotes wealth, and is an investment like any other, except that the returns on it cannot be measured or counted. What is sought is potency, life, health. In this sense the fiesta, like the gift and the offering, is one of the most ancient of economic forms.

This interpretation has always seemed to me to be incomplete. The fiesta is by nature sacred, literally or figuratively, and above all it is the advent of the unusual. It is governed by its own special rules, that set it apart from other days, and it has a logic, an ethic and even an economy that are often in conflict with everyday norms. It all occurs in an enchanted world: time is transformed to a mythical past or a total present; space, the scene of the fiesta, is turned into a gaily decorated world of its own; and the persons taking part cast off all human or social rank and become, for the moment, living images. And everything takes place as if it were not so, as if it were a dream. But whatever happens, our actions have a greater lightness, a different gravity. They take on other meanings and with them we contract new obligations. We throw down our burdens of time and reason.

In certain fiestas the very notion of order disappears. Chaos comes back and license rules. Anything is permitted: the customary hierarchies vanish, along with all social, sex, caste, and trade distinctions. Men disguise themselves as women, gentlemen as slaves, the poor as the rich. The army, the clergy, and the law are ridiculed. Obligatory sacrilege, ritual profanation is committed. Love becomes promiscuity. Sometimes the fiesta becomes a Black Mass. Regulations, habits and customs are violated. Respectable people put away the dignified expressions and conservative clothes that isolate them, dress up in gaudy colors, hide behind a mask, and escape from themselves.

Therefore the fiesta is not only an excess, a ritual squandering of the goods painfully accumulated during the rest of the year; it is also a revolt, a sudden immersion in the formless, in pure being. By means of the fiesta society frees itself from the norms it has established. It ridicules its gods, its principles, and its laws: it denies its own self.

The fiesta is a revolution in the most literal sense of the word. In the confusion that it generates, society is dissolved, is drowned, insofar as it is an organism ruled according to certain laws and principles. But it drowns in itself, in its own original chaos or liberty. Everything is united: good and evil, day and night, the sacred and the profane. Everything merges, loses shape and individuality and returns to the primordial mass. The fiesta is a cosmic experiment, an experiment in disorder, reuniting contradictory elements and principles in order to bring about a renascence of life. Ritual death promotes a rebirth; vomiting increases the appetite; the orgy, sterile in itself, renews the fertility of the mother or of the earth. The fiesta is a return to a remote and undifferentiated state, prenatal or presocial. It is a return that is also a beginning, in accordance with the dialectic that is inherent in social processes.

The group emerges purified and strengthened from this plunge into chaos. It has immersed itself in its own origins, in the womb from which it came. To express it in another way, the fiesta denies society as an organic system of differentiated forms and principles, but affirms it as a source of creative energy. It is a true "re-creation," the opposite of the "recreation" characterizing modern vacations, which do not entail any rites or ceremonies whatever and are as individualistic and sterile as the world that invented them.

Society communes with itself during the fiesta. Its members return to original chaos and freedom. Social structures break down and new relationships, unexpected rules, capricious hierarchies are created. In the general disorder everybody forgets himself and enters into otherwise forbidden situations and places. The bounds between audience and actors, officials and servants, are erased. Everybody takes part in the fiesta, everybody is caught up in its whirlwind. Whatever its mood, its character, its meaning, the fiesta is participation, and this trait distinguishes it from all other ceremonies and social phenomena. Lay or religious, orgy or saturnalia, the fiesta is a social act based on the full participation of all its celebrants.

Thanks to the fiesta the Mexican opens out, participates, communes with his fellows and with the values that give meaning to his religious or political existence. And it is significant that a country as sorrowful as ours should have so many and such joyous fiestas. Their frequency, their brilliance and excitement, the enthusiasm with which we take part, all suggest that without them we would explode. They free us, if only momentarily, from the thwarted impulses, the inflammable desires that we carry within us. But the Mexican fiesta is not merely a return to an original state of formless and normless liberty: the Mexican is not seeking to return, but to escape from himself, to exceed himself. Our fiestas are explosions. Life and death, joy and sorrow, music and mere noise are united, not to re-create or recognize themselves, but to swallow each other up. There is nothing so joyous as a Mexican fiesta, but there is also nothing so sorrowful. Fiesta night is also a night of mourning.

If we hide within ourselves in our daily lives, we discharge ourselves in the whirlwind of the fiesta. It is more than an opening out: we rend ourselves open. Everything—music, love, friendship—ends in tumult and violence. The frenzy of our festivals shows the extent to which our solitude closes us off from communication with the world. We are familiar with delirium, with songs and shouts, with the monologue . . . but not with the dialogue. Our fiestas, like our confidences, our loves, our attempts to reorder our society, are violent breaks with the old or the established. Each time we try to express ourselves we have to break with ourselves. And the fiesta is only one example, perhaps the most typical, of this violent break. It is not difficult to name others, equally revealing: our games, which are always a going to extremes, often mortal; our profligate spending, the reverse of our timid investments and business enterprises; our confessions. The somber Mexican, closed up in himself, suddenly explodes, tears open his breast and reveals himself, though not without a certain complacency, and not without a stopping place in the shameful or terrible mazes of his intimacy. We are not frank, but our sincerity can reach extremes that horrify a European. The explosive, dramatic, sometimes even suicidal manner in which we strip ourselves, surrender ourselves, is evidence that something inhibits and suffocates us. Something impedes us from being. And since we cannot or dare not confront our own selves, we resort to the fiesta. It fires us into the void; it is a drunken rapture that burns itself out, a pistol shot in the air, a skyrocket. . . .

CHAPTER 5

CONQUEST AND COLONIALISM

Any contact with the Mexican people, however brief, reveals that the ancient beliefs and customs are still in existence beneath Western forms. These still-living remains testify to the vitality of the pre-Cortesian cultures. And after the discoveries of archaeologists and historians it is no longer possible to refer to those societies as savage or primitive tribes. Over and above the fascination or horror they inspire in us, we must admit that when the Spaniards arrived in Mexico they found complete and refined civilizations.

Mesoamerica—that is, the nucleus of what was later to be New Spain—was a territory that included the central and southern parts of present-day Mexico and a portion of Central America. To the north, the Chichimecas wandered among the deserts and uncultivated plains. (Chichimeca is a generic term, without national distinctions, that was applied to the barbarians by the inhabitants of the Central Plateau.) The frontiers between were unstable, like those of ancient Rome, and the last centuries of Mesoamerican history can be summed up as the history of repeated encounters between waves of northern hunters—almost all of them belonging to the Náhuatl family—and the settled populations. The Aztecs were the last to enter the Valley of Mexico. The previous work of erosion by their predecessors, and the wasting away of the intimate springs of the ancient local cultures, made it possible for them to accomplish the extraordinary task of founding what Arnold Toynbee calls a Universal Empire, based on the remains of older societies. According to Toynbee, the Spaniards did nothing except act as substitutes, resolving through political synthesis the tendency toward dispersal that threatened the Mesoamerican world.

When we consider what Mexico was like at the arrival of Cortés, we are surprised at the large number of cities and cultures, in contrast to the relative homogeneity of their most characteristic traits. The diversity of the indigenous nuclei and the rivalries that lacerated them indicate that Mesoamerica was made up of a complex of autonomous peoples, nations and cultures, each with its own traditions, exactly as in the Mediterranean and other cultural areas. Mesoamerica was a historical world in itself.

In addition, the cultural homogeneity of these centers shows that the primitive individuality of each culture had been replaced, perhaps within a fairly recent period, by uniform religious and political structures. The mother cultures in the central and southern areas had in fact been extinguished several centuries before. Their successors had combined and re-created all that variety of local expression, and the work of synthesis had culminated in the erection of a model which, with slight differences, was the same for all.

Although historical analogies deserved the discredit they have suffered, it is almost impossible not to compare the Mesoamerican world at the beginning of the sixteenth century with the Hellenic world at the moment when Rome began its career of universal domination. The existence of several great states, and the survival of a great number of independent cities, especially in continental Greece and the islands, underscores rather than negates the prevailing cultural uniformity. The Seleucids, the Ptolemies, the Macedonians and many small and ephemeral states were not distinctive because of the diversity and originality of their respective societies, but rather because of the quarrels that fatally divided them. The same can be said of the Mesoamerican societies. In both worlds, differing traditions and cultural heritages mixed together and at last became one. This cultural heterogeneity contrasts strongly with the perpetual quarrels that divided them.

In the Hellenic world this uniformity was achieved by the predominance of Greek culture, which absorbed the Oriental cultures. It is difficult to determine the element that unified our indigenous societies. One hypothesis, valuable mainly as a theme for reflection, suggests that the role played by Greek culture in the ancient world was fulfilled in Mesoamerica by the great culture that flourished in Tula and Teotihuacán and that has inaccurately been called "Toltec." The influence of the cultures of the Central Plateau on those of the south, especially in the area occupied by the so-called Second Mayan Empire, justifies this idea. It is noteworthy that no Mayan influence has been found in the remains of Teotihuacán, whereas Chichén-Itzá was a "Toltec" city. Everything seems to indicate that at a certain time the cultural forms of central Mexico spread out and became predominant.

Mesoamerica has been described very generally as a uniform historical area characterized by the constant presence of certain elements common to all its cultures: an agriculture based on maize, a ritual calendar, a ritual ball-game, human sacrifices, solar and vegetation myths, etc. It is said that all of these elements originated in the south and were assimilated at various times by the immigrants from the north. If this were true, Mesoamerican culture would be the result of various southern creations that were adopted, developed and systematized by nomadic groups. But this scheme neglects the originality of each local culture. The resemblances among the religious, political and mythical conceptions of the Indo-European peoples, for instance, do not deny the originality of each one of them. But, apart from the particular originality of each culture, it is evident that all of them, because of decadence or debilitation, were on the point of being absorbed into the Aztec Empire, which was heir to the civilizations of the Central Plateau.

Those societies were impregnated with religion. The Aztec state was both military and theocratic. Therefore, political unification was preceded or completed by religious unification, or corresponded to it in one way or another. Each pre-Cortesian city worshiped gods who steadily became more alike: their names were different but the ceremonies honoring them were similar. The agrarian deities—the gods of the earth, of vegetation and fertility, like Tláloc—and the Nordic gods—celestial warriors like Tezcatlipoca, Huitzilopochtli and Mixcóatl—belonged to a single cult. The most outstanding characteristic of Aztec religion at the time of the Conquest was the incessant theological speculation that reformed, systematized and unified diverse beliefs, both its own and others. This synthesis was not the result of a popular religious movement like the proletarian religions that existed in the ancient world at the beginning of Christianity. It was the work of a caste located at the apex of the social pyramid. The systematizations, adaptations and reforms undertaken by the priestly caste show that the process was one of superimposition, which was also characteristic of religious architecture. Just as an Aztec pyramid often covers an older structure, so this theological unification affected only the surface of the Aztec consciousness, leaving the primitive beliefs intact. The situation prefigured the introduction of Catholicism, which is also a religion superimposed upon an original and still living religious base. Everything was prepared for Spanish domination.

The conquest of Mexico would be inexplicable without these antecedents. The arrival of the Spaniards seemed a liberation to the people under Aztec rule. The various city-states allied themselves with the conquistadors or watched with indifference—if not with pleasure—the fall of each of their rivals, especially that of the most powerful, Tenochtitlán. But the political genius of Cortés, the superior techniques of the Spaniards (lacking in such decisive actions as the battle of Otumba), and the defection of vassals and allies, could not have brought about the ruin of the Aztec Empire if it had not suddenly felt a sense of weakness, an intimate doubt that caused it to vacillate and surrender. When Moctezuma opened the gates of Tenochtitlán to the Spaniards and welcomed Cortés with gifts, the Aztecs lost the encounter. Their final struggle was a form of suicide, as we can gather from all the existing accounts of that grandiose and astounding event.

Why did Moctezuma give up? Why was he so fascinated by the Spaniards that he experienced a vertigo which it is no exaggeration to call sacred—the lucid vertigo of the suicide on the brink of the abyss? The gods had abandoned him. The great betrayal with which the history of Mexico begins was not committed by the Tlaxcaltecas or by Moctezuma and his group: it was committed by the gods. No other people have ever felt so completely helpless as the Aztec nation felt at the appearance of the omens, prophecies and warnings that announced its fall. We are unlikely to understand the meaning of these signs and predictions for the Indians if we forget their cyclical conception of time. As with many other peoples and civilizations, time was not an empty, abstract measurement to the Aztecs, but rather something concrete, a force or substance or fluid perpetually being used up. Hence the necessity of rites and sacrifices to reinvigorate the year or the century. But time—or, more precisely, each period of time—was not only something living that was born, grew up, decayed and was reborn. It was also a succession that returned: one period of time ended and another came back. The arrival of the Spaniards was interpreted by Moctezuma, at least at the beginning, not so much as a threat from outside than as the internal conclusion of one cosmic period and the commencement of another. The gods departed because their period of time was at an end, but another period returned and with it, other gods and another era.

This divine desertion becomes even more pathetic when we consider the youth and vigor of the nascent Aztec state. All of the ancient empires, such as Rome and Byzantium, felt the seduction of death at the close of their long histories. The people merely shrugged their shoulders when the final blow was struck. There is such a thing as imperial fatigue, and servitude see a light burden after the exhausting weight of power. But the Aztecs experienced the chill of death in their youth, while they were still approaching maturity. The Conquest of Mexico is a historical event made up of many very different circumstances, but what seems to me the most significant—the suicide of the Aztec people—is often forgotten. We should remember that fascination with death is not so much a trait of maturity or old age as it is of youth.

Noon and midnight are the hours of ritual suicide. At noonday everything stops for a moment, vacillating; life, like the sun, asks itself whether it is worth the effort to go on. At this moment of immobility, which is also the moment of vertigo, the Aztec people raise their eyes toward the heavens: the celestial omens are adverse, and the people feel the attraction of death.

> *Je pense, sur le bord doré de l'univers*
> *A ce goût de périr qui prend la Pythanise*
> *En qui mugit l'espoir que le monde finisse.*

One part of the Aztec people lost heart and sought out the invader. The other, betrayed on all sides and without hope of salvation, chose death. The mere presence of the Spaniards caused a split in Aztec society, a split corresponding to the dualism of their gods, their religious system and their higher castes.

Aztec religion, like that of all conquering people, was a solar religion. The Aztecs concentrated all their aspirations and war-like aims in the sun, the god who is the source of life, the bird-god who breaks through the mists and establishes himself in the center of the sky like a conquering army in the center of a battlefield. But the gods were not mere representations of nature. They also embodied the will and desire of society, which made itself divine in them. Jacques Soustelle has written that Huitzilopochtli, the warrior of the south, "is the tribal god of war and sacrifice . . . and his career begins with a massacre. Quetzalcóatl-Nanauatzin is the sun-god of the priests, who consider voluntary self-sacrifice the highest expression of their doctrine of life and the world: Quetzalcóatl is a priest-king who respects ritual and the decrees of destiny, refusing to fight and dying in order to be reborn. Huitzilopochtli, on the contrary, is the sun-hero of the warriors, defending himself and triumphing in battle: he is the *invictus sol* who destroys his enemies with the flames of his *xiucóatl*.[3] Each of these divine personalities corresponds to the ideal of some important segment of the ruling class."[4]

The duality of Aztec religion, reflected in its theocratic-military division and its social system, corresponds to the contradictory impulses that motivate all human beings and groups. The death-wish and the will-to-live conflict in each one of us. The profound tendencies impregnate the activities of all classes, castes and individuals, and in critical moments they reveal themselves in complete nakedness. The victory of the death wish shows that the Aztecs suddenly lost sight of their destiny. Cuauhtémoc fought in the knowledge that he would be defeated. The tragic nature of his struggle lies in this bold and intimate acceptance of defeat. The drama of a consciousness that sees everything around it destroyed—even the gods—appears to preside over our whole history. Cuauhtémoc and his people died alone, abandoned by their friends, their allies, their vassals and their gods. They died as orphans.

The fall of Aztec society precipitated that of the rest of the Indian world. All the nations that composed it were over-whelmed by the same horror, which almost always expresses itself as a fascinated acceptance of death. Few documents are as impressive as the remaining handful that describe this catastrophe. Here is an expression of the suffering of the Mayas, as recorded in the *Chilam Balam de Chumayel*: "II Ahan Katun: the blond-bearded strangers arrived, the sons of the sun, the pale-colored men. Ah, how sad we were when they arrived! . . . The white man's stick will fall, will descend from on high, will strike everywhere. . . . The words of Hunab-Ku,

---

[3]   The war-god and sun-god Huitzilopochtli was also a fire-god; in this latter role he wore the mask of the ancient fire-god Xiuhtecuhtli. The mask was called "xiucóatl" or "xiuhcóatl" ("fire-serpent").—*Tr.*

[4]   Jacques Soustelle: *La pensée cosmologique des anciens mexicains* (Paris: 1940).

our one god, will be words of sorrow when the words of the God of Heaven spread out over the earth. . . ." And later: "The hangings will begin, and lightning will flash from the white man's hands. . . . The hardships of battle will fall upon the Brothers, and tribute will be demanded after the grand entrance of Christianity, and the Seven Sacraments will be established, and travail and misery will rule this land."

The character of the Conquest is equally complex from the point of view expressed in the various accounts by the Spaniards. Everything is contradictory. Like the reconquest of Spain, it was both a private undertaking and a national accomplishment. Cortés and the Cid fought on their own responsibility and against the will of their superiors, but in the name of—and on behalf of—the king. They were vassals, rebels and crusaders. Opposing concepts fought within their own minds and those of their soldiers: the interests of the Monarchy and of individuals, the interests of the Faith and of personal greed for gold. Each conquistador and missionary and bureaucrat was a field of battle. Considered separately, each one represented the great powers that struggled for the control of society—feudalism, the Church and absolute Monarchy—but other tendencies struggled within them. These were the same tendencies that distinguished Spain from the rest of Europe and made her, in the literal sense of the word, an eccentric nation.

Spain was the defender of the Faith and her soldiers were soldiers of Christ. This circumstance did not prevent the Emperor and his successors from carrying on such heated disputes with the Papacy that the Council of Trent could not completely settle them. Spain was still a medieval nation, and many of the institutions she brought to the New World, like many of the men who established them, were also medieval. At the same time, the discovery and conquest of America was a Renaissance undertaking. Therefore Spain also participated in the Renaissance, although it is sometimes thought that her overseas conquests—the result of Renaissance science and technology, even Renaissance dreams and utopias—did not form a part of that historical movement.

On the other hand, the conquistadors were not merely repetitions of the medieval warriors who fought the Moors and infidels. They were adventurers, that is, men who opened new lands and risked the unknown. This was another Renaissance characteristic. The medieval knight, on the contrary, lived in a closed world. His great undertaking was the Crusades, a historical episode very different from the conquest of America. The former was a winning back; the latter, a discovery and a founding. Also, many of the conquistadors—Cortés, for example, or Jiménez de Quesada—are unimaginable in Middle Ages. Their literary tastes as well as their political realism, their awareness of the work they were doing as well as what Ortega y Gasset would call their "style of life," have small resemblance to the medieval sensibility.

If Spain renounced the future and closed herself off from the West at the moment of the Counter Reformation, she did not do so without first adopting almost all the artistic forms of the Renaissance: poetry, the novel, painting and architecture. These forms, along with certain philosophical and political ideas, all permeated with Spanish traditions of a medieval nature, were transplanted to our continent. It is significant that the most vital part of the Spanish heritage in America is made up of those universal elements that Spain assimilated during a period when her history was likewise universal. The absence of castes, traditionalism and Hispanism (in the medieval sense that has been given to the word: crust and husk of the Castilian caste[5]) is a permanent trait of Spanish-American culture, which is always open to the outside world and has a longing for universality. Juan Ruiz de Alarcón, Sor Juana Inés de la Cruz, Darío and Bello were none of them traditional, pure-bred spirits. The

---

[5] "Costra y cáscara de la casta Castilla."

Spanish tradition that we Spanish-Americans inherited is one that in Spain itself has been looked on with suspicion or contempt: that of heterodoxy, open to French or Italian influences. Our culture, like a certain portion of Spanish culture, is a free election by a few free spirits. Therefore, as Jorge Cuesta pointed out, it is a form of liberty contrasting with the passive traditionalism of our people. It is sometimes superimposed on or indifferent to the reality that sustains it. Its greatness results from this characteristic, but so does its occasional vacuity or impotence. The flowering of our lyricism—which is by nature a dialogue between the poet and the world—and the relative poverty of our epic and dramatic forms, reside perhaps in this alien, unreal aspect of our tradition.

The disparity of elements that can be observed in the Conquest does not obscure its clear historical unity. They all reflect the nature of the Spanish state, whose most notable characteristic was the fact that it was an artificial creation, a political construction in the strictest sense of the word. The Spanish monarchy was born from violence, the violence which the Catholic kings inflicted on the diversity of peoples and nations under their rule. Spanish unity was and still is the result of the political will of the state, which ignored the will of the elements that made it up. (Spanish Catholicism has always expressed the same will; hence, perhaps, its belligerent, authoritarian, inquisitorial tone.) The speed with which the Spanish state assimilated and organized the conquests made by many individuals demonstrates that a single will, pursued with a certain coherent inflexibility, animated both the European and overseas undertakings. In a brief time the Spanish colonies achieved a complexity and perfection that contrast sharply with the slow development of those founded by other countries. The previous existence of mature and stable societies undoubtedly facilitated the task of the Spaniards, but the Spanish will to create a world in its own image was also evident. In 1604, less than a century after the fall of Tenochtitlán, Balbuena told the world of the *Grandeza Mexicana.*

The Conquest, then, whether considered from the native or the Spanish point of view, must be judged as an expression of a will to unity. Despite the contradictions that make it up, it was a historical act intended to create unity out of the cultural and political plurality of the pre-Cortesian world. The Spaniards postulated a single language, a single faith and a single lord against the variety of races, languages, tendencies and states of the pre-Hispanic world. If Mexico was born in the sixteenth century, we must agree that it was the child of double violence, imperial and unifying: that of the Aztecs and that of the Spaniards.

The empire that Cortés founded on the remains of the old aboriginal cultures was a subsidiary organism, a satellite of the Spanish sun. The fate of the Indians could have been that of so many peoples who have seen their national culture humiliated but have not seen the new order—a mere tyrannous super-imposition—open its doors to the participation of the conquered. The state founded by the Spaniards was an open order, however, and deserves a sustained examination, as do the modes of participation by the conquered in the central activity of the new society, that is, in religion. The history of Mexico, and even that of each Mexican, derives precisely from this situation. Therefore a study of the colonial order is indispensable. By determining the salient features of colonial religion, whether in its popular manifestations or in those of its most representative spirits, we can discover the meaning of our culture and the origins of many of our later conflicts.

The rapidity with which the Spanish state recreated its new possessions in the image and likeness of the metropolis—despite the ambitions of its military commanders, the infidelities of its judges, and rivalries of every kind—is as amazing as the solidity of the social edifice it constructed.

Colonial society was an order built to endure. That is, it was a society designed in conformance with judicial, economic and religious principles that were fully coherent among themselves and that established a vital and harmonious relationship between the parts and the whole. It was a self-sufficient world, closed to the exterior but open to the other world.

It is very easy to laugh at the religious pretensions of colonial society. It is still easier to denounce them as empty forms intended to cover up the abuses of the conquistadors or to justify them to themselves and their victims. To a certain extent this accusation is true, but it is no less true that these other-worldly aspirations were more than a simple addition: they were part of a living faith which, like the roots of a tree, sustained other cultural and economic forms. Catholicism was the center of colonial society because it was the true fountain of life, nourishing the activities, the passions, the virtues and even the sins of both lords and servants, functionaries and priests, merchants and soldiers. Thanks to religion the colonial order was not a mere superimposition of new historical forms but a living organism. The Church used the key of baptism to open the doors of society, converting it into a universal order open to everyone. And when I speak of the Catholic Church I am not referring only to the apostolic labors of the missionaries but to the Church as a whole, with its saints, its rapacious prelates, its pedantic ecclesiastics, its impassioned jurists, its works of charity and its accumulation of riches.

It is quite clear that the reason the Spaniards did not exterminate the Indians was that they needed their labor for the cultivation of the vast haciendas and the exploitation of the mines. The Indians were goods that should not be wasted. It is difficult to realize that along with this consideration there were others of a humanitarian nature. Anyone who knows the treatment of the Indians by the military will laugh at this hypothesis, but the fate of the Indians would have been very different if it had not been for the Church. I am not thinking only of its struggle to improve their living conditions and to organize them in a more just and Christian manner, but also of the opportunity that baptism offered them to form a part of one social order and one religion. This possibility of belonging to a living order, even if it was at the bottom of the social pyramid, was cruelly denied to the Indians by the Protestants of New England. It is often forgotten that to belong to the Catholic faith meant that one found a place in the cosmos. The flight of their gods and the death of their leaders had left the natives in a solitude so complete that it is difficult for a modern man to imagine it. Catholicism re-established their ties with the world and the other world. It gave them back a sense of their place on earth; it nurtured their hopes and justified their lives and deaths.

It is unnecessary to add that the religion of the Indians was a mixture of new and ancient beliefs. It could not have been otherwise, because Catholicism was an imposed religion. From another point of view, this circumstance was of the very highest importance, but it lacked any immediate interest for the new believers. The important thing was that their social, human and religious relationships with the surrounding world and with the divine had been re-established. Their personal existence became part of a greater order. It was not out of simple devotion or servility that the Indians called the missionaries *tatas* (dads) and the Virgin of Guadalupe *madre* (mother).

The difference between colonial Mexico and the English colonies was immense. New Spain committed many horrors, but at least it did not commit the gravest of all: that of denying a place, even at the foot of the social scale, to the people who composed it. There were classes, castes and slaves, but there were no pariahs, no persons lacking a fixed social condition and a legal, moral and religious status. Its difference from the world of modern totalitarian societies was equally decisive.

It is true that New Spain, as a satellite society, did not create any original forms of art, thought, myth or government. (The only truly original creations of America—and of course I do not exclude the United States—were pre-Columbian.) It is also true that the technical superiority of the colonial world, and the introduction of richer and more complex cultural forms than those of the Mesoamericans, are not enough to justify an epoch. But the creation of a universal order, which was the most extraordinary accomplishment of colonialism, does justify that society and redeems it from its limitations. Colonial poetry, Baroque art, the Laws of the Indies, the chroniclers, historians and philosophers, and, above all, neo-Hispanic architecture—in which all things, even fantastic fruits and profane dreams, were harmonized within an order as rigorous as it was ample—are reflections of the equilibrium of a society in which all men and all races found a place, a justification and a meaning. That society was shaped by a Christian order no different from that which we can see in temples and in poems.

I am not attempting to justify colonial society. In the strictest sense, no society can be justified while one or another form of oppression subsists in it. I want to understand it as a living and therefore contradictory whole. In the same way, I refuse to regard the human sacrifices of the Aztecs as an isolated expression of cruelty without relation to the rest of that civilization. Their tearing-out of hearts and their monumental pyramids, their sculpture and their ritual cannibalism, their poetry and their "war of flowers," their theocracy and their great myths are all an indissoluble one. To deny this would be as infantile as to deny Gothic art or Provençal poetry in the name of the medieval serfs, or to deny Aeschylus because there were slaves in Athens. History has the cruel reality of a nightmare, and the grandeur of man consists in his making beautiful and lasting works out of the real substance of that nightmare. Or, to put it another way, it consists in transforming the nightmare into vision; in freeing ourselves from the shapeless horror of reality—if only for an instant—by means of creation. . . .

CHAPTER 9

THE DIALECTIC OF SOLITUDE

... Love is one of the clearest examples of that double instinct which causes us to dig deeper into our own selves and, at the same time, to emerge from ourselves and to realize ourselves in another: death and re-creation, solitude and communion. But it is not the only one. In the life of every man there are periods that are both departures and reunions, separations and reconciliations. Each of these phases is an attempt to transcend our solitude, and is followed by an immersion in strange environments.

The child must face an irreducible reality, and at first he responds to its stimuli with tears or silence. The cord that united him with life has been broken, and he tries to restore it by means of play and affection. This is the beginning of a dialogue that ends only when he recites the monologue of his death. But his relations with the external world are not passive now, as they were in his prenatal life, because the world demands a response. Reality has to be peopled by his acts. Thanks to games and fantasies, the inert natural world of adults—a chair, a book, anything—suddenly acquires a life of its own. The child uses the magic power of language or gesture, symbol or act, to create a living world in which objects are capable of replying to his questions. Language, freed of intellectual meanings, ceases to be a collection of signs and again becomes a delicate and magnetic organism. Verbal representation equals reproduction of the object itself, in the same way that a carving, for the primitive man, is not a representation but a double of the object represented. Speech again becomes a creative activity dealing with realities, that is, a poetic activity. Through magic the child creates a world in his own image and thus resolves his solitude. Self-awareness begins when we doubt the magical efficacy of our instruments.

Adolescence is a break with the world of childhood and a pause on the threshold of the adult world. Spranger points out that solitude is a distinctive characteristic of adolescence. Narcissus, the solitary, is the very image of the adolescent. It is during this period that we become aware of our singularity for the first time. But the dialectic of the emotions intervenes once more: since adolescence is extreme self-consciousness, it can only be transcended by self-forgetfulness, by self-surrender. Therefore adolescence is not only a time of solitude but also of great romances, of heroism and sacrifice. The people have good reason to picture the hero and the lover as adolescents. The vision of the adolescent as a solitary figure, closed up within himself and consumed by desire or timidity, almost always resolves into a crowd of young people dancing, singing or marching as a group, or into a young couple strolling under the arched green branches in a park. The adolescent opens himself up to the world: to love, action, friendship, sports, heroic adventures. The literature of modern nations—except Spain, where they never appear except as rogues or orphans—is filled with adolescents, with solitaries in search of communion: of the ring, the sword, the Vision. Adolescence is an armed watch, at the end of which one enters the world of facts.

Solitude is not characteristic of maturity. When a man struggles with other men or with things, he forgets himself in his work, in creation or in the construction of objects, ideas and institutions. His personal consciousness unites with that of others: time takes on meaning and purpose and thus becomes history, a vivid, significant account with both a past and a future. Our singularity—deriving from the fact that we are situated in time, in a particular time which is made up of our own selves and which devours us while it feeds us—is not actually abolished, but it is attenuated and, in a certain sense, "redeemed." Our personal existence takes part in history, which becomes, in Eliot's phrase, "a pattern of timeless moments." During vital and productive epochs, therefore, a mature man suffering from the illness of solitude is always an anomaly. This type of solitary figure is very frequent today, and indicates the gravity of our ills. In an epoch of group work, group songs, group pleasures, man is more alone than ever. Modern man never surrenders himself to what he is doing. A part of him—the profoundest part—always remains detached and alert. Man spies on himself. Work, the only modern god, is no longer creative. It is endless, infinite work, corresponding to the inconclusive life of modern society. And the solitude it engenders—the random solitude of hotels, offices, shops and movie theaters—is not a test that strengthens the soul, a necessary purgatory. It is utter damnation, mirroring a world without exit.

The dual significance of solitude—a break with one world and an attempt to create another—can be seen in our conception of heroes, saints and redeemers. Myth, biography, history and poetry describe a period of withdrawal and solitude—almost always during early youth—preceding a return to the world and to action. These are years of preparation and study, but above all they are years of sacrifice and penitence, of self-examination, of expiation and purification. Arnold Toynbee gives many illustrations of this idea: the myth of Plato's cave, the lives of St. Paul, Buddha, Mahomet, Machiavelli, Dante. And all of us in our own lives, and within our limitations, have lived in solitude and retirement, in order to purify ourselves and then return to the world.

The dialectic of solitude—"the twofold motion of withdrawal-and-return," to use Toynbee's words—is clearly revealed in the history of every people. Perhaps the ancient societies, less complex than ours, are better illustrations of this double motion.

It is not difficult to imagine the extent to which solitude is a dangerous and terrifying condition for the persons we refer to—complacently and inaccurately—as "primitives." In archaic societies, a complex and rigid system of prohibitions, rules and rituals protects the individual from solitude. The group is the only source of health. The solitary man is an invalid, a dead branch that must be lopped off and burned, for society as a whole is endangered if one of its components becomes ill. Repetition of secular beliefs and formulas assures not only the permanence of the group but also its unity and cohesion; while religious ritual, and the constant presence of the dead, create a center of relationships which restrict independent action, thus protecting the individual from solitude and the group from dissolution.

To the primitive man, health and society are synonymous terms, and so are death and dispersion. Lévy-Bruhl says that anyone who leaves his native region "ceases to belong to the group. He dies, and receives the customary funeral rites."[6] Permanent exile, then, is the same as a death sentence. The social group's identification with the spirits of its ancestors, and its identification of these with the land, is expressed in this symbolic African ritual: "When a native brings back a wife from Kimberley, they carry with them a little dirt from his home place. Every day she has to eat a bit of this dirt . . . to accustom herself to this change of residence." The social solidarity of these people has "a vital, organic character. The individual is literally part of a body." Therefore individual conversions are rare. "No one is either saved or damned on his own account," and each person's actions affect the entire group.

Despite all these safeguards, the group is not immune to dispersion. Anything can break it up: wars, religious schisms, changes in the systems of production, conquests. . . . As soon as the group is divided, each of its fragments is faced with a drastic new situation. When the source of health—the old, closed society—is destroyed, solitude is no longer merely a threat or an accident: it is a condition, the basic and ultimate

---

6   Lucien Lévy-Bruhl *La mentalité primitive* (Paris: 1922).

condition. And it leads to a sense of sin—not a sin resulting from the violation of some rule, but rather one that forms a part of their nature. Or, to be more precise, one that now *is* their nature. Solitude and original sin become one and the same. Also, health and communion again become synonymous, but are located in a remote past. They constitute the golden age, an era which preceded history and to which we could perhaps return if we broke out of time's prison. When we acquire a sense of sin, we also grow aware of our need for redemption and a redeemer.

A new mythology and a new religion are then created. The new society—unlike the old—is open and fluid, since it is made up of exiles. The fact of having been born within the group no longer assures a man that he belongs: he has to be worthy of belonging. Prayer begins to take the place of magic formulas, and initiation rites put more and more emphasis on purification. The idea of redemption fosters religious speculation, theology, asceticism and mysticism. Sacrifice and communion cease to be totem feasts (if that is what they actually were) and become means of entering the new society. A god—almost always a god who is also a son, a descendant of ancient creation-gods—dies and is resurrected at fixed periods. He is a fertility god but he is also a redeemer, and his sacrifice is a pledge that the group is an earthly prefiguration of the perfect society awaiting us on the other side of death. These hopes concerning the next life are in part a nostalgic longing for the old society. A return to the golden age is implicit in the promise of salvation.

Of course it is difficult to discover all these factors in the history of any one society. Nevertheless, there are various societies that fit the scheme in almost every detail. Consider, for instance, the birth of Orphism. The Orphic cult arose after the destruction of Achaean civilization, which caused a general dispersion of the Greek world and a vast reaccommodation of its peoples and cultures. The necessity of reforging the ancient links, both social and sacred, created a number of secret cults in which the only participants were "uprooted, transplanted beings . . . who dreamed of fashioning an organization from which they could not be separated. Their only collective name was that of 'orphans.'"[7] (I should mention that *orphanos* means both "orphan" and "empty." Solitude and orphanhood are similar forms of emptiness.)

The Orphic and Dionysiac religions, like the proletarian religions that flourished during the collapse of the ancient world, show very clearly how a closed society becomes an open one. The sense of guilt, of solitude and expiation, plays the same dual role as it does in the life of an individual.

The feeling of solitude, which is a nostalgic longing for the body from which we were cast out, is a longing for a place. According to an ancient belief, held by virtually all peoples, that place[8] is the center of the world, the navel of the universe. Sometimes it is identified with paradise, and both of these with the group's real or mythical place of origin. Among the Aztecs, the dead returned to Mictlán, a place situated in the north, from which they had emigrated. Almost all the rites connected with the founding of cities or houses allude to a search for that holy center from which we were driven out. The great sanctuaries—Rome, Jerusalem, Mecca—are at the center of the world, or symbolize and prefigure it. Pilgrimages to these sanctuaries are ritual repetitions of what each group did in the mythical past before establishing itself in the promised land. The custom of circling a house or city before entering it has the same origin.

The myth of the labyrinth pertains to this set of beliefs. Several related ideas make the labyrinth one of the most fertile and meaningful mythical symbols: the talisman or other object, capable of restoring health or freedom to the

---

[7]   Amabel Audin: *Les Fêtes Solaires* (Paris, 1945).

[8]   On the idea of "sacred place," see Mircia Eliade: *Histoire des Religions* (Paris: 1949).

people, at the center of a sacred area; the hero or saint who, after doing penance and performing the rites of expiation, enters the labyrinth or enchanted palace; and the hero's return either to save or redeem his city or to found a new one. In the Perseus myth the mystical elements are almost invisible, but in that of the Holy Grail asceticism and mysticism are closely related: sin, which causes sterility in the lands and subjects of the Fisher King; purification rites; spiritual combat; and, finally, grace—that is, communion.

We have been expelled from the center of the world and are condemned to search for it through jungles and deserts or in the underground mazes of the labyrinth. Also, there was a time when time was not succession and transition, but rather the perpetual source of a fixed present in which all times, past and future, were contained. When man was exiled from that eternity in which all times were one, he entered chronometric time and became a prisoner of the clock and the calendar. As soon as time was divided up into yesterday, today and tomorrow, into hours, minutes and seconds, man ceased to be one with time, ceased to coincide with the flow of reality. When one says, "at this moment," the moment has already passed. These spatial measurements of time separate man from reality—which is a continuous present—and turn all the presences in which reality manifests itself, as Bergson said, into phantasms.

If we consider the nature of these two opposing ideas, it becomes clear that chronometric time is a homogeneous succession lacking all particularity. It is always the same, always indifferent to pleasure or pain. Mythological time, on the other hand, is impregnated with all the particulars of our lives: it is as long as eternity or as short as a breath, ominous or propitious, fecund or sterile. This idea allows for the existence of a number of varying times. Life and time coalesce to form a single whole, an indivisible unity. To the Aztecs, time was associated with space, and each day with one of the cardinal points. The same can be said of any religious calendar. A fiesta is more than a date or anniversary. It does not celebrate an event: it *reproduces* it. Chronometric time is destroyed and the eternal present—for a brief but immeasurable period—is reinstated. The fiesta becomes the creator of time; repetition becomes conception. The golden age returns. Whenever the priest officiates in the Mystery of the Holy Mass, Christ descends to the here and now, giving himself to man and saving the world. The true believers, as Kierkegaard wished, are "contemporaries of Jesus." And myths and religious fiestas are not the only ways in which the present can interrupt succession. Love and poetry also offer us a brief revelation of this original time. Juan Ramón Jiménez wrote: "More time is not more eternity," referring to the eternity of the poetic instant. Unquestionably the conception of time as a fixed present and as pure actuality is more ancient than that of chronometric time, which is not an immediate apprehension of the flow of reality but is instead a rationalization of its passing.

This dichotomy is expressed in the opposition between history and myth or between history and poetry. In myth—as in religious fiestas or children's stories—time has no dates: "Once upon a time . . ." "In the days when animals could talk . . ." "In the beginning . . ." And that beginning, which is not such-and-such a year or day, contains all beginnings and ushers us into living time where everything truly begins every instant. Through ritual, which realizes and reproduces a mythical account, and also through poetry and fairy tales, man gains access to a world in which opposites are reconciled and united. As Van der Leeuw said, "all rituals have the property of taking place in the now, at this very instant."[9] Every poem we read is a re-creation, that is, a ceremonial ritual, a fiesta.

The theater and the epic are also fiestas. In theatrical performances and in the reciting of poetry, ordinary time ceases to operate and is replaced by original time. Thanks

---

[9]   Van der Leeuw: *L'homme primitif et la Religion* (Paris: 1940).

to participation, this mythical time—father of all the times that mask reality—coincides with our inner, subjective time. Man, the prisoner of succession, breaks out of his invisible jail and enters living time: his subjective life becomes identical with exterior time, because this has ceased to be a spatial measurement and has changed into a source, a spring, in the absolute present, endlessly re-creating itself. Myths and fiestas, whether secular or religious, permit man to emerge from his solitude and become one with creation. Therefore myth—disguised, obscure, hidden—reappears in almost all our acts and intervenes decisively in our history: it opens the doors of communion.

Contemporary man has rationalized the myths, but he has not been able to destroy them. Many of our scientific truths, like the majority of our moral, political and philosophical conceptions, are only new ways of expressing tendencies that were embodied earlier in mythical forms. The rational language of our day can barely hide the ancient myths behind it. Utopias—especially modern political utopias (despite their rationalistic disguises)—are violently concentrated expressions of the tendency that causes every society to imagine a golden age from which the social group was exiled and to which man will return on the Day of Days. Modern fiestas—political meetings, parades, demonstrations and other ritual acts—prefigure the advent of that day of redemption. Everyone hopes society will return to its original freedom, and man to his primitive purity. Then time will cease to torment us with doubts, with the necessity of choosing between good and evil, the just and the unjust, the real and the imaginary. The kingdom of the fixed present, of perpetual communion, will be re-established. Reality will tear off its masks, and at last we will be able to know both it and our fellow men.

Every moribund or sterile society attempts to save itself by creating a redemption myth which is also a fertility myth, a creation myth. Solitude and sin are resolved in communion and fertility. The society we live in today has also created its myth. The sterility of the bourgeois world will end in suicide or a new form of creative participation. This is the "theme of our times," in Ortega y Gasset's phrase; it is the substance of our dreams and the meaning of our acts.

Modern man likes to pretend that his thinking is wide-awake. But this wide-awake thinking has led us into the mazes of a nightmare in which the torture chambers are endlessly repeated in the mirrors of reason. When we emerge, perhaps we will realize that we have been dreaming with our eyes open, and that the dreams of reason are intolerable. And then, perhaps, we will begin to dream once more with our eyes closed.

W. E. B. DU BOIS

1868-1963

THE SOULS OF BLACK FOLK

1903

William Edward Burghardt Du Bois was born in Great Barrington, Massachusetts; his ancestors were Africans and Europeans (probably in about equal proportions). He probably never knew his father, but was very close to his mother, who died in the year of his high school graduation. The only black in his high school graduating class, Du Bois received financial support to attend Fisk University, a black college in Tennessee, although he wanted to study at Harvard. After graduation from Fisk he did go on to graduate work at Harvard and at the University of Berlin in Germany, attaining his Ph.D. from Harvard in Economics in 1895. He was eager to introduce students to the newly emerging discipline of sociology in which his studies, especially in Europe, had immersed him. Great was his disappointment when his first teaching appointment, at Wilberforce College in Ohio, allowed him only to teach Greek and Latin. When Du Bois was offered funding to conduct a sociological survey of blacks in the Philadelphia area, he quickly accepted and produced a model study which he hoped to replicate with an entire series of studies on the conditions of blacks in

America. It was with this goal that he accepted a teaching appointment at Atlanta University, a black school in Georgia. In Atlanta Du Bois had to face the racism of Jim Crow laws in the South; rigid color barriers had become established throughout the entire region and threatened to perpetuate the inequality produced by economic differences and the legacy of slavery. In 1896, Du Bois was married to Nina Gomer. They were married for more than fifty years and had two children. After Nina's death Du Bois married Shirley Graham, a writer of the Harlem Renaissance and a political activist.

Du Bois always spoke out with bold candor, regardless of the personal cost. Throughout his life, he fought for racial equality and an end to oppression of all sorts in society. He stressed the African heritage of his people, and argued eloquently for the unique contribution that African Americans had made and would make to American society. *The Souls of Black Folk*, published in 1903, is Du Bois's greatest work, a powerful indictment of the evils of racial prejudice, documented with carefully researched data, but written with the eloquence of poetry. In 1905, to fight against racism he helped found the Niagara movement of black leaders who insisted on full political and economic equality. Then in 1910 he was the leading African American founder of the National Association for the Advancement of Colored People (NAACP), and for many years was editor of the journal *Crisis*, the NAACP's official publication.

Du Bois was also a world leader in the struggle of Africans for independence from European colonialism. Known as the "father of Pan-Africanism," he organized and chaired a series of Pan-African Congresses, which brought together black leaders from all parts of the globe. In later years Du Bois became increasingly disillusioned about the chances for racial equality in the capitalist society of the United States. In his nineties he joined the Communist Party and accepted President Kwame Nkrumah's invitation to move to Ghana, becoming a Ghanaian citizen in the year of his death, 1963. Soon after his death, at the historic March on Washington, the leaders of the African American civil rights movement remembered his contributions with deep appreciation.

SOURCE

Du Bois, W.E.B. 1903. *The Souls of Black Folk: Essays and Sketches.* Third Edition. Chicago, A.C. McClurg & Co.

Selections from:
> Chapter 1: Of Our Spiritual Strivings (1-12)
> Chapter 14: Of the Sorrow Songs (excerpted 250-251, 254, 255, 260-264)

CHAPTER 1

OF OUR SPIRITUAL STRIVINGS

O water, voice of my heart, crying in the sand,
 All night long crying with a mournful cry,
As I lie and listen, and cannot understand
 The voice of my heart in my side or the voice of the sea,
O water, crying for rest, is it I, is it I?
 All night long the water is crying to me.

Unresting water, there shall never be rest
 Till the last moon drop and the last tide fail,
And the fire of the end begin to burn in the west;
 And the heart shall be weary and wonder and cry
 like the sea,
All life long crying without avail,
 As the water all night long is crying to me.

         ARTHUR SYMONS

[melody]

BETWEEN me and the other world there is ever an unasked question: unasked by some through feelings of delicacy; by others through the difficulty of rightly framing it. All, nevertheless, flutter round it. They approach me in a half-hesitant sort of way, eye me curiously or compassionately, and then, instead of saying directly, How does it feel to be a problem? they say, I know an excellent colored man in my town; or, I fought at Mechanicsville; or, Do not these Southern outrages make your blood boil? At these I smile, or am interested, or reduce the boiling to a simmer, as the occasion may require. To the real question, How does it feel to be a problem? I answer seldom a word.

And yet, being a problem is a strange experience,—peculiar even for one who has never been anything else, save perhaps in babyhood and in Europe. It is in the early days of rollicking boyhood that the revelation first bursts upon one, all in a day, as it were. I remember well when the shadow swept across me. I was a little thing, away up in the hills of New England, where the dark Housatonic winds between Hoosac and Taghkanic to the sea. In a wee wooden schoolhouse, something put it into the boys' and girls' heads to buy gorgeous visiting-cards—ten cents a package—and exchange. The exchange was merry, till one girl, a tall newcomer, refused my card,—refused it peremptorily, with a glance. Then it dawned upon me with a certain suddenness that I was different from the others; or like, mayhap, in heart and life and longing, but shut out from their world by a vast veil. I had thereafter no desire to tear down that veil, to creep through; I held all beyond it in common contempt, and lived above it in a region of blue sky and great wandering shadows. That sky was bluest when I could beat my mates at examination-time, or beat them at a foot-race, or even beat their stringy heads. Alas, with the years all this fine contempt began to fade; for the worlds I longed for, and all their dazzling opportunities, were theirs, not mine. But they should not keep these prizes, I said; some, all, I would wrest from them. Just how I would do it I could never decide: by reading law, by healing the sick, by telling the wonderful tales that swam in my head,—some way. With other black boys the strife was not so fiercely sunny: their youth shrunk into tasteless sycophancy, or into silent hatred of the pale world about them and mocking distrust of everything white; or wasted itself in a bitter cry, Why did God make me an outcast and a stranger in mine own house? The shades of the prison-house closed round about us all: walls strait and stubborn to the whitest, but relentlessly narrow, tall, and unscalable to sons of night who must plod darkly on in resignation, or beat unavailing palms against the stone, or steadily, half hopelessly, watch the streak of blue above.

After the Egyptian and Indian, the Greek and Roman, the Teuton and Mongolian, the Negro is a sort of seventh son, born with a veil, and gifted with second-sight in this American world,—a world which yields him no true self-consciousness, but only lets him see himself through the revelation of the other world. It is a peculiar sensation, this double-consciousness, this sense of always looking at one's self through the eyes of others, of measuring one's soul by the tape of a world that looks on in amused contempt and pity. One ever feels his two-ness—an American, a Negro; two souls, two thoughts, two unreconciled strivings; two warring ideals in one dark body, whose dogged strength alone keeps it from being torn asunder.

The history of the American Negro is the history of this strife,—this longing to attain self-conscious manhood, to merge his double self into a better and truer self. In this merging he wishes neither of the older selves to be lost. He would not Africanize America, for America has too much to teach the world and Africa. He would not bleach his Negro soul in a flood of white Americanism, for he knows that Negro blood has a message for the world. He simply wishes to make it possible for a man to be both a Negro and an American, without being cursed and spit upon by his fellows, without having the doors of Opportunity closed roughly in his face.

This, then, is the end of his striving: to be a co-worker in the kingdom of culture, to escape both death and isolation, to husband and use his best powers and his latent genius. These powers of body and mind have in the past been strangely wasted, dispersed, or forgotten. The shadow of a mighty Negro past flits through the tale of Ethiopia the Shadowy and of Egypt the Sphinx. Throughout history, the powers of single black men flash here and there like falling stars, and die sometimes before the world has rightly gauged their brightness. Here in America, in the few days since emancipation, the black man's turning hither and thither in hesitant and doubtful striving has often made his very strength to lose effectiveness, to seem like absence of power, like weakness. And yet it is not weakness,—it is the contradiction of double aims. The double-aimed struggle of the black artisan—on the one hand to escape white contempt for a nation of mere hewers of wood and drawers of water, and on the other hand to plough and nail and dig for a poverty-stricken horde—could only result in making him a poor craftsman, for he had but half a heart in either cause. By the poverty and ignorance of his people, the Negro minister or doctor was tempted toward quackery and demagogy; and by the criticism of the other world, toward ideals that made him ashamed of his lowly tasks. The would-be black *savant* was confronted by the paradox that the knowledge his people needed was a twice-told tale to his white neighbors, while the knowledge which would teach the white world was Greek to his own flesh and blood. The innate love of harmony and beauty that set the ruder souls of his people a-dancing and a-singing raised but confusion and doubt in the soul of the black artist; for the beauty revealed to him was the soul-beauty of a race which his larger audience despised, and he could not articulate the message of another people. This waste of double aims, this seeking to satisfy two unreconciled ideals, has wrought sad havoc with the courage and faith and deeds of ten thousand thousand people,—has sent them often wooing false gods and invoking false means of salvation, and at times has even seemed about to make them ashamed of themselves.

Away back in the days of bondage they thought to see in one divine event the end of all doubt and disappointment; few men ever worshipped freedom with half such unquestioning faith as did the American Negro for two centuries. To him, so far as he thought and dreamed, slavery was indeed the sum of all villainies, the cause of all sorrow, the root of all prejudice; Emancipation was the key to a promised land of sweeter beauty than ever stretched before the eyes of wearied Israelites. In song and exhortation swelled one refrain—Liberty; in his tears and curses the God he implored had Freedom in his right hand. At last it came—suddenly, fearfully, like a dream. With one wild carnival of blood and passion came the message in his own plaintive cadences:—

> "Shout, O children!
> Shout, you're free!
> For God has bought your liberty!"

Years have passed away since then,—ten, twenty, forty; forty years of national life, forty years of renewal and development, and yet the swarthy spectre sits in its accustomed seat at the Nation's feast. In vain do we cry to this our vastest social problem:—

> "Take any shape but that, and my firm nerves
> Shall never tremble!"

The Nation has not yet found peace from its sins; the freedman has not yet found in freedom his promised land. Whatever of good may have come in these years of change, the shadow of a deep disappointment rests upon the Negro people,—a disappointment all the more bitter because the unattained ideal was unbounded save by the simple ignorance of a lowly people.

The first decade was merely a prolongation of the vain search for freedom, the boon that teemed ever barely to elude their grasp,—like a tantalizing will-o'-the-wisp, maddening and misleading the headless host. The holocaust of war, the terrors of the Ku-Klux Klan, the lies of carpet-baggers, the disorganization of industry, and the contradictory advice of friends and foes, left the bewildered serf with no new watchword beyond the old cry for freedom. As the time flew, however, he began to grasp a new idea. The ideal of liberty demanded for its attainment powerful means, and these the Fifteenth Amendment gave him. The ballot, which before he had looked on as a visible sign of freedom, he now regarded as the chief means of gaining and perfecting that liberty with which war had partially endowed him. And why not? Had not votes made war and emancipated millions? Had not votes enfranchised the freedmen? Was anything impossible to a power that had done all this? A million black men started with renewed zeal to vote themselves into the kingdom. So the decade flew away, the revolution of 1876 came, and left the half-free serf weary, wondering, but still inspired. Slowly but steadily, in the following years, a new vision began gradually to replace the dream of political power,—a powerful movement, the rise of another ideal to guide the unguided, another pillar of fire by night after a clouded day. It was the ideal of "book-learning"; the curiosity, born of compulsory ignorance, to know and test the power of the cabalistic letters of the white man, the longing to know. Here at last seemed to have been discovered the mountain path to Canaan; longer than the highway of Emancipation and law, steep and rugged, but straight, leading to heights high enough to overlook life.

Up the new path the advance guard toiled, slowly, heavily, doggedly; only those who have watched and guided the faltering feet, the misty minds, the dull understandings, of the dark pupils of these schools know how faithfully, how piteously, this people strove to learn. It was weary work. The cold statistician wrote down the inches of progress here and there, noted also where here and there a foot had slipped or some one had fallen. To the tired climbers, the horizon was ever dark, the mists were often cold, the Canaan was always dim and far away. If, however, the vistas disclosed as yet no goal, no resting-place, little but flattery and criticism, the journey at least gave leisure for reflection and self-examination; it changed the child of Emancipation to the youth with dawning self-consciousness, self-realization, self-respect. In those sombre forests of his striving his own soul rose before him, and he saw himself,—darkly as through a veil; and yet he saw in himself some faint revelation of his power, of his mission. He began to have a dim feeling that, to attain his place in the world, he must be himself, and not another. For the first time he sought to analyze the burden he bore upon his back, that dead-weight of social degradation partially masked behind a half-named Negro problem. He felt his poverty; without a cent, without a home, without land, tools, or savings, he had entered into competition with rich, landed, skilled neighbors. To be a poor man is hard, but to be a poor race in a land of dollars is the very bottom of hardships. He felt the weight of his ignorance,—not simply of letters, but of life, of business, of the humanities; the accumulated sloth and shirking and awkwardness of decades and centuries shackled his hands and feet. Nor was his burden all poverty and ignorance. The red stain of bastardy, which two centuries of systematic legal defilement of Negro women had stamped upon his race, meant not only the loss of ancient African chastity, but also the hereditary weight of a mass of corruption from white adulterers, threatening almost the obliteration of the Negro home.

A people thus handicapped ought not to be asked to race with the world, but rather allowed to give all its time and thought to its own social problems. But alas! while sociologists gleefully count his bastards and his prostitutes, the very soul of the toiling, sweating black man is darkened by the shadow of a vast despair. Men call the shadow prejudice, and learnedly explain it as the natural defence of culture against barbarism, learning against ignorance, purity against crime, the "higher" against the "lower" races. To which the Negro cries Amen! and swears that to so much of this strange prejudice as is founded on just homage to civilization, culture, righteousness, and progress, he humbly bows and meekly does obeisance. But before that nameless prejudice that leaps beyond all this he stands helpless, dismayed, and well-nigh speechless; before that personal disrespect and mockery, the ridicule and systematic humiliation, the distortion of fact and wanton license of fancy, the cynical ignoring of the better and the boisterous welcoming of the worse, the all-pervading desire to inculcate disdain for everything black, from Toussaint to the devil,—before this there rises a sickening despair that would disarm and discourage any nation save that black host to whom "discouragement" is an unwritten word.

But the facing of so vast a prejudice could not but bring the inevitable self-questioning, self-disparagement, and lowering of ideals which ever accompany repression and breed in an atmosphere of contempt and hate. Whisperings and portents came borne upon the four winds: Lo! we are diseased and dying, cried the dark hosts; we cannot write, our voting is vain; what need of education, since we must always cook and serve? And the Nation echoed and enforced this self-criticism, saying: Be content to be servants, and nothing more; what need of higher culture for half-men? Away with the black man's ballot, by force or fraud,—and behold the suicide of a race! Nevertheless, out of the evil came something of good,—the more careful adjustment of education to real life, the clearer perception of the Negroes' social responsibilities, and the sobering realization of the meaning of progress.

So dawned the time of *Sturm und Drang:* storm and stress to-day rocks our little boat on the mad waters of the world-sea; there is within and without the sound of conflict, the burning of body and rending of soul; inspiration strives with doubt, and fruit with vain questionings. The bright ideals of the past,—physical freedom, political power, the training of brains and the training of hands,—all these in turn have waxed and waned, until even the last grows dim and overcast. Are they all wrong,—all false? No, not that, but each alone was over-simple and incomplete,—the dreams of a credulous race-childhood, or the fond imaginings of the other world which does not know and does not want to know our power. To be really true, all these ideals must be melted and welded into one. The training of the schools we need to-day more than ever,—the training of deft hands, quick eyes and ears, and above all the broader, deeper, higher culture of gifted minds and pure hearts. The power of the ballot we need in sheer self-defence,—else what shall save us from a second slavery? Freedom, too, the long-sought, we still seek,—the freedom of life and limb, the freedom to work and think, the freedom to love and aspire. Work, culture, liberty,—all these have need, not singly but together, not successively but together, each growing and aiding each, and all striving toward that vaster ideal that swims before the Negro people, the ideal of human brotherhood, gained through the unifying ideal of Race; the ideal of fostering and developing the traits and talents of the Negro, not in opposition to or contempt for other races, but rather in large conformity to the greater ideals of the American Republic, in order that some day on American soil two world-races may give each to each those characteristics both so sadly lack. We the darker ones come even now not altogether empty-handed: there are today no truer exponents of the pure human spirit of the Declaration of Independence than the American Negroes; there is no true American music but the wild sweet melodies of the Negro slave; the American fairy tales and folk-lore are Indian and African; and, all in all, we black men seem the sole oasis of faith and reverence in a dusty desert of dollars and smartness. Will America be poorer if she replace her brutal dyspeptic blundering with light-hearted but determined Negro humility? or her coarse and cruel wit with loving jovial good-humor? or her vulgar music with the soul of the Sorrow Songs?

Merely a concrete test of the underlying principles of the great republic is the Negro problem, and the spiritual striving of the freedmen's sons is the travail of souls whose burden is almost beyond the measure of their strength, but who bear it in the name of an historic race, in the name of this the land of their fathers' fathers, and in the name of human opportunity.

And now what I have briefly sketched in large outline let me on coming pages tell again in many ways, with loving emphasis and deeper detail, that men may listen to the striving in the souls of black folk.

Chapter XIV

THE SORROW SONGS

> I walk through the churchyard
>   To lay this body down;
> I know moon-rise, I know star-rise;
> I walk in the moonlight, I walk in the starlight;
> I'll lie in the grave and stretch out my arms,
> I'll go to judgment in the evening of the day,
> And my soul and thy soul shall meet that day,
> When I lay this body down. [**][1]

NEGRO SONG

---

[1] In the 1903 edition, musical notes on a staff follow the verse for each of 5 songs; where those songs with notes are here included, the musical notation is indicated by [**].

THEY that walked in darkness sang songs in the olden days—Sorrow Songs—for they were weary at heart. And so before each thought that I have written in this book I have set a phrase, a haunting echo of these weird old songs in which the soul of the black slave spoke to men. Ever since I was a child these songs have stirred me strangely. They came out of the South unknown to me, one by one, and yet at once I knew them as of me and of mine. Then in after years when I came to Nashville I saw the great temple builded of these songs towering over the pale city. To me Jubilee Hall seemed ever made of the songs themselves, and its bricks were red with the blood and dust of toil. Out of them rose for me morning, noon, and night, bursts of wonderful melody, full of the voices of my brothers and sisters, full of the voices of the past.

Little of beauty has America given the world save the rude grandeur God himself stamped on her bosom; the human spirit in this new world has expressed itself in vigor and ingenuity rather than in beauty. And so by fateful chance the Negro folk-song—the rhythmic cry of the slave—stands to-day not simply as the sole American music, but as the most beautiful expression of human experience born this side the seas. It has been neglected, it has been, and is, half despised, and above all it has been persistently mistaken and misunderstood; but notwithstanding, it still remains as the singular spiritual heritage of the nation and the greatest gift of the Negro people. . . .

The songs are indeed the siftings of centuries; the music is far more ancient than the words, and in it we can trace here and there signs of development. My grandfather's grandmother was seized by an evil Dutch trader two centuries ago; and coming to the valleys of the Hudson and Housatonic, black, little, and lithe, she shivered and shrank in the harsh north winds, looked longingly at the hills, and often crooned a heathen melody to the child between her knees, thus:

Do bana coba, gene me, gene me!
Do bana coba, gene me, gene me!
Ben d' nuli, nuli, nuli, nuli, ben d' le. [**]

The child sang it to his children and they to their children's children, and so two hundred years it has traveled down to us and we sing it to our children, knowing as little as our fathers what its words may mean, but knowing well the meaning of its music.

This was primitive African music; it may be seen in larger form in the strange chant which heralds "The Coming of John":

"You may bury me in the East,
You may bury me in the West,
But I'll hear the trumpet sound in that morning,"

—the voice of exile.

Ten master songs, more or less, one may pluck from this forest of melody—songs of undoubted Negro origin and wide popular currency, and songs peculiarly characteristic of the slave. One of these I have just mentioned. Another whose strains begin this book is "Nobody knows the trouble I've seen." When, struck with a sudden poverty, the United States refused to fulfil its promises of land to the freedmen, a brigadier-general went down to the Sea Islands to carry the news. An old woman on the outskirts of the throng began singing this song; all the mass joined with her, swaying. And the soldier wept. . . .

As in olden time, the words of these hymns were improvised by some leading minstrel of the religious band. The circumstances of the gathering, however, "the rhythm of the songs" and the limitations of allowable thought, confined the poetry for the most part to single or double lines, and they seldom were expanded to quatrains or longer tales, although there are some few examples of sustained efforts, chiefly paraphrases of the Bible. Three short series of verses have always attracted me,—the one that heads this chapter, of one line of which Thomas Wentworth Higginson has fittingly said, "Never, it seems to me, since man first lived and suffered was his infinite longing for peace uttered more plaintively." The second and third are descriptions of the Last Judgment,—the one a late improvisation, with some traces of outside influence:

> "Oh, the stars in the elements are falling,
> And the moon drips away into blood,
> And the ransomed of the Lord are returning
>   unto God,
> Blessed be the name of the Lord."

And the other earlier and homelier picture from the low coast lands:

> "Michael, haul the boat ashore,
> Then you'll hear the horn they blow,
> Then you'll hear the trumpet sound,
> Trumpet sound the world around,
> Trumpet sound for rich and poor,
> Trumpet sound the Jubilee,
> Trumpet sound for you and me."

Through all the sorrow of the Sorrow Songs there breathes a hope—a faith in the ultimate justice of things. The minor cadences of despair change often to triumph and calm confidence. Sometimes it is faith in life, sometimes a faith in death, sometimes assurance of boundless justice in some fair world beyond. But whichever it is, the meaning is always clear: that sometime, somewhere, men will judge men by their souls and not by their skins. Is such a hope justified? Do the Sorrow Songs sing true?

The silently growing assumption of this age is that the probation of races is past, and that the backward races of today are of proven inefficiency and not worth the saving. Such an assumption is the arrogance of peoples irreverent toward Time and ignorant of the deeds of men. A thousand years ago such an assumption, easily possible, would have made it difficult for the Teuton to prove his right to life. Two thousand years ago such dogmatism, readily welcome, would have scouted the idea of blond races ever leading civilization. So woefully unorganized is sociological knowledge that the meaning of progress, the meaning of "swift" and "slow" in human doing, and the limits of human perfectability, are veiled, unanswered sphinxes on the shores of science. Why should Æschylus have sung two thousand years before Shakespeare was born? Why has civilization flourished in Europe, and flickered, flamed, and died in Africa? So long as the world stands meekly dumb before such questions, shall this nation proclaim its ignorance and unhallowed prejudices by denying freedom of opportunity to those who brought the Sorrow Songs to the Seats of the Mighty?

Your country? How came it yours? Before the Pilgrims landed we were here. Here we have brought our three gifts and mingled them with yours: a gift of story and song—soft, stirring melody in an ill-harmonized and unmelodious land; the gift of sweat and brawn to beat back the wilderness, conquer the soil, and lay the foundations of this vast economic empire two hundred years earlier than your weak hands could have done it; the third, a gift of the Spirit. Around us the history of the land has centred for thrice a hundred years; out of the nation's heart we have called all that was best to throttle and subdue all that was worst; fire and blood, prayer and sacrifice, have billowed over this people, and they have found peace only in the altars of the God of Right. Nor has our gift of the Spirit been merely passive. Actively we have woven ourselves with the very warp and woof of this nation,—we fought their battles, shared their sorrow, mingled our blood with theirs, and generation after generation have pleaded with a headstrong, careless people to despise not Justice, Mercy, and Truth, lest the nation be smitten with a curse. Our song, our toil, our cheer, and warning have been given to this nation in blood-brotherhood. Are not these gifts worth the giving? Is not this work and striving? Would America have been America without her Negro people?

Even so is the hope that sang in the songs of my fathers well sung. If somewhere in this whirl and chaos of things there dwells Eternal Good, pitiful yet masterful, then anon in His good time America shall rend the Veil and the prisoned shall go free. Free, free as the sunshine trickling down the morning into these high windows of mine, free as yonder fresh young voices welling up to me from the caverns of brick and mortar below—swelling with song, instinct with life, tremulous treble and darkening bass. My children, my little children, are singing to the sunshine, and thus they sing:

> Let us cheer the weary traveller,
> Cheer the weary traveller, Let us
> Cheer the weary traveller
> Along the heavenly way. [**]

And the traveller girds himself, and sets his face toward the Morning, and goes his way.

INDEX

B

C

G

H

N

O

P

T

thrift 80

Tikar legend 118

time 117, 119, 120, 122, 123, 125,
127, 128, 129, 133, 135, 136,
137, 138, 139

tobacco 145, 148

tortoises 122

Toynbee, Arnold 357, 373

trader 149, 154

tradition 14, 16, 17, 92, 93, 96,
98, 100, 109, 133, 134, 138,
139, 182, 209, 217, 218, 237,
349, 357, 358, 365

tranquility 135

transmigration of souls 151

trees 39

Tristan 279, 280, 281, 282, 283

triumph 298, 300

Trojan 57, 58, 60, 65, 68

Trojan War 15, 51

Troy 51, 57

trust 32, 105, 225

truth 37, 56, 60, 64, 172, 175, 177,
221, 225, 226, 227, 288, 291,
298, 307, 315, 317, 397

truthfulness 225, 226

twin sisters 274

two sons in one birth 265

two souls 385

tyrants 170

Tzu Lu 34, 35, 42, 43, 48

U

United Fruit Company 21

United States 182, 184, 187, 189,
191, 206

unity 206, 208, 209, 217

universal human dilemma 348

universal virtues 19

University of Berlin 381

upright 31, 40, 43, 44

useless members of 170

Utopia 110, 112

V

vanity 167, 177, 180

Vassa, Gustavus 140, 141

Vassar College 83

vegetables 145, 148

Venus 244, 245

Virgin of Guadalupe 350, 369

virtue 19, 26, 29, 32, 33, 34, 40,
42, 44, 45, 50, 78, 91, 110,
112, 119, 154, 166, 167, 168,
169, 170, 171, 172, 173, 175,
176, 177, 178, 179, 180, 185,
190, 204, 206, 207, 208, 209,
210, 211, 212, 213, 214, 215,
216, 217, 218, 223, 224, 225,
226, 231, 300, 302, 303, 306,
307, 317, 368

W

war 58

War of 1812 181

warrior 15, 150, 152, 179, 211,
213, 359, 362, 365

wartime 113

water 29, 62, 63, 65

Edwards Brothers, Inc.
Thorofare, NJ USA
July 15, 2011